THE INVESTING
REVOLUTIONARIES

TO NANCY —
FELLOW PATRIOT!

DISCLAIMER

JWA Financial Group, Inc. (JWA), makes notice that there are no warranties, expressed or implied, as to the accuracy, completeness, or results obtained from any information in this book.

No part of this book should be interpreted to state or imply past results as an indication of future performance. This book is in no way a solicitation or an offer to sell securities or investment advisory services except, where applicable, in states where JWA Financial Group, Inc., is a registered investment advisor.

Information within this book is assumed by JWA Financial Group, Inc., to be reliable, but JWA does not guarantee the timeliness or accuracy of this information. JWA Financial Group, Inc., shall not be liable for any errors or inaccuracies, regardless of cause.

Data and charts are copyrighted by their respective owners; they are reproduced in this book as supportive research data and not as endorsements of their respective owners to the content contained.

Quotes in this book are for educational and illustrative purposes only and in no way imply an endorsement of goods or services from JWA Financial Group, Inc., or *The Investing Revolution*.

THE INVESTING REVOLUTIONARIES

How the World's Greatest Investors Take on Wall Street and Win in Any Market

JAMES N. WHIDDON
with Nikki Knotts

New York   Chicago   San Francisco   Lisbon   London   Madrid   Mexico City
Milan   New Delhi   San Juan   Seoul   Singapore   Sydney   Toronto

1 2 3 4 5 6 7 8 9 0   DOC/DOC   0 1 5 4 3 2 1 0 9

ISBN-13: 978-0-07-162394-0
ISBN-10: 0-07-162394-9

This publication is designed to provide accurate and authoritative information in regard to the subject matter covered. It is sold with the understanding that neither the author nor the publisher is engaged in rendering legal, accounting, futures/securities trading, or other professional service. If legal advice or other expert assistance is required, the services of a competent professional person should be sought.

—From a Declaration of Principles jointly adopted by a Committee
of the American Bar Association and a Committee of Publishers

McGraw-Hill books are available at special quantity discounts to use as premiums and sales promotions, or for use in corporate training programs. To contact a representative, please visit the Contact Us pages at www.mhprofessional.com.

This book is printed on acid-free paper.

CONTENTS

* **v** *

PREFACE

Many years ago, I launched a weekly Internet radio show, *The Investing Revolution*, from a makeshift studio in our corporate offices in Dallas, Texas. Since then, the equipment has become more sophisticated, and we have expanded to a daily syndicated radio program available throughout the United States, but our message has stayed the same: free market investment returns are there for the taking—for all. The tyrants of Wall Street must be tyrants no more. Freedom of commerce leads to all other freedoms, and we will not succumb to the institutional confinement in which the financial giants, as well as many willing accomplices in government and the media, long to subject us.

If there is an issue in the financial or investing realm of any import, then we have likely talked about it on our program. Authors, professors, economists, media personalities, columnists, politicians, and Nobel Laureates have all joined us to give our listeners the insights they need to help them create wealth without worry.

The Investing Revolutionaries offers a prism through which I explored ideas and concepts with these influencers, and it is designed to enhance your understanding of the financial world as it really is—not the way it appears in the media or in Wall Street advertisements. This is a book I hope you will eagerly recommend and pass along to friends and associates.

At times you will find this book challenging and sometimes humorous, but always enlightening. Your reactions will include disbelief on some topics and excitement on others. You will be incredulous and infuriated at some of the notions, and in other cases, surprised and intrigued. I know this all sounds quite different for an investing book; these books typically generate as much excitement as fruitcakes during the holidays. But I am confident that you will not only enjoy this offering but you will learn much in the process.

I start out with conversations with several free market and passive investing patriots. I visit with Vanguard founder John Bogle, Burton Malkiel of Princeton, efficient market expert Eugene F. Fama, author William Bernstein, and Nobel Laureates Edmund Phelps and Edward Prescott.

In Chapter 2, I'll tell you what Wall Street doesn't want you to know concerning its many conflicts of interests. Then we'll take a clear look at the issues with John Stossel from *ABC News*, and we'll unveil our favorite investing experiment of all time—the D.U.M.B. funds.

We will delve into the methods of Wall Street in Chapter 3, including the real role that advertising plays and whether to invest in Spam (the meat) or the latest cell phone technology. I will also check in with radio show regular Weston Wellington as he takes a look at some of the most incredible stock picks of the last decade.

In Chapter 4, I will review the topics associated with understanding markets as they really are—not as you read about them in the newspapers and see on television. "Are markets really that volatile, historically speaking?" "What are the advantages of market cycles like the dot.com boom and bust?" "What will the 2008 financial crisis do to the market?" Daniel Gross and Robert Samuelson of *Newsweek* join the discussion and make some great analogies between finance and real life.

In Chapter 5, I continue with the practical applications of investment principles by taking a look at economic forecasts and owning gold in difficult markets. *Stocks for the Long Run* author Jeremy Siegel and financial news commentator Jane Bryant Quinn weigh in on these and other important issues including the worst financial products to avoid.

In Chapter 6, I will enter into a deeper discussion of investing principles that you can use for your own portfolio. I will address international markets with *When Markets Collide* author Mohamed El-Erian and geoeconomic-political matters with Marvin Zonis. I'll also address the issues of what countries are best to invest in now, and I'll discuss the oil crisis with T. Boone Pickens.

The fascinating field of human behavior plays a major role in investing. In Chapter 7, I review an enjoyable collection of subjects such as the *Paradox of Choice* with author Barry Schwartz. In this chapter I include some of Nobel Prize winner Gary Becker's thinking on human capital and Ori Brafman's thinking on what will try to SWAY you. And I'll show you why losses hurt so much with the help of bestselling author Peter Bernstein. I'll also introduce the tax we have all paid at one time or another: the fear tax.

The last chapter—"What's in It for Me?"—brings it all home with conversations concerning socially responsible investing options, the right benchmark to track for your money and the eight-point portfolio check-up. I also bring you inspiring conversations with the great Ken Blanchard of *The One Minute Manager* fame and Dr. Arthur Brooks, as we discuss happiness and money.

Leonardo da Vinci once said, "Simplicity is the ultimate sophistication." My ultimate objective is to help you wade through all of the financial nonsense that is so pervasive today and allow you to simplify your life. There should be no bad news when it comes to your money *if* you have the proper long-term strategy in place. Free capital markets prevail if you use them wisely and harness their power. This book is an important step in your quest to do just that—and thus experience wealth without worry.

Now on behalf of all those who worked so hard to bring you this message, we invite you to recline yourself, grab a beverage, and prepare to join the Investing Revolutionaries.

ACKNOWLEDGMENTS

Aristotle said many centuries ago, "Education is the best provision for the journey to old age." As the son of public school teachers, I led a humble life as a youngster from an economic standpoint but a rich life in terms of learning academic lessons — and more importantly, life's lessons. Education is what we do at *The Investing Revolution*. And "we" is the key word as it is undoubtedly a team effort.

Gratitude must first of all go to all of the guests that have made our program successful over the years with the valuable information they have proffered for your benefit. Their combined efforts and contributions in academia, politics, journalism, and research are immeasurable. Without each of them, this book could never have come about. I appreciate the willingness of all of those who gave us their time and permission to share their stories and advice. They are all brilliant at their craft, and I thank them for allowing me to be the messenger.

A dedicated team is behind every successful project, and this one is no different. Thank you to all of our manuscript readers; your thoughtful suggestions allowed us to hone this book into a compilation of the best ideas we have heard over the five years of our radio broadcasts. Your interest in our efforts is always flattering and humbling.

Thank you to my long-time partner Lance Alston for your continued encouragement and your invaluable research for both the radio program and this written effort. Your guidance and suggestions have always proved helpful.

Thanks also to John Hetzel, Micky Reeves, Tiffany Finney-Johnson, Zac Beckerley, Brittany Farris, and our summer interns for your painstaking research and data checking. You all deserve to have your names on the front cover.

Thank you to Jeanne Glasser and her team at our publisher, McGraw-Hill Professional, for giving us this humbling opportunity to tell our story. Your finishing touches on the book made it better than I ever believed possible. My deepest gratitude is extended to you all.

I want to offer a heartfelt thank-you to our listeners and readers. Without you, there is no career, no profession, no radio program, no book, and no revolution. Your loyalty and relationships are what make our professional lives so fulfilling.

Thanks to my companion and sweetheart—my wife Nizie—and our four children: Johnathan, Daniel, Analiese, and Alexandra. You are all my inspiration. Thank you for sacrificing time with me for unusually long hours as I engaged in a project you knew I was passionate about. You may now have me back.

Finally, thank you to Nikki Knotts, my producer, coauthor, and the one who gets things done around here. I told you this was easier said than done; I know now you believe me. Your guidance and encouragement made it all happen. Congratulations.

THE INVESTING
REVOLUTIONARIES

one

INVESTING PATRIOTS

Everything that is really great and inspiring is created
by the individual who can labor in freedom.
—Albert Einstein

E very great cause has at its core men and women whose hearts run in front of their heads. They are the patriots who are often maligned or cast off by the establishment as wannabes or zealots who have no real foundation. I begin by telling you about several individuals who have taken a stand with the greatness of free markets and used their brains, time, and talents to better the cause of economic freedom and champion the individual investor's liberty. What an honor it has been to have had them as guests on our radio program named aptly for the work they have done: *The Investing Revolution.*

John Bogle, a Founding Father

John C. Bogle is one of the most gracious people I have ever had the honor of engaging. He is of the George H. W. Bush ilk of gentlemen—the type that responds to inquiries with personal handwritten notes, using a style that connotes the integrity of America's Greatest Generation. Born in 1929 in Verona, New Jersey, just 21 miles from Wall Street, and 175 days before Black Tuesday (the worst day in stock market history), it seems that bringing an approach to investing defined by simplicity and common sense was not only his life's mission but his destiny as well. Having developed difficulty with a genetic heart condition as a young adult, he received a heart transplant in 1986. Given his enthusiasm, quick-witted responses, and air of optimism and idealism, I can only suspect that the heart he received must have come from a young person—perhaps even a teenager. Whether or not it did, I know this: the doctors attending him certainly put it in the right place.

John Bogle is a legend in the world of investing. He founded the Vanguard Group in 1974, and under his leadership, it grew to be the second-largest mutual fund company in the world. He was named as one of "the world's most powerful and influential people" by *Time* magazine in 2004, and he is currently president of the Bogle Financial Markets Research Center. He is the author of several books, including one of my favorites: *The Battle for the Soul of Capitalism*. He joined our radio program *The Investing Revolution* in 2005, in 2007, and again in January 2009 with his insights on the state of the financial services industry.[1]

Bogle started the first index fund back in 1974, and since then investors have experienced some incredible success in passive investing. Passive mutual fund investing is characterized by low costs and a buy-and-hold mentality. The funds actually track selected indexes such as the Standard & Poor's 500.

Thirty years later, passive low-cost investing is still only a tiny part of the mutual fund business. Active fund managers who pick stocks for their mutual funds and try to time entries and exits from the stock market continue to have great success marketing their products. Bogle responds to the relative nonuse of passive methods in this way: "The [mutual] fund business is based on selling something to somebody, and it's easier to sell an actively managed fund because you can always find an actively managed fund that is shooting the lights out. If people would only understand that the past is not a prologue to the future, they would be much more successful investors. It's really quite as simple as that."

The title of Bogle's book is an intriguing one: *The Battle for the Soul of Capitalism.*[2] On the cover there is the subtitle *How the Financial System Undermined Social Ideals, Damaged Trust in the Markets, Robbed Investors of Trillions, and What to Do about It.* It is clearly not difficult to surmise how he feels about the matter at hand. I felt that a historical perspective would be beneficial for those of our listeners that were perhaps not fully familiar with the passive-active debate. When asked what had gone wrong with the financial system since he started using a passive approach 30 years ago, Bogle responded with a strong comparison between how the system is designed to work and what it has become—or as he says, how it has "mutated."

"We have taken a wonderful system of capitalism in which rewards went to the owners (those who put up the capital and took the risk) and moved to a system of managers' capitalism, in which the rewards largely went to the corporate managers. I call it in the book a pathological mutation from owners' to managers' capitalism, where far too much of the reward is going to the managers and far too little, therefore, going to the owners.

"You see this in CEO compensation. Where the CEO of 25 years ago was making maybe 40 times the salary of the average worker, it's been as high as 500 times [as of late]. And people say, 'They should get that kind of money if they do a good job.' Well, the fact of the matter is, these CEOs, as a group, have predicted over the last 25 years that their [company] earnings would grow at 11.5% per year. They've delivered 6% a year, and the economy's been growing at 6.5%. Does that sound like good performance, to fall halfway short of your expectations and half a point behind simply being in the economy? Not at all."

On the program, we do a great deal of watchdogging the financial services industry. Consolidation is one trend we have noted often in recent years. I wanted to get a feel from Bogle as to the degree to which the merging of various financial companies was exacerbating the problems of the management incentive. His perspective on this issue was frank. In fact, I believe it to be one of the most important points to consider when evaluating the supposed worth of active investment management.

Bogle explained, "The big incentive is, of course, to get big. Mutual fund managers don't make a lot of money when they perform well. They make a lot of money when they run a lot of assets, and as the inestimable Warren Buffett says, 'A fat wallet is the enemy of superior returns.' The bigger you get, the harder it is to deliver the results that attracted investors in the first place. It doesn't come back. It's astonishingly difficult to outperform once you get to this giant size. And this is an industry of huge companies: $50 billion, $100 billion, $500 billion in assets managed.

There are two firms that are managing $1 trillion of assets. How can they differentiate themselves when the U.S. stock market is around $13 trillion, and here they are managing 1 trillion of those dollars? They [active managers] cannot do well at that level.

"The Fidelity Magellan Fund is a classic example of that. It was great, it got big, [then] it stopped being great, and in the last 10 years it has lagged the market by around 2 percentage points a year, the amount of all of its transaction and management fees and all those costs. In the meanwhile, the fund's investors have paid Fidelity around $4 billion for below-average returns. It's a lot of money. A lot of money—for nothing."

Another of Bogle's passions in the financial industry, and one he often speaks about in speeches, is the subject of fiduciary responsibility. Being a fiduciary is generally defined as acting in the highest good faith and with integrity. Arthur Levitt, former chairman of the Securities and Exchange Commission (SEC), defines a fiduciary as an "individual entrusted with investing decisions on behalf of another who is obligated to make decisions in the client's best interest."[3] The acknowledgment and fulfillment of this obligation seem to be lacking in the relationship that most investors have with mutual fund companies.

I explored the notion of getting back to the point where there is a fiduciary relationship between investors and the people who invest their money. Bogle's response on this issue was particularly pointed and insightful: "[We need] a federal statute of fiduciary duty. We do not have that now. We have state statutes, [and] they're loosely enforced. State regulation isn't the solution because it's a little like a race to the bottom. [If one state has] tough fiduciary standards, corporations or mutual funds will move to a state that has easy ones. So there's not a lot of market discipline in enforcing fiduciary duty. The SEC is trying to accomplish [a federal statute of fiduciary duty] by having an independent mutual fund chairman, independent of the management company. Managers have been known to appraise bad results with rose-colored glasses on. As you can probably imagine, they can't be objective, and the hope is that an independent chairman will be. So [that's an] important step. [It's] being fought tooth and nail by the Investment Company Institute and by the U.S. Chamber of Commerce because they don't want mutual funds to be controlled by their own investors. I hope the courts will see through all that double-talk and allow these very important reforms to go through. We need the federal statute of fiduciary duty. That's one of the policy recommendations in the book."

One of my favorite questions to ask guests on the show is, "If we were to make you king for a day, what one thing would you change?" Predictably, Bogle's response did not disappoint.

"Wake up, investors. If investors could understand clearly what I'm talking to you about today, [if they] could realize that all this trading, moving in and out, all this expense is a deadweight on their return and a devastating weight over a lifetime. If they were merely educated enough to know we have a failed system, a fleecing operation, a skimming machine, a giant scam (these are some of the words that responsible people have used to describe the mutual fund industry). If they would realize that and understand the relentless rules of humble arithmetic, they would move their money only to people who recognize their fiduciary duty and give them a fair shake."

We owe much to revolutionaries like John Bogle. Passive investing has made great strides over the years. The free capital market environment that we enjoy has made it possible for individual investors to take advantage of diversification and share in the progress of the overall economy with the very first dollar they invest in a passively managed mutual fund. Passive mutual funds have become more commonplace. But more needs to be done to ensure education and access for all investors. The movement Bogle helped start continues to march forward in this investing revolution.

A Random Walk with Burton Malkiel

Professor Burton Malkiel's A *Random Walk Down Wall Street* is the quintessential investing classic.[4] I had the distinct privilege of interviewing the famed professor of economics at Princeton University on our show in August 2005.[5] Malkiel is also the author or coeditor of eight other books, the most recent of which is *From Wall Street to the Great Wall*.[6] He is a past appointee to the Council of Economic Advisors, and he holds BA and MBA degrees from Harvard and a Ph.D. degree from Princeton University. He's also a frequent contributor to the *Wall Street Journal*.

I began our conversation by asking Professor Malkiel about a quote from the eighth edition of *Random Walk*: "On Wall Street the term 'random walk' is an obscenity. It is an epithet coined by the academic world and hurled insultingly at the professional soothsayers. Taken to its logical extreme, it means that a blindfolded monkey throwing darts at a newspaper's financial pages could select a portfolio that would do just as well as one carefully selected by the experts. Financial analysts in pin-striped suits do not like being compared with apes."

Active management is still alive and well. So I asked him why investors are still so enamored with picking and timing if financial markets are in fact efficient.

"Because the financial community makes money from selling you a very high expense mutual fund so that the salespeople can get a big commission or from making you do a lot of trading so that your broker can get some share of the commission. So I think it's basically that one of the things investors have to realize is there is a real conflict of interest here. Your broker [or] your financial advisor's interest is not necessarily your interest. And what I recommend is that you get into the market with as efficient and low-cost instruments as possible. Incidentally, on the quote, which I appreciate, I don't really suggest that you throw darts at the pages. I suggest you throw a towel over the page and you buy an index fund, and you don't buy [only] a Standard & Poor's 500 Index fund, because that's just the large-cap stocks. You want the small-cap stocks as well. You want the value. You want the growth. And my suggestion for an index fund is that you buy a total stock market index fund that includes large and small and value and growth. You don't just want a part of the market. You want the whole market."

Professor Malkiel has a knack for relying on empirical data while at the same time considering behavioral factors as well. He commented about what the combination of the two means to the average investor.

"Look, there's nobody who puts chapters in his book about tulip bulbs and how in seventeenth-century Holland people went absolutely crazy and were paying as much for a tulip bulb as a nobleman's castle. And the new chapter 'The Biggest Bubble of All: Surfing the Internet' in [my] book [A *Random Walk Down Wall Street*, ninth edition]—nobody writes about these things without under-standing that, sure, the market is by and large rational but sometimes it goes nuts. That's the kind of thing the behavioralists talk about, and frankly, avoiding those kinds of mistakes, getting swept up in some kind of euphoria about the Internet or about anything else, that's the kind of thing that can really hurt the investor. So I think those are the big lessons from behavioral finance.

"I'm an efficient market guy. I think by and large the market gets it right, but when I have debates with the behavioral people, we both come to the same conclusion—namely, that the best thing for an individual to do is to buy a low-cost index fund and don't do a lot of buying and selling."

Professor Malkiel makes a point in the book that there's a differ-ence between statistical significance and economic significance. I asked him to explain the difference.

"There's no question that those guys who follow charts will tell you that charting works. That is to say, if a stock's been going up, there's a slight tendency for it to keep going up. You know, you hear this all the time. This stock is acting well. This stock is acting poorly. There is a slight statistical tendency for that to be true, but I don't think people should act on that basis because if they do, they're going to be doing a lot of buying and selling. One of the great pieces of the behavioral finance literature suggests that people get overoptimistic about their ability to predict. They do too much buying and selling, and the more buying and selling you do, the richer your broker gets, but the poorer you get."

Malkiel had recently written in the *Wall Street Journal* that "a frequent criticism of the proposal to allow individuals to invest a portion of their Social Security contributions in the private accounts is that it would subject retirees to unconscionable risk that could leave many of them in poverty."[7] The AARP [formerly the American Association of Retired Persons] advertises that private accounts will turn Social Security into "Social Insecurity." Since this is a political debate that is not likely to go away, I wanted to get his take on the matter.

"Well, I'm a supporter of private accounts, and I think that the argument that they're simply too risky is wrong. A couple of things we know about the stock market. There's no question that if you have got some money that you need to send your kid to college next year, you don't put it in the stock market because nobody knows what the return of the stock market is going to be over the next year. But if you've got money to invest for 25 years, 30 years, 35 years, the stock market is much less risky.

"If you look back in history, and you look at what was the lowest 25-year return that anybody ever got, even if you started this before the Great Depression, you got a 6%, 7% return. So first point [is that the] stock market is less risky for the long-term investor because these invariable ups and downs cancel one another out. Second, if you dollar cost average—by which I mean you put a little money in periodically—and you do it religiously, you know, you don't stop in October 2002 when it looks like the sky is falling, and you don't put more in March 2000 when it looks like you're going to the sky. You put in a regular amount in each quarter or each pay period as you would do with the Social Security system. So [then] my answer would be that if you diversify broadly, you pay lower investment expenses, you invest over the long pull, and you dollar cost average, you take a lot of risk out of investing, and if you do it that way, I don't think being in the stock market is too risky at all. Quite the contrary. I think it would give the average American a chance to really build some wealth, some wealth that could be given to your heirs if you wanted. I happen to be a big supporter of private accounts and think that a lot of the arguments against them are simply incorrect."

One troubling trend that was gaining momentum at the time of our visit was the entrance by many individual investors into hedge funds. These products are marketed as the "place to be" when the stock market is not providing the returns investors have come to expect. I asked Professor Malkiel what some of the problems are with hedge funds and why they are becoming so popular with the inaptly named "smart money."

"I think they're not good for the average investor. I think they're very good for the hedge fund manager. You can see why so many people are going into hedge funds. The general pay for the manager is something called '2 and 20.' Now, what that means is the manager gets 2% of the amount that you've invested. The '20' refers to the fact that if there are any profits, the manager gets 20% of the profits. Now, you may wonder, 'Even if the hedge fund does well, how much is going to be left for me?'

"My analyses of the returns suggest that the average investor, in fact, will get less than a simple index investment in the stock market by going into hedge funds. It's also very risky because these hedge fund returns are all over the place. If instead you buy a fund of funds [hedge funds] so you get the diversification to take away some of the risk, then it's even a worse deal for the investor. The fund of funds buys hedge funds where the managers get this 2 and 20, and then the fund-of-funds manager gets 1 and 10. He gets an extra 1% on the top, and then 10% of any profits that the hedge funds make in this diversified fund of funds. It's great for the hedge fund manager. I think the individual investor should absolutely stay away."

I then asked Professor Malkiel the king-for-a-day question.

"I think some of the [fund] disclosure is about as opaque as it possibly could be. It's just very hard if you pick up a prospectus for a mutual fund to really figure out what are all the costs that you're paying. So I think [there has to be] better disclosure of the conflicts of interest in this financial game, of the costs the individuals are paying. It's not that I want more paperwork. Quite the contrary. I'm a big believer in a one-page prospectus. Less may be even more, but [there needs to be] very clear information on what the conflicts are, what the expenses are. I'd like less paperwork, but more clarity."

Professor Burton Malkiel—another one of the great patriots of the revolution.

Efficient Economist: Eugene F. Fama

Eugene F. Fama is the Robert R. McCormick Distinguished Service Professor of Finance at the University of Chicago Graduate School of Business. He coined the term "efficient market," which gained widespread use following the publication of his paper on efficient capital markets in the *Journal of Finance* in 1970.[8]

In addition to being a windsurfer and a tennis fanatic, Fama and his wife of over 50 years, Sally, have 4 children and 10 grandchildren. Understanding efficiency may have been more of a necessity around his house than an academic endeavor. One of his children, Gene F. Fama Jr., is a vice president of Dimensional Fund Advisors following in his father's "efficient market" footsteps.

Professor Fama's work has essentially redefined our understanding of which types of stocks pay the greatest returns. He joined us on *The Investing Revolution* radio program in April 2007 to discuss his groundbreaking work.[9]

I asked Professor Fama what he had meant by the term "efficient capital markets" in its application four decades earlier. I found his response interestingly practical: "If you interpret the term strictly, what it means is that everything knowable about the future is already built into prices, so there's not much you can do to beat the information in the current price. And as a consequence, what you can expect from investing is just normal relation between expected return and risk. I never took that strict definition that seriously. Nothing's ever perfectly efficient. That's just kind of the extreme by which you judge things. My practical definition would be that most people can't come up with information that isn't already in the price, so as far as they are concerned, the market is efficient. It's very difficult to find a person for whom that's not true."

Our listeners, like most individual investors, have been so influenced by the financial media's emphasis on investing in sectors (recognized large functional sectors of the economy such as technology, oil and gas, and pharmaceuticals) that they know much less about the concept of asset class investing. Therefore, I wanted to get a good explanation from Fama. So I asked him how he defined an asset class.

"Well, you can begin with bonds versus stocks. Then within the stock category, the research of the last 20 years that Ken French and I have been doing says that basically there are two kinds, or two divisions, of stocks that are interesting and seem to be related to average returns. One is small stocks versus big stocks, where small stocks seem to generate higher average returns than big stocks. The other is between value stocks and growth stocks. Growth stocks are stocks of companies that are profitable and fast growing, and they look really good, and they're strong companies typically, especially the big ones. Value stocks tend to be the other end of the spectrum. They're not so profitable; they're not growing that rapidly. A simple way to think about it is that growth stocks have very high prices relative to fundamentals like earnings or book values because they're expected to grow a lot in the future, whereas ratios of prices to fundamentals are lower for value stocks because they're not expected to grow, and they might actually be restructuring, and so might be declining in size for a while."

While he did not list them all, I also appreciated the simplification that he used to break down asset classes into large versus small, and value versus growth. If you cast this template over international and emerging markets also, then you basically have the 8 to 10 asset classes you need for the equity side of your portfolio.

If we had ended our discussion at this point, you might have had the impression that Fama was endorsing the use of large-cap growth stocks. The description he used sounds like the kind of investments you would want to buy for your own portfolio. However, I pressed Professor Fama further on the topic to bring out the research he has done that shows the long-term advantages to tilting your portfolio toward small-cap and value stocks.

Along with Ken French, Professor Fama wrote several articles in the early 1990s on the size and value effects. In our interview, Fama reflected on how that research evolved since he wrote his earlier papers.

"One of the things we did was to test in detail whether the same phenomena [with value and small stocks] showed up if you looked at different time periods other than the one we studied initially. We started in 1964 in the initial study, and we extended it back to 1926, and then we looked at foreign markets to see if we observed the same thing. It seems to show up around the world in pretty much the same way and in different time periods. In our view, this is all reward for risk. Value stocks are basically riskier, and they have higher cost of capital than growth stocks; and small stocks are basically riskier, and they have higher cost of capital than big stocks. But risk is risk, and you can't expect these things to pay off on a year-by-year basis. In fact, there may be long periods of time when they don't pay off. That's just the essential nature of risk and return. If you want to see these things on a reliable basis, basically you're talking about investment lifetimes, 35-year periods."

Since Professor Fama first introduced the concept of efficient markets, a debate has been going on between the behavioral theorists and the efficient market theorists. I asked Fama where he felt the debate stood now and why he felt that the other side has it wrong.

"Take the value and growth stuff. In our theory, that's just risk and return. The value stocks are from relatively distressed companies, and they have a higher cost of capital, which means they're going to have higher expected stock returns. In their [behavioral theorists'] view, the spread in returns between growth and value stocks comes about because both are mispriced. The prices of growth stocks are too high, and the prices of value stocks are too low. [Again] in their view, what happens is that these price imbalances get corrected, and as a consequence, the value stocks end up with higher returns than the stronger growth stocks. So they don't disagree on the outcome; they disagree on the source. In their world, people never learn. There's always market overreaction to past performance, and the next generation of investors is as bad as the last. There's never any learning in the investment process. To an economist, that doesn't ring true. We don't expect people to be forever fooled."

I saved the most important question for last: What are the one or two most important aspects or points you would want individual investors to learn from your work and remember as they invest throughout the rest of their lives?

"I think what they should remember is they're probably not informed about much of anything. I don't think I'm informed enough to say that markets aren't efficient as far as I'm concerned. I've been studying markets for 45 years now, and I don't think I can forecast which stocks are going to beat other stocks, except based on the fact that some stocks are riskier than others. So [investors] should focus on asset allocation, how much risk they want to take for potentially higher or lower reward, and then they should stick to whatever plan they choose. Don't do a lot of switching around. And diversification is your buddy. Always hold a diversified portfolio."

I believe Professor Fama is on his way to a Nobel Prize in economics. He has been considered a front runner for several years now. His work on the efficiency of markets is world renowned, and I believe it places him squarely in the category of an investing revolutionary. It was a privilege to be able to share his straightforward approach to markets with our listeners and now with you. His research

and message have profound implications for all individual investors: tilting a portfolio toward small-cap and value companies will
pay off in the long run.

William Bernstein Talks Trade

Dr. William J. Bernstein is an extraordinarily bright fellow and a
passive investing patriot in his own right. He took a very unusual
path to becoming a financial theorist. Bernstein holds a Ph.D. in
chemistry, and he is an MD specializing in neurology, which he
practiced until retiring from the field. His first book, *The Intelligent
Asset Allocator,* clearly makes the case that most investment return
is determined by the asset allocation of the portfolio rather than the
asset selection.[10] His second book, *The Four Pillars of Investing:
Lessons for Building a Winning Portfolio,* is aimed at those less comfortable with statistical thought.[11] It also puts asset class returns into
long-term historical perspective. Both tomes are quickly becoming
classics in the investing arena, and his thoughtful and honest
approach to investing has been an important influence in shaping
my own ideas and positions concerning wealth management.

In his most recent book, A *Splendid Exchange: How Trade
Shaped the World,* Bernstein shifts gears a bit and launches into an
expansive look at trade throughout all of recorded history.[12]

Dr. Bernstein joined us on the show in August 2008, and the
first question we asked concerned a new concept that had really
grabbed me.[13] It was the idea that there is a difference in the average (or the mean) versus the median. This is not a new or
revolutionary thought, I know, but I was interested to hear how

trade has affected people over the last 50 years relative to the mean and also to the median. Here are his remarks:

"Well, first of all, we have to define for the listeners what you mean by those terms. The *mean* is simply the average. The *median*, on the other hand, is the person right in the middle at the 50th percentile. The way to understand this is the classic example of what happens when Bill Gates walks into or out of a room: the average income of that room rises dramatically or falls dramatically. He's adding a couple hundred billion dollars of net worth to that room every time he walks in, and he subtracts it when he walks out. But he doesn't do anything significant to the median if there are 100 or 200 people in the room. He might change the median just a small amount—the person at the 50th percentile is probably earning $50,000 or $60,000 a year, and that's not going to change much when Bill Gates walks in or out. So the mean and the median carry a lot of ideological freight.

"The average [income in the United States] has done very well because a relatively small number of people are doing extremely well, and that raises the average of the mean considerably. But the income of the average person at the median, that is to say at the 50th percentile, has not increased dramatically over the past generation or so. In fact, if you look at male workers and you adjust for inflation, you find that his median income has actually fallen."

As I pondered his answer—although it was referring to how we can look at differing income statistics—I considered how this also might be applied in the investing world. We often talk about the average return for a particular fund or investment. But as Dr. Bernstein pointed out, the average (mean) and the median are almost always two different numbers. This is why knowing how an investment strategy is performing in regards to its peers is an important component of understanding that strategy.

You may well be satisfied with an average return of 8%. But if that 8% return is in the bottom quartile of funds in the same asset class, then you have fallen victim to what I call the "dumb-and-happy" or "ignorance-is-bliss" syndrome of investing. You can, and should, be doing better, but you do not know it because you are happy with the average and you are unaware of the median (and above). Bill Gates has walked out of the room, and you are still getting a below-average return.

Given Dr. Bernstein's reputation for critical research, the interview continued to be quite a primer on free trade as the following narrative attests.

"In countries that have a relative abundance of something, that something will do well with trade. If they have a relative scarcity of it, that something will do poorly with free trade. So, for example, if you look at the United States, we have an abundant amount of capital relative to the rest of the world, so our capitalists do well with trade. We have a relatively abundant amount of land. We have probably the best-quality land in [the world here in] America. So the people who own the land, that is, the farmers, tend to do relatively well with free trade. We have a relatively small amount of labor compared to the rest of the world. Labor in the rest of the world is relatively more abundant than it is in the United States. So U.S. laborers tend not to do as well with free trade. You can break that down further and look just at skilled labor. We actually have a large amount of skilled labor relative to the rest of the world, so skilled laborers tend to do well.

And unskilled laborers, people who are working on the floor in the factories at minimum wage jobs, tend not to do well with free trade.

"And so, when you look at the polling data, what you see is that if your income is more than $100,000 a year, you like free trade because you're the relatively abundant factor in the United States. And if you're someone who is a blue-collar worker who has a high school education, then you probably do not favor free trade because you don't benefit from it all that much.

"Now, there's no question that nations as a whole benefit from free trade. When you average it all together, almost all nations benefit. It's hard to find an example of a nation that doesn't. But it's certainly true that significant minorities of people do not do well with free trade. Now, [I can give] you all sorts of examples in the United States of people who don't do well with free trade, but remember that we lead the world in any number of industries, starting with agriculture, medical equipment, pharmaceuticals, aircraft, military equipment—just all sorts of industries where we really have a comparative advantage over just about every other nation on the face of the earth. And so if you're going to impede free trade, what you're going to be doing is damaging our most productive and profitable industries. So I don't want to give the impression that I'm a protectionist."

As a follow-up, Bernstein then was asked about the underdeveloped countries. Of course this topic speaks to the importance of investing a portion of your portfolio in emerging markets. Does free trade benefit these markets in the long run?

"Oh, there's no question that it does. About 10 years ago Jeffrey Sachs, of all people, and Andrew Warner did a study that they published under the aegis of the Brookings Institution. They looked at all nations, but particularly at developing nations. And there's no question that the ones that opened up to free trade prospered and the ones that kept themselves closed did not develop at all. They stayed poor. All you have to do to convince yourself of that anecdotally is to look at India, which for about 40 years after its independence closed itself down, shut itself off from the world in terms of trade, and stayed poor. And then sometime around the late 1980s they decided to open themselves up. The results speak for themselves."

Finally, we asked about the benefits of trading with our friends and neighbors—and enemies. His answer was surprising as well as fascinating.

"The benefits of free trade are very real in an economic sense, but the real value of trade is in the intangibles. The counterexample or the negative example of that is what happened with Smoot-Hawley. Smoot-Hawley is the tariff that was passed in 1930, and it's still named [that], but it's actually the Hoover Tariff because that's what Hoover ran on in 1928. Smoot and Hawley were the legislators who pushed through Hoover's Tariff, and it plunged the world into a commercial trade crisis. It didn't really greatly worsen the Great Depression, but what it did do was precipitate World War II because Germany couldn't repay its reparations at Versailles that it owed after World War I, and without Smoot-Hawley, Hitler probably wouldn't have become chancellor, and there wouldn't have been a World War II. The people in our State Department looking over the wreckage in 1945 realized that this should never be allowed to happen again, and that's how we got the GATT, the General Agreement on Tariffs and Trade."

William Bernstein's research and the communication of such is a treasure to individual investors. He not only provides valuable and convincing arguments concerning the passive approach to investing but also provides precise arguments and interesting reading when he ventures outside the investing lines to other important financial topics such as trade and the world's standard of living. I always look forward to his next project and will undoubtedly add it to my free market library collection upon its release.

A Nobel Perspective: Capitalism Finding Direction

Edmund S. Phelps is the McVickar Professor of Political Economy at Columbia University, director of Columbia's Center on Capitalism and Society, and the winner of the 2006 Nobel Prize for Economics.[14] His research has spanned the gamut of economic growth, including the Golden Rule of Saving.

He says, "Economic success is tied to a country's entrepreneurial spirit."[15] Ultimate success in free markets is derived from the entrepreneurial form of capitalism. Where innovation and creativity are embraced and encouraged, the economy will thrive. Where those same tendencies are squelched by the system, the economy can easily grow stagnant.

Consider the case of Europe and the United States. Phelps told *The Investing Revolution* that the story of capitalism is a European history.[16]

"Well, begin with going back to ancient times [when] there was quite a discussion of the good life, and the good life involved applying yourself, studying and learning and understanding things, and that became quite influential not just in ancient Greece but also in Italy where the farmers who studied how to tend their crops and so forth were very celebrated and considered important people, . . . and then in Britain you had the property rights and government property. In France in the eighteenth century, [you] had a lot of respect for business entrepreneurs. And Germany came up with a lot of financial institutions at the end of the nineteenth century, so I think that the history of capitalism is basically a European history." It appears that competition and free markets were not overly encouraged by any means, and yet capitalism triumphed.

"Fast forward to today. The United States has an economy that is outpacing those in Europe. Germany, France, and Italy now suffer higher unemployment, along with lower productivity and job satisfaction than the United States. One could argue that each of these trends influences the others. For example, low job satisfaction could lead to low productivity." Phelps, however, ties each of these trends to a lack of what he calls "economic dynamism," meaning, in his words, "how fertile the country is in coming up with innovative ideas, how adept it is at identifying and nourishing the ideas, and how prepared it is in evaluating and trying out the new products and methods that are launched onto the market." In other words, its entrepreneurial spirit.

Countries that fail to encourage, nurture, and support new innovations will suffer economically. Where there are new ideas, there are new jobs created that are engaging and fulfilling. But what about whether a country encourages—or discourages—entrepreneurship? Institutions, for their part, can discourage innovation through

excessive regulation and taxation. It is a country's values—or attitudes—
however, that hold special interest. Phelps says a cultural shift is in
order before better economic performance can occur.

"I think there is an understanding that there has to be more
competition [in] Europe; otherwise, the system won't be open to
new ideas and the development of new ideas. I think it is not just
economic institutions in the sense of practices and legal stuff. It is
all also attitudes. There are a lot of workplace attitudes that are
probably not very friendly to start-up entrepreneurs that are trying
to create something new."

Along these lines, perhaps Western Europe is taking note. Interestingly, several European political and economic trends are moving
toward an entrepreneurial free market system and away from a
more left-leaning big-firm form of capitalism. This was borne out
with the general elections in France, Italy, and Great Britain in
the years 2005 to 2008 as the leaders that were elected moved to
the right of the political landscape.[17]

For U.S. workers and investors, this trend leads to a new appreciation for the entrepreneurial spirit that America fosters. While
the wheels of capitalism have trouble gaining traction worldwide,
they are still fully engaged here in the United States, regularly providing new opportunities for workers and keeping our free market
system relevant and dynamic.

For investors, it's "full speed ahead." By embracing a marketplace that implements innovative ideas, investors can reap the
reward in U.S. firms. As fledgling free economies move to a more
entrepreneurial form of capitalism, opportunities for individual
investors to take advantage of growing international companies is
going to be tremendous.

Free capital markets are alive and well. There will always be a natural ebb and flow throughout the economies of the world. You can rest assured that as long as capitalism and the rewards for innovative ideas are in place, free markets survive and thrive. That means you will have ample opportunity to invest your money and get the return you need and desire.

Edward Prescott on Tax Rates and Economic Growth

Work to live, or live to work? It seems Americans are asking this question daily, in search of the holy grail of "work-life balance." Contrast this struggle with the fact that by about October 24 each year, Americans will have worked as many hours as Europeans do in a full year—there's a reason their gross domestic product (GDP) per capita is less than all but four of the poorest states in the United States.[18] The average American works 25 hours a week; the average French person, 18; the average Italian, a bit more than 16.5. Even the hardest-working Europeans—the British, who put in an average of 21.5 hours—are far more laid-back than their American cousins.

Compared with Europeans, Americans are not only more likely to be employed and more likely to work longer hours but they are also more likely to take fewer (and shorter) vacations. The average American takes off less than 6 weeks a year; the average French worker, almost 12.[19] The world champion vacationers are the Swedes, at 16 weeks per year. Of course, Europeans pay a price for their extravagant leisure. The average French worker produces only three-quarters as much as the average American worker, even though productivity per hour is slightly higher in France.[20]

So are Americans preprogrammed to work longer hours, and if so, do they work longer hours for cultural reasons? Nobel Laureate Edward C. Prescott has published many articles on this topic, and world policymakers and leaders have been discussing his findings in relation to global economies for the last several years.[21] Prescott's premise is that our current low income tax rates encourage people to work more hours because we can keep more for consumption. We are consciously choosing spending over leisure.

Prescott visited with us on *The Investing Revolution* in 2007 to discuss the topic.[22] Here's a startling fact: Based on labor market statistics from the Organisation for Economic Co-operation and Development (OECD), American workers aged 15 to 64 work 50% more than French workers.[23] Comparisons between Americans and Germans or Italians are similar. What's going on here? What can possibly account for these large differences in the hours people work? It turns out that the answer is not related to cultural differences or institutional factors like unemployment benefits. Rather, "marginal tax rates explain virtually all of this difference," says Prescott. He goes on to say, "I've made this point about tax rates before, but it bears repeating because it reflects a fundamental economic insight that gets to the heart of policymaking: People respond to incentives. You don't make economic policy for nations; you make it for people. And it's the responses of those people, when aggregated, that give us those data that we all love to analyze."

In fact, the current marginal income tax rate in the United States shown in Figure 1-1 rewards dual-income households more than it did in the 1970s when the average tax rate doubled when a spouse joined the workforce.[24] Now that more people are working, there is a greater need for labor to do some of the things people often don't

Denmark	59%
The Netherlands	52%
Belgium	50%
France	48%
Italy	43%
United States	35%

Figure 1-1 Highest Marginal Income Tax Rates

have time to do for themselves—like provide child care, prepare meals, clean the house, and run errands. Prescott goes on to say, "The bottom line is that a thorough analysis of historical data in the United States and Europe indicates that, given similar incentives, people make similar choices about labor and leisure. Free European workers from their tax bondage and you will see an increase in gross domestic product. The same holds true for Americans and Europeans who live and work in America."[25]

Arthur Godfrey once said, "I'm so proud to pay taxes in the United States; the only thing is, I could be just as proud for half the money." Nobody likes taxes. But we are blessed to live in a free market economy that rewards entrepreneurship and hard work and that fosters a relatively plentiful job supply. We also have one of the lowest marginal income tax schedules in the industrialized world. Hopefully our elected officials will understand the positive fiscal relationship between low taxes and a strong economy—and stay the course.

Dinesh D'Souza on What's So Great about America

In September 2008 and again in early 2009, I invited Dinesh D'Souza to join me on the program.[26] D'Souza is a charming fellow with an enthusiastic appeal. His passion for the topic at hand was clear. He has been called one of the top young policy-makers in the country by *Investor's Business Daily*.[27] The *New York Times Magazine* named him as one of America's most influential conservative thinkers, and he was a former policy analyst in the Reagan White House. D'Souza has served at the American Enterprise Institute and the Hoover Institution. His book *The Enemy at Home*, published in 2007, stirred up a furious debate both on the left and on the right.[28] Even so, it became a national bestseller. I decided to take him back a few years to his 2000 bestseller, *The Virtue of Prosperity*, because I enjoyed it so much and I think it is one of those books that should be required reading for all first-year college students.[29] I opened the conversation by asking D'Souza about his statement "Reaganism produced great changes."

"The changes were very dramatic in the area of public policy. Most people forget now, but in 1980 when Reagan was elected, the top marginal tax rate in America was about 70%, and Reagan brought it down over a period of six years to 28%. Now it's gone up to about 35%, but my point is from 70 to 28, that's a huge change.

"And I think it goes beyond that. It wasn't just that Reagan supported tax cuts, privatization, and so on; but he was also pushing a bigger cultural change. You know, I'm an immigrant to America, and when I first came to this country in the late 1970s, a sort of ethos had been set by John F. Kennedy, who had said earlier that if you're young, if you're idealistic, and if you care, join the Peace Corps. Become a public servant. So the idea was that if you work for yourself or if you're an entrepreneur or an investor, well, you're kind of a greedy, selfish guy, but if you go work for the Department of Education, you're a noble person putting the public good ahead of your own.

"Reagan challenged all that, and he said, it's not the public servant—who would be called, by the way, the bureaucrat—but rather the entrepreneur who is the embodiment of the American dream. And so Reagan was pushing for a cultural shift. And I think we've seen that. We've seen a cultural shift in America today, so more parents today would probably like their kids to be like Bill Gates rather than, say, Bill Clinton. And that's going beyond politics. So when I look back at Reaganism, most people would focus on the Cold War and so on, but I think Reagan also produced an economic and a sort of cultural shift in the United States."

At the time of our discussion, we were in the midst of the heated 2008 presidential campaign. You may recall a question that came up concerning Senator John McCain and the number of houses he owned. I expressed how I was pounding the table in my own breakfast nook pleading with McCain to tell the interviewers that he wants houses for everybody—that there's nothing wrong with being prosperous. That's what the American dream is all about. I told D'Souza that it seems there's a reemergence of this idea that there may be no virtue in prosperity. I asked him if I was reading it wrong.

"No. In fact, one reason I wanted to tackle that topic is because I saw that in the twentieth century everyone was celebrating the triumph of capitalism. And capitalism did win the economic debate against socialism in the same way that it won the economic debate against mercantilism a couple of centuries earlier. But although capitalism wins the economic debate, it never seems to win the moral debate. It almost always seems that at the end of the day, people say, we admit that capitalism produces efficiency and so on, but we don't care about that. It undermines family and community and morality and equality. It wrecks the environment. So the basic idea here is that capitalism may be efficient, but it's not really a very decent system. And politics takes advantage of that, the prejudice against the rich guy, the successful guy, the entrepreneur. The basic idea is that they must be succeeding at the expense of everybody or they must be succeeding by finagling their way to success, and I think ultimately entrepreneurs are in some ways always on the defensive against this kind of thing."

D'Souza describes two sets of people in his book: the party of "yeah" versus the party of "nah." I asked him to tell us what the difference between those two groups is.

"We often think of political debates in ideological terms, the conservatives against the liberals, or the Republicans against the Democrats, or even the free market views against the socialist views. But I think behind all that is that there's almost, you might say, a temperamental difference, and you can always test it even with friends of yours when you raise a lot of the new things that are happening in the economy.

"For example, 'we're living in a global market,' or 'technology is changing our everyday life right before our eyes,' or 'we'll soon have the ability to implant little chips in our arm so people can find us if we get lost,' and so on. There's one type of people where whenever you describe these new developments, they're superexcited, and so I call them the 'party of yeah' because it's almost like you can hear them pounding their fists on the table and going, 'Yeah, that's great! The future will be better than the past. We have reasons to be optimistic. Things are looking up.' Then there's another group of people where whenever you describe one of these developments, cloning or technological change, or so on, immediately they focus on the negative. They're going, 'Nah, that's not going to do it. No. You're dreaming.' Or 'You're missing out on the costs of this, and it's going to make our life so much worse, and we're going to have no privacy left.' So you've got these two parties, one that is gung ho about the future, about capitalism, about globalization, about technology. The other group is very pessimistic and thinks in a sense that all of this is eroding our sense of community, that it is making inequality even greater, that it is destroying the American middle class, and so on."

After this answer, I could not resist stepping on the soap box. I told him that I say that "the optimist is always eventually correct" and asked him to comment.

"Well, I think that's certainly true in economic terms. I keep hearing people say, 'The rich are getting richer and the poor are getting poorer.' But when I actually looked at American living standards over the past generation—let's say from World War II, or even from 1980—what you see is that the rich get richer, and the poor also get richer, although not at the same pace. So, yes, inequality does rise, but it's rising because more people from the middle class are moving up. So economically, yes. I think the optimist is always right.

"The deeper criticism—which requires a little more examination—is that there's a widespread feeling in America supported by a lot of surveys that over the past half century, you might say portfolios and living standards have gone up, but there's a sense that values have gone down. And that's not strictly an economic issue, but in some ways I think the deeper critics of the market are basically saying, 'Yeah, it makes us better off, but does it actually make us better people?'"

His comments on "being better people" gave me pause. Biblical literature, as well as secular writings throughout history, has wrestled with the questions and afflictions of two economic states for individuals—prosperity and scarcity. Both have equal but differing challenges. I, like perhaps many of you, have experienced both economic states in my lifetime. I wanted to explore the values topic a little further so I asked D'Souza if maybe we as Americans are a bit spoiled and will always complain that we are not well enough off.

"I think it was Warren Buffett who was asked, 'Do you attribute your success to luck or to achievement,' and initially Buffett said, 'To luck.' And everyone was a little startled, but what Buffett meant wasn't that he wasn't a careful or thoughtful investor. What he meant was that 'I'm lucky to be born in the United States of America where I can be Warren Buffett. If I was born in Afghanistan, there's a very small chance that I would be doing what I'm doing now.' So in a sense, we often forget that it's not only markets but it's also America that makes possible the tangent of opportunity that makes our lives so much better."

If you have had any exposure to religion in your life at all, you are familiar with the adage that "money is the root of all evil." D'Souza has stated that he feels that "money is the root of all good." I was curious how he would approach telling my listeners what he means by that statement.

"Well, I think that what the Bible is condemning, first of all, isn't money. It's what the Bible calls the 'love of money.' But even that's stated in a clear context. The basic idea here is that money is a means and not an end. People often condemn capitalism for selfishness, and selfishness is to be condemned. But the thing is that the selfishness is not in capitalism. The selfishness is in human nature. What capitalism does is channel that selfishness in such a way that it makes you a better person, and it also serves the public betterment of society.

"In *The Virtue of Prosperity* I put it this way. Capitalism civilizes greed in much the same way that marriage civilizes lust. I mean, you can think of lust as part of the human condition too. Now, it would be crazy for someone to say, 'Well, let's just get rid of it. Let's root it out.' That's impractical. So what do we do? We figure out social institutions that take human nature as it is and try to say that there is a way that we can steer this impulse, which might otherwise act out in destructive ways, steer it in such a way that it leads to the raising of children, mutual love, [and] the betterment of society. And the same, I think, is true with markets. It's a way of channeling self-interest in a way that's productive for you, productive for society, and also makes the entrepreneur spend a lot of his day or her day thinking about what's going to serve the wants and needs of other people. That can't be a bad thing."

Bottom Line

Capitalism has its faults, but it is indisputably the most efficient and marvelous economic invention of all time. Markets work well if allowed to do so. As citizens of this great free market nation, we must be willing to stand up for freedom of choice in making decisions involving commerce and finances. In doing so, we protect all other freedoms as well. These free market patriots have set the stage—and in many ways paid the price—for you to benefit from their capital market thinking. Take advantage of their wisdom and you will undoubtedly reap the benefits in your own financial life.

two

WHAT WALL STREET WON'T TELL YOU

A great deal of intelligence can be invested in ignorance
when the need for illusion is deep.
—Saul Bellow

H alf truths are like half bricks. They can be thrown much
further." This is one of those sayings I heard as a youngster that
has always stuck with me. I think you would agree that one of life's
frustrations is that we really never have all of the facts concerning
a situation before we have to make a decision. We have all been
taken advantage of by being told only part of the story.

In this chapter I will explore some of the rest of the story—the
parts of the story Wall Street would rather not share. You will learn
about the biggest cost that investors unwittingly pay. I will also
show you how mutual funds are created and marketed through our
own little "dumb" experiment. I will bring to light the conflicts of
interest that are so rampant in the financial services industry but
that somehow stay hidden from most investors. My goal, once you
have become aware of the other half of the story, is for you to use

this information to break free of the system that seeks to dominate your financial life.

The House Always Wins

Seventeenth-century Spanish poet Joaquin Setanti famously said, "Be wary of the man who urges an action in which he himself incurs no risk." Wall Street knows the risk. And it wants you to take it all.

Gambling has become mainstream entertainment. Most states have lotteries, poker tournaments air on prime time television, and online gambling has become a billion-dollar industry. What once many considered undesirable is now commonplace. The gambling industry makes, for many, an easy comparison to the financial services industry. While not a gambler myself, it is a comparison that I use often on *The Investing Revolution*.

Here's how it breaks down. From Wall Street's perspective, you—the investors—are the gamblers. With dollar signs in your eyes, you put your money into its system (the stock market) that can potentially return big bucks. Wall Street depends on your knowing that the system doesn't always work in your favor while at the same time believing that you can come out on top with enough patience and practice. This realization can lower your expectations, which keeps Wall Street off the hook for your failures (most casino visitors don't really expect to win big, after all), and at the same time it appeals to your hope and anticipation of winning the jackpot—your greedy side.

A significant amount of time, energy, and money must be committed to the game in hopes of creating payoffs. But even with great effort, the returns are usually well below your expectations. (The investment performance you experience is also usually well below the return freely given by the market without such effort. More on that in a moment.) Nevertheless, you ultimately decide the chance of winning big outweighs the risk of losing big, and you choose to roll the dice.

In a casino, the house sets the rules and runs things behind the scenes. Casinos have large staffs and marketing budgets that hype the glitz and glamour of winning big. They invite people in, knowing they themselves hold the keys to success for the players. Some players may win a jackpot here and there, but in the long run, it's the house that will come out on top. Casinos also have very extensive and expensive surveillance systems that keep players in check and protect the system. Additionally, they are known for using freebies, many in the form of low-priced meals and hotel rooms, to get their patrons to the slot machines.

In the same way, Wall Street has its own systems in place that keep investors coming back and keep Wall Street raking in the profits. It too has the information that could allow you to win big. But it disseminates just enough to make you interested and hopeful while at the same time trading in its own house accounts (ironic name these firms use, huh?) with information it may or may not have shared with its clients. In the casino hotel tradition, Wall Street operatives (brokers and "advisors") like to offer you free seminar dinners and discounted trading platforms for "preferred" clients.

Wall Street also protects its system through massive war chests it has accumulated over the decades. A battalion of lobbyists keep political campaigns funded on both sides of the aisle. Wall Street knows that many of its own will likely end up in high government positions one day and keep its interests protected. Wall Street also knows that many of those holding public office will be interviewing for jobs among its ranks after their political careers are over. It is not difficult to see why politicians and the financial titans are so mutually congenial.

Casinos have tinted glass because they don't want to lose your attention. They don't want you looking outside. They, like Wall Street, want to keep you hypnotized with their games of chance and all of their bells and whistles. Like the casino, Wall Street does not care how many numbers (stocks) you decide to put your chips on. In fact, go ahead and play as much as you wish. They still get paid no matter what your results are. If you win occasionally—all the better! Now they have another story to tell to attract even more players. And get this—it is even better for Wall Street than the casinos in that Wall Street doesn't even have to pay the winners. Wall Street firms are simply the facilitators of the bets (transactions).

Whoever is making the rules and running the business of the game will always come out ahead. The promoters always make more money, don't they? The realms of sports and entertainment are other good examples. Professional athletes, movie stars, and musicians make huge money nowadays. No one can argue this. But their earnings pale in comparison to what team owners, movie producers, and event organizers make. Yet most often we don't even think about them. Furthermore, what are the odds of "making it big" in those fields of entertainment as a player or a performer? Dreamers come and go, yet the facilitators continue to get paid.

Now for the good news. The key to success for you as an investor does not lie in trying to beat the house at its own game but in owning the house. You can take matters into your own hands and turn the proverbial tables on Wall Street. How does this happen? You don't have to be confined to Wall Street's casino where you have to play on its slot machines and on its blackjack tables. In fact, you don't have to gamble at all.

If you own the casino, then your odds of winning are turned upside down. Capitalism gives everyone a chance to own the market, which, in its efficiency, expands and grows more than 80% of the time. Just like "owning the house," it's a system that lets you always eventually win.

How do you "own the house"? By owning the entire market. This is best accomplished by using a passive asset class approach to building your portfolio. You own the market by including thousands of securities (10,000 to 13,000) in a wide variety of asset classes, including many—micro-cap, small-cap international and emerging markets—not commonly seen in investor portfolios. This eliminates the burden of picking the winners. You own all of the winners. Yes, you own some losers too. But which side will you bet on concerning public companies: those whose stock value will go to $0 or those whose stock value will grow and thrive and make a profit in a free economy? Which happens more often? I believe history and the power of free markets make this a rhetorical question.

While there will always be those who try their hand at beating the system, ironically, it's the stock pickers and market timers (the gamblers) in Wall Street's game who keep the system efficient. In order for investors to win by owning the house, there must be those who also participate in losing games. In every casino, there are people who spend all day putting coins in the slot machine or rolling dice at the craps table, and most walk away empty-handed but still return the next day. These same individuals also know that the overwhelming majority of gamblers do not win more than they lose. The opposite is true if you own the market. Each day millions of gamblers walk into your "house," and by virtue of the power of the free market, you will eventually always win.

Investing should not be a gamble. It's only a gamble when you try to win playing by Wall Street's rules. Wall Street will take its experience and your money and turn them into your experience and its money. But when you take control, the system works in your favor—as it was meant to! Yes, the house will still win. But you will be the house.

Wall Street's Conflicts of Interest

I talk continuously on my program about the goals and motives of Wall Street. The hype inherent in Wall Street's marketing message must be there in order to create fear or greed and thus achieve success for itself. This is unfortunate for the unwary audience that is misled—or at minimum, receives biased opinions from Wall Street's "experts." To help prevent you from being misled, the following are several conflicts that perhaps you have not been aware of or you have not considered lately.

Incubator Funds

The incubator fund strategy works something like this: A fund company opens up several new funds, each with a slightly different strategy. The company may rely heavily on market timing, data mining, or the fair-haired manager with the golden touch. After each investment strategy runs its course, the odds are that one or two funds have hit a random hot streak and shown impressive one-year returns. These survivors can now be marketed and promoted for their high performance. The money starts flowing in.

After large amounts have been gathered from early investors, there is a clear incentive to drop high-risk stocks and replace them with lower-risk stock positions. Managers know that whatever stock picking good fortune has come their way will likely not stay. However, by taking chances on riskier stocks with other people's money, they stand to profit by being able to show higher-than-benchmark returns early in the life of the fund. Once they have those higher returns, they can tout them in advertisements and then migrate to safer stock positions. These incubator funds also present investors with higher internal fund expenses due to higher advertising costs and frequent trading. This is done in an effort to find the supposed winners and attract new money. This lab experiment usually ends up clobbering investors.

Active managers know that passive investing works, so they will often retreat to a passive portfolio to preserve those lucky early returns. This technique of eventually creating a closet index fund that maintains reasonable performance may sound a bit fishy. That's because it is. But the math—from the active manager's perspective—is sound. Once you start with a return higher than your benchmark—say, in the first 12 months—then if you go to a group of stocks that then mirrors your benchmark, you will forever have historical returns higher than your benchmark returns (less your fees). It is a mathematical certainty. Pretty shrewd of them, isn't it?

The incubation of funds is another method used by managers to feed the return-chasing desires of the general public. And for what?

So that the fund company can generate more revenue at the fund-holders' expense. The focus on short-term results is rarely spelled out in the fund prospectus per se. The prospectus will tout "long-term investing" and "diversification" and then trade frequently, searching for the right security mix for the fund company's funds to generate that early return. Numerous studies have shown that higher turnover in funds generally leads to below-average performance because of higher expenses. Timing strategies also exacerbate this problem as they try to predict up and down market moves.

To add insult to injury, it has been reported that less than half (43%) of the managers in U.S. stock funds own, in their personal portfolio, the fund they manage.[1] This is insulting and a plain example of the misaligned interests that exist between Wall Street and you as an individual investor.

Survivorship Bias

Another area within the world of active management that is little publicized is that of survivorship bias. This occurs when mutual funds fail to perform and are swept under the rug like dust bunnies.

According to a *Wall Street Journal* report in March 2004, mutual funds closed and/or merged at an astonishing rate in the previous three years.[2] They reported that 4,117 funds were either merged into other funds or closed in the combined years of 2001 through 2003. This eliminated more than 4,000 track records that were most likely below average.[3] When these track records are purged, a mutual fund family sees the average returns on all remaining funds go up—thus skewing the average and creating the survivorship bias. Now you might think because of the very difficult markets that occurred in this time frame (especially in 2001 and 2002 when the S&P 500 Index, for example, lost a combined 34%), that some mutual fund families might have had trouble staying in business. But that wasn't the story. Incredibly, during this same 2001 through 2003 period, an additional 6,161 new funds were created.[4]

I looked at this issue again to update the numbers and found that mutual fund company tactics did not change. An additional 6,902 new funds were created in the three-year period from 2005 through 2007.[5] This bull market period in the markets (the S&P 500 earned 26.2% during this three-year period) apparently inspired even more fund incubation in order to exploit investor greed at the time. After the dust settles from the financial crisis of 2008, I expect to see the same behavior from Wall Street when I check on fund mergers, closings, and new offerings in 2009 through 2010. This ongoing mutual fund shell game makes it more difficult to get accurate performance information. So beware of vanishing funds and the survivorship bias their demise causes.

Brokerage House Rating Systems

For stock pickers, "buy," "sell," and "hold" are three little words that have big meanings. (Hopefully, by the time you finish this book, they will mean nothing whatsoever to you.) It was reported in May 2008 that one of the giants in the industry, Merrill Lynch, was creating new internal rules which require that no more than 70% of its stock recommendations can be rated "buy," and no more than 30% can be rated "neutral."[6] This is an effort to reduce its optimistic recommendations and make its firm look more bearish— or objective—than its rivals.

There is an inherent conflict of interest between research and investment banking. In other words, brokerage firms would recommend the very stocks they were underwriting or "taking public." Those new offerings make the most money for the underwriters when they are bought—not sold—thus driving up the price and their take of the pot. There is a predisposition to push the stock with a "buy" recommendation. Studies have suggested analysts still have a bullish tendency that is out of touch with reality.

This idea of capping the percentage of picks in each category seems quite conflicting. I thought these brilliant stock pickers were supposed to be making recommendations based on the merit of each individual stock for the purposes of recommending it for your portfolio. How can they impose limits? Are there really artificially imposed quotas for stock picks? Yet another nonsensical example of how Wall Street's interests are not aligned with yours.

Financial Research

"Firms Pressure Mutual Fund Messenger" was a headline (in the back pages) that got my attention.[7] It was an obvious signal of a conflict of interest that would hurt the investing public. Sure enough, as we explored the story, it outlined that pressure had been brought to bear on data provider Financial Research Corporation (FRC). This company is a financial industry information source that reports inflows and outflows to mutual fund companies. The *Wall Street Journal* article indicated that this company would stop disclosing net sales information to the public. The article cautioned that "the decision shuts the door to the news media and other fund observers who want to know how fund sales are doing."

Why would such a decision be made? Whom is this information hurting? Possibly Fidelity Investments, Barclays Global Investors, and State Street Global Advisors. These are three big players that all posted year-to-date net outflows through February 2008. Apparently they did not like the information making its way to the general public. The Financial Research Corporation said the decision to cease this reporting practice was based on a backlash from fund companies who are its clients.[8] The FRC also said it wanted to shift resources to broaden services into industry commentary. Sam Campbell, director of research at the FRC, said, "We want to become more of an advocate to clients, and if part of that is shielding them from negative press, it's probably good for us and for them."[9] Translation: They want to hide factual, objective information if it doesn't suit the mutual fund company's marketing objective. Instead, the company appears to be delving into the business of "industry commentary" (that is, into subjective analysis to benefit its clients). Hasn't it forgotten about the individual investor?

Conflicts of interests are rampant in the financial services industry. It is always enlightening to learn what goes on behind the proverbial "curtain." Once you understand where the conflicts lie, you can make informed—and thus better—decisions about your money. One of the goals at *The Investing Revolution* is to monitor the financial industry for those conflicts that affect you and your individual portfolio and expose any that we feel pose a threat to your investing well-being.

The D.U.M.B. Funds

In January 2004, we started what turned out to be a very interesting five-year experiment. I charged my team with creating and incubating a family of hypothetical mutual funds.

Even though it was to be hypothetical, the pressure was on to come up with something that would have a chance at success—if only on paper. With this in mind, we charged into the fray, and after 20 minutes of painstaking research, we came up with the strategy that would have allowed us to beat virtually every actively managed domestic fund in the universe.

Rather than waste time with fundamental analysis or stock charting, we used a single criterion. We simply divided all of the stocks on the U.S. exchanges into state categories. We placed the companies into mutual funds based on their corporate headquarters' location. Naturally, we ended up with 50 funds in the incubator grouping. We named our new endeavor the Diversified United States Mutual Fund Balderdash—D.U.M.B.—Funds.

This hypothetical experiment allowed us to analyze the original 50 funds over a five-year time frame and observe how the 50 funds might have fared. As shown in Figure 2-1, the winner for the calendar year 2003 turned out to be the Wyoming Fund with an incredible one-year performance of 168.2%.[10] This was good enough to have beaten every one of the 2,121 actively managed U.S. mutual funds in the Morningstar universe with its sophisticated timing and picking strategies.[11]

These phenomenal one-year results would have allowed us to blow our own horn, and we could have advertised our tremendous results in every major media forum in the country. The average return of our 50 funds that year was a whopping 74.8%. Only one of our funds—Vermont at 22.2%—would have trailed the S&P 500 Index, which returned a very healthy 26.3% (not including dividends).[12] Can you imagine the kind of money that would have rolled into our fund family with this kind of story to tell?

Rank	Fund Name	1-Year Total Return, %	Rank	Fund Name	1-Year Total Return, %
1	Wyoming Fund	168.22	26	Michigan Fund	64.10
2	Oklahoma Fund	156.79	27	Nevada Fund	61.84
3	Arizona Fund	147.15	28	Louisiana Fund	60.93
4	Colorado Fund	145.18	29	Connecticut Fund	60.81
5	Utah Fund	140.44	30	North Dakota Fund	60.65
6	Washington Fund	118.33	31	New Hampshire Fund	59.53
7	California Fund	109.83	32	Pennsylvania Fund	59.04
8	Massachusetts Fund	106.61	33	Maine Fund	58.81
9	Georgia Fund	103.73	34	Arkansas Fund	56.90
10	Florida Fund	103.41	35	Iowa Fund	55.50
11	Minnesota Fund	99.78	36	Alabama Fund	55.36
12	Oregon Fund	91.87	37	Tennessee Fund	50.69
13	New York Fund	90.48	38	Wisconsin Fund	48.89
14	Alaska Fund	87.05	39	Delaware Fund	47.92
15	North Carolina Fund	86.37	40	Nebraska Fund	47.83
16	Idaho Fund	86.21	41	Indiana Fund	45.93
17	New Jersey Fund	84.17	42	Kansas Fund	45.66
18	Texas Fund	83.27	43	West Virginia Fund	45.30
19	Mississippi Fund	78.40	44	South Carolina Fund	43.92
20	Hawaii Fund	77.73	45	Ohio Fund	43.78
21	Illinois Fund	71.63	46	New Mexico Fund	42.91
22	Maryland Fund	69.73	47	Missouri Fund	41.15
23	Virginia Fund	66.37	48	Montana Fund	30.07
24	Rhode Island Fund	65.99	49	South Dakota Fund	29.55
25	Kentucky Fund	65.93	50	Vermont Fund	22.21

Figure 2-1 D.U.M.B. Funds Performance for 2003

But playing the role of the greedy mutual fund marketers, we went even further. By lopping off the bottom 10 funds, we could bring our average fund return up 9.0% to 83.8%. As we liquidate Indiana, Kansas, West Virginia, South Carolina, Ohio, New Mexico, Missouri, Montana, South Dakota, and Vermont, the average return of the fund skyrockets. This is an example of how funds are liquidated and merged with other funds—otherwise known as "creating survivorship bias." Now the lower returns would be forever invisible to the investing public.

We could advertise these incredible returns for the next two years until we could get to our next marketing milestone—the three-year returns. Because of the tremendous performance year in which we started this venture (2003), the three-year numbers were almost guaranteed to be superb as well. And they were, as shown in Figure 2-2.

Rank	Fund Name	3-Year Annualized, %	Rank	Fund Name	3-Year Annualized, %
1	Nevada Fund	85.94	26	New York Fund	21.64
2	Wyoming Fund	59.31	27	Maryland Fund	21.17
3	Oklahoma Fund	39.07	28	Rhode Island Fund	20.54
4	Delaware Fund	35.67	29	Mississippi Fund	20.34
5	Texas Fund	33.89	30	Kentucky Fund	20.23
6	Colorado Fund	32.96	31	Virginia Fund	20.15
7	Alaska Fund	31.83	32	California Fund	20.01
8	Arizona Fund	29.79	33	Missouri Fund	19.92
9	Tennessee Fund	29.33	34	Pennsylvania Fund	19.91
10	North Dakota Fund	29.22	35	Ohio Fund	19.73
11	Montana Fund	27.74	36	Georgia Fund	19.71
12	Washington Fund	27.11	37	Wisconsin Fund	19.66
13	Connecticut Fund	24.95	38	Louisiana Fund	19.44
14	Alabama Fund	24.59	39	North Carolina Fund	18.89
15	Arkansas Fund	24.54	40	Kansas Fund	18.75
16	South Dakota Fund	24.52	41	Maine Fund	18.66
17	New Mexico Fund	24.19	42	Iowa Fund	18.63
18	Illinois Fund	23.91	43	Nebraska Fund	18.44
19	Massachusetts Fund	23.71	44	Utah Fund	15.60
20	Hawaii Fund	23.46	45	South Carolina Fund	15.42
21	Idaho Fund	23.02	46	Indiana Fund	14.31
22	Oregon Fund	22.99	47	New Jersey Fund	14.20
23	Florida Fund	22.60	48	Michigan Fund	12.23
24	West Virginia Fund	22.28	49	New Hampshire Fund	5.08
25	Minnesota Fund	21.66	50	Vermont Fund	3.31

Figure 2-2   D.U.M.B. Funds Performance for 2005

Of the original 50 funds, the top 40 funds had an average three-year annualized return of 25.4%. This compared again quite favorably to the most watched of index barometers—the S&P 500—which returned 14.4% for the same three-year period.[13]

But while beating the S&P by 11% was outstanding, we wanted more. So we simply dropped our 40 funds down to the top 25; the shaded funds are again liquidated from the fund return. This move increased the average return of the remaining funds to 30.3%. Why settle for 11% when you can bury them with 16% and market the heck out of it? We could have bought full-page ads in the *Wall Street Journal* and *USA Today* at about $250,000 a pop, for starters. Our PR director could have easily booked us on all the major financial talking-head programs. What a tour of triumph it would have been for us—the geniuses of the investing world—and it would only get better.

At long last our experiment was now going to really pay off. It would be one thing to have one- or three-year averages that looked good. But our credibility would be greatly increased at the five-year mark. Five years means stability and creates a perception of a methodology that works throughout different market cycles.

But not unexpectedly, a reversion to the mean occurred as our average for 25 funds shrunk to only 12.6% annualized. This would be compared to 12.8% for the S&P 500 for the five-year period.[14]

Uh oh. The jig was up. Or maybe not. Time for our old friend survivorship bias to enter the scene again. After all this hard work and gathering assets for five years, we would not let a little thing like a drop in returns undermine our efforts. So it was time to again repackage our 50 funds and roll out the "Top 10 U.S. Funds" (see Figure 2-3). So we folded the bottom 15 remaining funds, changed the name of our fund family, and revamped all of our marketing materials to reflect our superiority. The average return for our top 10 would be a whopping 18.7% per year—almost a full 6% higher than the S&P 500. So not only would we have already gathered hundreds of millions of dollars over the last five years with the returns we had published but now we could say the following:

"Five years of intense research has led us to develop a foolproof strategy for selecting the top 10 states in the union for your investment dollars. Based on our average annual return of nearly 20% per year for the group of funds, we believe our methodology has proven to be the best way to invest. We anticipate that these funds will remain open to new investors for at least the remainder of this calendar year and probably until the end of 2010."

Rank	Fund Name	5-Year Annualized, %	Rank	Fund Name	5-Year Annualized, %
1	Wyoming Fund	31.05	26	Illinois Fund	9.96
2	North Dakota Fund	21.73	27	Missouri Fund	9.92
3	Idaho Fund	20.79	28	Tennessee Fund	9.09
4	Oklahoma Fund	20.01	29	North Carolina Fund	9.02
5	South Dakota Fund	19.60	30	Pennsylvania Fund	8.93
6	Alaska Fund	18.97	31	Rhode Island Fund	8.61
7	Louisiana Fund	18.84	32	South Carolina Fund	8.52
8	Texas Fund	16.03	33	Kansas Fund	8.40
9	Nevada Fund	15.84	34	Arizona Fund	8.23
10	Delaware Fund	15.42	35	Georgia Fund	7.52
11	Kentucky Fund	13.37	36	New York Fund	6.48
12	Colorado Fund	13.23	37	Hawaii Fund	6.31
13	Iowa Fund	13.13	38	Virginia Fund	6.16
14	Connecticut Fund	12.33	39	Arkansas Fund	6.13
15	Washington Fund	11.54	40	California Fund	5.99
16	Maryland Fund	11.38	41	New Mexico Fund	5.69
17	West Virginia Fund	11.16	42	Indiana Fund	5.57
18	Wisconsin Fund	11.12	43	Utah Fund	4.66
19	Ohio Fund	10.95	44	Oregon Fund	4.29
20	Nebraska Fund	10.94	45	Florida Fund	3.10
21	Massachusetts Fund	10.82	46	New Jersey Fund	2.22
22	Maine Fund	10.80	47	Alaska Fund	2.09
23	Vermont Fund	10.69	48	Michigan Fund	1.52
24	Mississippi Fund	10.45	49	Montana Fund	1.27
25	Minnesota Fund	10.12	50	New Hampshire Fund	−2.90

Figure 2-3 D.U.M.B. Funds Performance for 2007

That last little sense of urgency would bring in the money in a hurry. Not only that, we could have rolled out the compelling five-year performance chart showing how an investor would have an additional $5,303, or 29%, more money in our Top 10 U.S. Funds versus the S&P 500 Index on an initial investment of $10,000 (Figure 2-4).

This is all a quite sad depiction of some of the thinking that goes on inside the heads of Wall Street tyrants as they try to remove you from your money. You may say, "Well, it is somewhat tricky, but didn't investors get good returns?" Maybe, but probably not.

The chances of picking 1 of the 50 funds that beat the top 10 group average were 6 out of 50, or 12%. Obviously those were not very good odds. Therefore, the vast majority of investors would not have experienced the higher early returns of the eventual top 10. But Wall Street marketers know that a small chance is still just

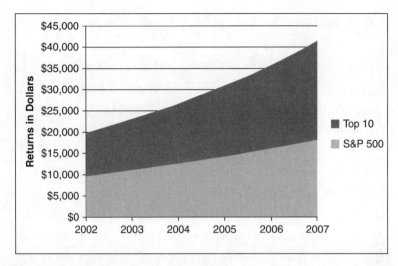

Figure 2-4 Five-Year Performance of the Top 10 U.S. Funds versus the S&P 500 Index for 2003 through 2007

enough to coax investors into trying. So goes the world of actively managed mutual funds and exchange-traded funds (ETFs).

It is also notable that the mutual fund incubators don't care about the "ones they missed." For example, our South Dakota Fund was actually dismissed after year 1 because it finished number 49 in the rankings of 50. Had it been kept all five years, it would have ended up number 5 with a 19.6% average annual return. But this casualty of the process would not have mattered because we still would have ended up with what we wanted—returns we could tout as real even though no investor had likely ever received them.

As time goes on and I continue to report on this experiment, the returns will continue to revert to the mean. They will get closer and closer to market return and the common indexes such as the S&P 500. However, in real life, the money managers in this experiment would likely have been long gone to another mutual fund family trying to parlay their superstar status and reputation into bigger salaries and higher positions.

By the way, lest you think this incubation and survivorship bias business is not a common reality, here is an excerpt from a *Wall Street Journal* article entitled "Claymore Plans to Cut Its ETFs by about Half":

> Claymore Securities, Inc., announced Friday that it has decided to shut down almost half of its 37 funds. . . . The funds will be closed to new investment on February 20 and will be "liquidated," or dissolved, about a week later. The 11 funds being shuttered represent less than 2% of the firm's U.S. ETF assets, with many recently holding less than $5 million in assets each. "No one wanted" the products that are closing, says Christian Magoon, senior managing director and head of the ETF group at Claymore. In fact, much of the current money in the funds is "seed capital," or the original start-up assets, rather than new investor cash.[15]

Hopefully, you will read reports such as this with just a little different perspective after taking another look behind "the curtain" of Wall Street.

If you see a very active manager with superior results in the short run, it is either just plain dumb luck or quite likely the result of an incubator type of strategy. This exercise shows how one ridiculously simple and random criterion can outperform the best-funded investment management teams on Wall Street.

P.S.: This was just an experiment. It is hypothetical. Neither the D.U.M.B. nor the Top 10 U.S. Funds exist. Sorry. We know you return chasers are disappointed. And so am I—because boy, could we have made a lot of money! Extending the time frame through 2008 might have changed the data, but the marketing ploy would have remained intact. In fact, stay tuned to *The Investing Revolution* for the announcement of how we used the 2008 election year to capitalize on red and blue states for a six-year return success, even during the most difficult downturn in American history.

John Stossel's Clear Look at the Issues

John Stossel is the award-winning news anchor and correspondent for *20/20* on ABC. His programs take a skeptical look at a wide array of issues, from education to gun control, and they have earned him 19 Emmy Awards and recognition as "the most consistently thought provoking TV reporter of our time."[16] Stossel joined *The Investing Revolution* to discuss his book *Myths, Lies, and Downright Stupidity: Get Out the Shovel—Why Everything You Know Is Wrong.*[17]

While the interview was not focused on investing issues alone, I thought his insight would be good for our listeners because the topics we discussed with Stossel demonstrated how people's thinking about various issues can be skewed by world events—especially as they are reported by the media. Here are his thoughts as he expressed them to us in our 2006 interview on several practical economic issues of our day.[18]

On why we shouldn't restrict the outsourcing of jobs:

"It would kill jobs. It's the freedom of trade, of goods, and of jobs that have created the millions of jobs we have in America. We have lost 390 million jobs over the past 10 years, and some of that's because of outsourcing. But during that same time we gained 410 million jobs, 20 million more than we lost, and it's outsourcing that partly makes that possible. A study at Dartmouth found that the companies that outsource the most are the ones that hire the most Americans. The money they save on that Indian engineer does get reinvested in American workers and things that Americans do better. And people say, 'Well, all the leftover jobs are hamburger-flipping service jobs,' but that's not true. If it were true, average wages would be going down in America and they're not."

On price gouging:

"Nobody in economics calls it 'gouging'; they just call it 'sudden price spikes.' It's only dumb politicians and reporters that call it 'price gouging.' When there's a disaster, it's common for prices to go up because [goods and even some services are] in short supply, and that's good because that's what encourages people to bring more stuff in. I interviewed a guy who after Hurricane Katrina saw that people had no power in Mississippi. So he bought 20 generators, loaded them into his truck, and drove 600 miles to Mississippi. People surrounded his truck eager to buy them—he was going to sell them for twice what he paid for them—but Mississippi authorities locked him up for four days and confiscated his generators. Now, who did that benefit? The Mississippi attorney general proudly bragged of how they'd enforced their law against evil price rises during the time of an emergency. But people needed the generators. It was the big price spike that got him to drive there. Likewise the 'kind' store that doesn't raise the price for water, batteries, and things like that after the disaster, sells out. Soon the shelves are empty. People stock up; they buy more than they need.

By raising the price, he makes sure that the batteries go to the people who really need them, and by raising the price, he inspires other people to get off their butts and bring new batteries in. Milton Friedman, the economist, was the one who in my 20/20 program summed it up by saying the price gougers are heroes. It's tough to explain to people, but prices are more than just prices; they're information—and when government locks them into place, they just create shortages."

On people paying more than they ever have for gas:

"[Consider] what it takes to get gas here: It's got to be dug out of the ground from five miles beneath the earth (the drills even bend to get to it), and then it gets shipped across an ocean, refined into three types of gasoline, put in trucks that cost $100,000 each, [then] shipped to stations that have all this expensive equipment so you don't blow yourself up. And it still costs less than the bottled water they sell at these gas stations. The government's take—the taxes— are far greater than the profits of the oil companies."

On raising the minimum wage:

"We all want poor workers to make more, but if government could do that with a minimum wage, why stop at $7 an hour? That's not very much. Why not $12, why not $30 an hour? When government artificially raises wages above the market price, above supply and demand, then some of those employers won't hire those workers, or they'll ship the jobs to India or they'll buy a machine instead. It's the low minimum wage that allows entry-level workers to get a start in the workforce. We used to have people washing our windshields in gas stations. We don't now because it doesn't pay the gas station to hire a kid because they have to pay the higher wage. Kids can't learn construction on the job because they have to be paid a minimum wage and because of all the regulations. We're taking the bottom rung off the opportunity ladder by passing these laws."

On investing "experts":

"All kinds of people make these predictions and act like they know what they're talking about, and you would think they would. They work at it full time, they're smart guys, they went to good colleges, and they study the stocks long hours every day. Who should know better? And yet, Morningstar, which keeps track of the actively traded mutual funds, found that 95% of them do worse than the averages, than the S&P. In other words, blindfolded, throwing darts at the stock table or having a monkey pick the stocks for you would do better than 95% of the professional stock traders. It's because all the information is out there. Everybody has the same information, and to beat it, you have to be unbelievably smart. Only 5% of them are able to do that, and because you invest with these funds that do a lot of trading—and they all want you to trade because that's where they make their commission money—odds are you're going to do worse than just buying an index fund."

On Americans' becoming more gullible:

"I don't think we have evidence that we're more gullible than we were. People have always been gullible about some things. Some things are just intuitive and wrong. The idea that more weird stuff happens on the night of the full moon is because we remember patterns. If you're at the police station and it's pretty wild and you look out the window and you see a full moon, you draw conclusions. And if it's wild on some night when there's no full moon, you don't remember that. So, there's always been misinformation. What's surprising now is that even with all the new media we have, there's still so much garbage out there; but that's because reporters by and large are ignorant when it comes to economics. They're not interested. They're interested in what happened today, they're interested in politics, theater, but not economics. People interested in economics tend not to go into journalism."

John Stossel brings a unique perspective to all of his work. It is hard not to love his straightforward approach to getting to the bottom of things. His joining us on the program was a real treat. He cuts through the sound bite world in which we live as few people can. I was so encouraged to hear someone with his reputation for candor and objectivity endorse a passive approach to investing.

Reconstituting Index Funds and ETFs with Gene Fama Jr.

Your main goal as an investor should be to capture the return of the entire stock market, a universe composed of different asset classes. Investors frequently attempt to capture the returns of the market by investing in index funds. While index funds are a good solution for achieving broad exposure, they have potential shortfalls that investors must face.

By definition, index investing outsources the investment blueprint to a third-party source and relies on that source to define the asset class. Many indexes were originally created to serve as an average of all the managers of a particular style rather than to serve the purpose of an investment strategy. As such, frequently, the securities that make up a particular index may not accurately represent an entire asset class or the market. In many cases, an index utilizes a smaller group of stocks and may represent only a portion of the market.

Given this reality, the results tend to be different as well.

Gene Fama Jr. adapts academic research of efficient market philosophies to the real world of investing at Dimensional Fund Advisors. When I visited with Gene Fama Jr. in December 2006, he explained, "Index funds are just an arbitrary definition of an asset class.[19] It is hard to represent the 8,000 stocks in the market with just 500 stocks. By nature, an index manager's mandate is to ensure that his holdings mimic the makeup of an index exactly."

In addition to focusing solely on tracking error, another problem potentially arises when those indexes, such as the S&P 500, are reconstituted. Reconstitution is the process by which a commercial index makes a decision to add or subtract companies from the index. Indexes have discretion on the process and timing of making and carrying out this decision. This reconstitution of indexes is something we refer to as "active management light."

As traditional index funds attempt to replicate commercial benchmarks, reconstitution may result in greater inefficiencies and higher costs in a portfolio. When an index sponsor announces the securities to be added or deleted from its composition, managers seeking to closely track the index must buy and sell to adjust their portfolios on the reconstitution date. Prices may be temporarily distorted by the spike in demand from numerous index managers seeking to buy or sell securities on the same day. Other market participants will then take advantage of this temporary demand.

Market impact is a zero-sum game; to the extent that one investor is penalized by the reconstitution effect, someone else enjoys a benefit. In any negotiated transaction, the party in a hurry to make the deal is at a disadvantage. Although index managers may successfully track the index, their trading strategy may penalize the return of the index itself. Investors, because they often make low tracking error a priority, bear the costs of this activity. (Having a low tracking error means mimicking as closely as possible the index in question.) As Gene Fama Jr. put it in our discussion, "When you make a stock trade, you want to make it based on price and not time."

The prices of securities added to an index rise before the effective date—then decay after the effective date. As you can see in Figure 2-5, international indexes, such as the MSCI EAFE Index, also experience the same problem. And the amount of decay in the price at which stocks must be purchased is even more significant.[20]

Stocks that are added to an index commonly enter a period of abnormal price escalation after the announcement and through the effective date. This results from speculative buying pressure. After the effective date, stocks experience a price decay resulting from lightened demand. Traditional index managers with rigid tracking policies must acquire the stock when the price is climbing. Buying the stock before the effective date may reduce tracking errors, but it also raises both acquisition and transaction costs.

A more flexible trading policy enables passive portfolio managers to avoid the heaviest trading days and higher prices by deferring the

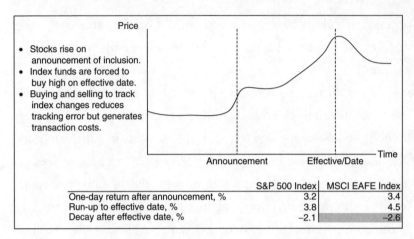

Figure 2-5 The Effect of Index Reconstitution on Stock Prices
Source: Dimensional Fund Advisors (DFA), Santa Monica, Calif.

transactions to more opportune times. Following this strategy can add value through the resulting cost reductions and lower acquisition prices. The flexibility that is present with asset class funds is a major reason why there is more consistency and a greater return potential with them than there is with traditional index funds.

Exchange-traded funds (ETFs) are a popular index-type of investment vehicles that have made their way to the stage in recent years. Like other index funds, the costs associated with these vehicles are typically low, but they have the same issue in regards to replication and reconstitution of an index. They were created in a bid to attract smaller investors as well as anyone who might wish to trade in and out of the market on a daily or even minute-by-minute basis. This is because they are treated like stocks whose prices fluctuate during the trading day—versus mutual funds, in which a transaction is conducted based on the day's closing market value. This real-time trading characteristic of ETFs inherently creates the idea that investors should watch the market closely and buy or sell at just the right moment to take advantage of market moves. This sends an unusual mixed message of "actively traded indexes."

ETFs are also touted as a good way to gain sector exposure in various industries or countries. However, often these types of ETFs can be highly concentrated; with the majority of their holdings in just a few stocks. This lack of diversification creates a real vulnerability to changes in the price of a single security. Additionally, ETFs and other sector-specific investment vehicles are subject to "event risk"—that is, untimely, and sometimes catastrophic, events that adversely affect particular industry sectors or regions of the world. There is no need to expose a portfolio to these types of risks.

Unfortunately, ETFs will likely remain popular with pickers and timers as they continue to be cleverly marketed. Remember also that ETFs were invented by Wall Street because passive investments such as index funds were taking away a substantial amount of business. The ETFs provided a way of acting passively but keeping that element of active trading intact. In recent years, the newer ETFs flooding the financial marketplace are presenting more overt active stock picking and market timing strategies. So while the early ETFs were designed to rival other passive approaches, Wall Street has gravitated back to investment products that are designed to capitalize on your greed or your fear of missing out.

The reconstitution of index funds and ETFs forces money managers to buy at a higher price on behalf of their fundholders. These investment vehicles also do not usually provide adequate representation of the full depth and breadth of the securities markets—either domestically or internationally. In my book *Wealth Without Worry*, I said that on a scale of 1 to 10, index funds are at a 7 and active management is a 1 or 2.[21] Obviously, indexing is far preferable to the myriad alternatives that Wall Street firms offer at a much greater profit margin for them. So while indexing is a far better way to invest as compared to active stock picking and market timing, it still falls short of being the optimum strategy available to most individual investors—that is, asset class investing.

Bottom Line

Many of Wall Street's conflicts of interest are obvious and have been in public view for years. Others are not as evident, and we take it as our mission to continue to point out all conflicts that affect your investing life.

The financial mess we have all witnessed in the large storied financial firms such as Bear Stearns, Lehman Brothers, Merrill Lynch, and AIG (the list could unfortunately go on and on) is a testament, I believe, to the out-of-touch, bulletproof mentality of today's Wall Street executives. My hope is that you will be able to see through the incredibly clever marketing campaigns that tug at your emotions and play on your greed or fear in the years to come. The Wall Street salespeople are not going away, regardless of market extremes—whether high or low. Your financial future depends on your sifting through the noise generated by the financial tyrants. You must do so if you are to experience wealth without worry.

three

WALL STREET'S METHODS

Subtlety may deceive you; integrity never will.
—Oliver Cromwell

The financial shenanigans that came to light in 2008 have rightly brought into question the motives and integrity of Wall Street's leadership. While I believe unflinchingly that our financial system, and thus our markets, will be restored, the toll inflicted by Wall Street's Ponzi schemes is likely to be incalculable.

As markets recover and over time as folks forget what has happened, Wall Street minions will creep back in to take advantage of individual investors as they always do. That means convincing you that they will help you time the market ups and downs and pick winners in the stock market in spite of their consistent abject failure in these efforts over the decades. The tyrants dwelling on Manhattan's lower end depend on you to place your confidence in these methods of producing wealth in order to create their own. Every action they take is geared toward making you believe that they have the answers and that you do not have a prayer without their direction. They will spare no expense to craft this message in a compelling and convincing manner. Fighting this misleading guidance is central to *The Investing Revolution's* cause.

Chief among Wall Street's methods is the use of advertising to communicate its "expertise."

Tuned In and Freaked Out

The following quote was posted at editorandpublisher.com in March 2008:

> According to new data released by the Newspaper Association of America, total print advertising revenue in 2007 plunged 9.4% to $42 billion compared to 2006—the most severe percent decline since the association started measuring advertising expenditures in 1950.[1]

Why was this bad news for individual investors? What possible effect could a loss in advertising revenue have on your portfolio unless your investments are biased toward public media firms and therefore have an abnormally large allocation to such stocks?

I was concerned that this 2007 report was bad news for investors because I am always afraid that the Wall Street media partners will ratchet up the fear (or greed) even more when they see the opportunity to do so. One of Wall Street's most effective methods for achieving its goals is to make sure you are tuned in and freaked out. Headlines are often influenced by salacious storylines to attract more viewers. You may have difficulty differentiating between true objective journalism in which both sides are fairly presented and subjective journalism in which only one side is presented.

How do all media organizations make money? They sell advertising—pure and simple. But there is a misconception that the personalities in the media—including the financial media—are in their profession to give helpful information and solid advice. While they may provide helpful tidbits and guidance in some instances, that is really not what they get paid to do. They get paid to attract an audience so that their employers can sell ad space. If they can also disseminate helpful information, then that is great. But the bottom line is the bottom line. And by the way, who can blame them for that? There is nothing inherently wrong with knowing your revenue source and meeting the demand for a product or service. Let them sell all they can in the name of free capital markets. I just don't want you to watch the market ticker shows and get the impression that the content and intent of these financial programs is purely benevolent.

So what sells advertising? Numbers. Specifically the number of readers, listeners, and viewers. How do those numbers grow? They grow by getting you to tune in. Their primary method for accomplishing this is by using hype (short for "hyperbole," by the way). Unfortunately the easiest news to hype is bad news. "If it bleeds it leads"—so goes the broadcast news mantra. It is no different in the financial media. In fact, it may be even worse in the financial services realm. That is why the truth about the media's motives— when understood—could actually lead to investing success with consistency and far less volatility in your own portfolio. The hype that elicits more emotion boosts the possibility of making panic decisions to sell low and buy high—the exact opposite of what you want to do and know you should do. When you realize that the talking-head financial channels are there to accomplish one goal—sell advertising—then you can learn to ignore the noise that comes from these sources and thus avoid making the bad decisions that can often result from allowing the media to influence you.

What is even more disturbing about the whole arrangement is that Wall Street firms tend to be the most frequent advertisers on the financial shows. Partnering in this manner makes good business sense, of course. The media is in the business of selling advertising, and the big financial firms want an audience to whom they can sell their services. Wall Street giants eagerly pay for the hype that inevitably occurs in a doom-and-gloom bear market or a bull market run wild. (They don't care which it is—remember the dot-com craze?) Advertising naturally avoids concrete promises and cultivates a sort of vagueness that charms us. This all plays out very well for Wall Street firms who are some of the very best at producing emotional ads that tug at the audience's heart strings and present a message of a bright future—using their products and services, of course.

Wall Street firms also spend millions of dollars each year studying your buying habits. They know that you most often make money decisions when you are in one of two emotional states: feeling scared to death or feeling invincible. Translation: They use the old dependable standbys of fear and greed. How many times have you made your wisest decisions when you were in a highly emotional state in any realm of life? You get the point. Wall Street firms depend on your moving your money in one direction or the other frequently. Most investors are more than willing to comply when they are in an emotional dither. And when you move money, the firms rake in fees, commissions, and transaction charges.

In this savvy, media-rich world in which we find ourselves, investors can easily be manipulated. The best way to avoid being manipulated is to completely cast off the mainstream financial media and their schemes of hype, half-truths, and conflicts of interest. If you can't break away cold turkey, at least maybe you can see them now more for their entertainment value (à la *Mad Money with Jim Cramer*) than for their serious advice.

Weston Wellington Reviews *Fortune*'s Top Stocks for the Decade

In early July 2008, the markets were tumbling. The Dow had fallen about 13.5% in the last 60 days or so, and I felt it was time to relax a bit, take a deep breath, allow our audiences to get a little perspective on the markets, and have a little fun.[2] What better way to have some fun than to check in on Mr. Weston Wellington.

Weston J. Wellington has joined us frequently on our radio program.[3] He is an engaging speaker, and I secretly covet his perfectly toned radio voice. He is a Yale-educated bloke from Boston with a gregarious personality combined with intelligence and a supreme wit. His talents include singing a cappella comical songs about the dark side of the financial industry (his gangly stature and facial expressions always add to the humor of his gig). As vice president with Dimensional Fund Advisors, one of his duties finds him in charge of media research—and nobody does it better.

Besides the ability to time the market, there is no skill more touted up and down Wall Street than the brokerage firms' abilities to pick stocks. In 2008, Wellington shared with our listeners his professional hobby of recycling old news for current analysis. In a follow-up to *Fortune* magazine's recommended stock picks for the decade, we were able to discuss some of the not-so-hot picks previously reported.[4] *Fortune* has published an annual *Retirement Guide* issue for many years. Wellington used the retirement issue appearing back in mid-1999, and he found that it had followed a very concentrated approach and had suggested only 10 stocks (interestingly, *Fortune* had changed to a 40-stock selection by 2002). Relying on both outside experts and in-house quantitative analysis, *Fortune* at that time had assembled a collection of firms "with the size, stability, and earnings power to carry investors through whatever the market throws their way in the decades to come."

I am confident that when *Fortune* publishes these stock picks on occasion, the magazine is not counting on someone like 'ole Weston Wellington keeping track of these predictions year by year. I am sure the publisher figures that nearly everyone throws these old magazines out. That is what I do. Wellington keeps them, and I am glad he does. He considers them his "wine list." He likes to put them away and let them mature and age, and then he opens them up to test whether the aroma is sweet or sour.

Concerning the 10 stocks that *Fortune* selected, the publication said it had worked hard to select companies with "the right business plan and the right management." As Wellington understates, "Time has not been kind to most of their recommendations." How unkind? Out of the 10 stocks, 9 have underperformed the S&P 500 Index including 2 of the selections whose shares have been determined as worthless in bankruptcy court.

So we conducted our own research, between *Fortune*'s quoting date of July 14, 1999, and Friday, June 13, 2008, and we found the

Fortune 10 had underperformed 50.7%, on average, while the S&P 500 Index (excluding dividends) fell only 3%.[5]

Further findings from our own research gave us the parallel findings and bad news for investors. Ouch!

Isn't this always the story? Stock picking "gurus" are looking for the "right management and the right business plan" in a concentrated set of 10 stocks or 25 or 50. It does not matter. Wellington's analysis was genius, and it provides such a great microcosm view of what happens when investors try to pick individual stocks using advice from the financial media. These are folks that supposedly know what they are talking about. After all, they have careers at one of the premier financial publications in the world. Let's look closer at their "chosen 10."

> *American International Group.* Here was the quote in the *Fortune* article: "A diverse product mix and an international presence should enable this insurance giant to grow earnings consistently into the next decade. AIG has maintained a 15% annual growth rate over the last 2 decades and shows no signs of slowing down." What was AIG's return over the nine-year period? Negative 46%.[6] Evidently their decade-long earnings growth ended early. Not only that but we (taxpayers) took an 85% stake in the company—like it or not—when the U.S. government had to bail out AIG in September 2008. Bad start for the *Fortune* list.

> *How about Bristol-Myers Squibb?* Everyone wants to buy health care and big pharma. *Fortune* called it "a smart prescription for long-term investors." If you are going to

make a sector bet, here is the company for the health-care sector. Results? Down 72%.[7]

Cisco Systems was hailed in this manner. "The king of networking should continue to thrive thanks to the explosive growth of the Internet and rising demand for its communication products." Wow, that sounds right, doesn't it? Down 21% for the period.[8]

Ford Motor Company. "A flurry of acquisitions has given Ford a high level of stable margin luxury brands including Lincoln, Volvo, Jaguar, and Aston Martin." Down 80%.[9]

Home Depot. How many times to you go there each month? I go twice a weekend! This has got to be a reasonable recommendation, right? Down 37%.[10]

IBM. It was down only 8%.[11]

Concerning Tyco International. *Fortune* magazine stated, "Strategic acquisitions have helped propel earnings." How did it do? Down 78%.[12]

Johnson & Johnson. *Fortune* finally had a pick that found plus territory. It was up 38%.[13] However, unfortunately that is the only positive pick they had out of the 10. And furthermore, that 38% return, when annualized, is only 3.6% per year. Not too exciting.

We saved the worst two for last:

UAL Corporation. *Fortune* asked, "Can an airline be a growth stock? This one can thanks to a strong domestic hub network and the signs of recovery in Asia." Down 100%.[14]

MCI WorldCom.   Worthless. And *Fortune* said, "When it comes to the fast-growing telecom sector and the technology solution, it is hard to find a better bet than MCI World-Com." Down 100%.[15] That is a hard number to look at. Especially if you had been an employee who had put your faith and money in MCI WorldCom's future.

What can you say? This is the kind of thing that happens in the stock picking world every day—literally. Investors anchor on the most recent trend. Ford was coming back, technology looked good. Health care was where everyone wanted to be. So those trends looked like good investments. Those 10 stocks that *Fortune* recommended at the time were all losers with the exception of Johnson & Johnson (if you call 3.6% per year winning). How could anyone have possibly missed on all of them?

I challenge any human on earth—"professional" stock picker or not—to find 10 companies that will lose value the way these did. If we had a contest in which the worst stock pickers would be the winners, there is no way the winner-loser (I am confused too) could perform as poorly as *Fortune* did! Furthermore, if we had set up two groups and charged one group with finding the 10 best stocks and the other with finding the 10 worst, I would submit that the average of the two groups would be close to equal. It would be a great investing and social experiment.

The point is that there is no one smart enough to have picked this poorly even if he or she had tried. And yet incredibly—as Wellington so ably pointed out to us—it happened. I mentioned that *Fortune*'s 10 stocks dropped in value as a group by 50.7%. Your $100,000 retirement account was worth about $49,300 if you had the misFortune of picking up that magazine at your doctor's office that summer in 1999 and thought it was giving you credible advice.[16] (I shudder to think how many investors did just that.)

Wellington has stated that his motivation was "not to skewer the stock picking skills of Fortune editors. Many of these stocks were also recommended by some of the world's most prominent analysts and money managers. Fortune editors in 1999 were well aware that many investors were fixated on Internet stocks and emphasized the importance of holding a diversified list of proven companies. Considering the widespread conviction at the time that growth stocks in general and technology stocks in particular were destined to outperform for the indefinite future, Fortune's choices, drawn from a wide array of industries, looked quite sensible. But time and time again, market participants are blindsided by unexpected events. Even today, it's difficult to find fault with the reasoning behind the various recommendations."

As for the perspective we wanted to give our listeners on The Investing Revolution, I investigated the question of what happened in the market in general during this same nine-year time frame. The answer is charted in Figure 3-1.

Real estate investment trusts (REITs)	199.08%
Emerging markets	209.65%
U.S. small-cap value	155.47%
International small-cap value	225.85%
International large-cap value	140.43%

Figure 3-1 A Comparison of Total Returns for the Period of July 1, 1999, through June 30, 2008

Investors may look at these results and say, "Sure, those areas of the market did much better, but how could we have known to select those areas to invest in any more than *Fortune* knew which individual stocks to pick?" Well, you couldn't. However, just about any area of the market that was more diversified than having only a few stocks would have fared much better. In other words, if you had put all your money in an asset class consisting of international small-cap value funds, it may have been a wild ride, but it would not have been as difficult as it was for *Fortune's* chosen 10 by any means.

The main understanding I hope you can glean from this analysis is that diversification is key. A stock portfolio that utilized an asset class approach to diversification for 100% of its holdings would have grown by 114.27% during this nine-year time frame.[17] No picking, no timing, no worries. Ponder that for a moment.

Spam (the Meat) versus Technology

I know I put myself alongside a relatively small number of people when I tell you that I have always liked canned meat—deviled ham, corned beef, and especially Spam. Yes, that is the meat product produced by Hormel Foods Corporation. I remember as a boy growing up in the Texas panhandle smelling the aroma of the Spam on the stove top as my grandfather ("Big Daddy") was making Spam and tomato and mayonnaise sandwiches on toasted bread. That sandwich along with a half-plate of Fritos and Texas sweet tea was a gourmet meal. My stomach growls and my mouth waters even to this day when I think of it. The Hormel people claim they've sold over 5 billion cans of Spam since its introduction in 1937, so someone else out there must like the stuff too.[18]

Boring stocks like Hormel sometimes generate impressive returns. Wall Street leads you to believe that when you consider buying a stock, you should carefully assess the product or service the company provides in order to judge its worthiness. If you had a hunch in the mid-1980s that one day almost every single American would walk around with a cell phone on his or her ear, then you would have naturally been attracted to the mobile telecommunications sector. Furthermore, you would have sought the best companies therein. But there is more to it than that. What about the firm's management team? Is there an internal legal issue brewing that could undermine the whole operation? Is there an unscrupulous CEO in charge? Is the sector in its infancy, and has the fallout from the inevitable new industry bubble not occurred yet? How will industry consolidation affect the stock's price when it occurs? Is the company susceptible to systematic (market) risk to a greater degree than other companies in other sectors?

If the only factor were determining whether or not a firm had a good product or service, stock picking would be easier than it is. In fact, the value of a stock depends on many factors.

To illustrate the point, we observed the long-term results of Hormel and a company that most investors would likely consider a more exciting offering—Motorola, maker of electronics, cell phones, and so on. Expanding on this idea, in Figure 3-2 we present for comparison purposes two portfolios of stocks that include Hormel and Motorola and their respective performances for the 27-year period from January 1, 1981, through December 31, 2007.[19]

We daresay that few professional money managers would have passionately defended a position that included snack foods instead of high-tech products in the 1980s and 1990s. Would you have

Snack Foods Portfolio		Technology Portfolio	
Tootsie Roll Industries	8,471.42%	IBM	1,354.54%
Dreyer's Grand Ice Cream	2,080.37%	Hewlett-Packard	1,287.02%
Hormel Foods	3,675.81%	Motorola	1,100.65%

Figure 3-2 A Comparison of the Total Returns for Two Portfolios over the 27-Year Period of January 1, 1981, through December 31, 2007

touted Tootsie Rolls as the "place to be in the market" at your neighborhood dinner party? Yet, the results are there. And there are hundreds of other examples we could cite.

I am not suggesting that technology stocks be avoided or that snack food stocks be the foundation of a portfolio. Rather, the numbers demonstrate that stocks making an important contribution to portfolio returns can be those you least expect. This is just one more example of why stock picking is such a futile endeavor. Since you never know which companies will be successful or why, you should own them all. Own capitalism. And then, when someone asks your opinion of a particular stock at the next potluck, you can say, "Why, yes, I do own that stock." Here's to fried Spam sandwiches!

OK, Let's Pick Stocks

Suppose *The Investing Revolution* decided to put together the 10 best stock pickers on the planet in the form of an experiment. We'd go to the *Wall Street Journal*'s annual list of the top money managers and use a tough set of criteria to select our panel. The money managers must have made the list at least 5 years in a row and have at least 20 years of experience in the money management business. Having met this standard will ensure that they have had success in the past and that they have seen several bull and bear market cycles. We would then instruct them to analyze the S&P 500 Index and narrow it down to the 25 best domestic stock selections. The panel must have a supermajority to keep or cut a stock. That means 7 out of 10 money managers must be in agreement. We would provide a substantial stipend for their time as well as a full staff of MBAs, CFAs, and Ph.D.s at their beck and call for one week. They would stay in the finest hotel with the best food, and they would have access to any and every type of research and technology they might require. It would be a spare-no-expense project.

The S&P 500 is the most popular index in the investing world. More people own it as an index fund than any other single type of mutual fund. We thought if we could, with the help of our experts, whittle it down to the best 25 stocks, then we would have a great all-star portfolio.

The first step would likely be pretty easy: cut the list in half to the best 250. Then we would ask the expert contingent to get it down to the best 125. A little more difficulty and discussion would likely ensue. Continue the process to get the list down to 50, 40, and finally 25. If experts and investors are confident in the S&P 500 as a good solid investment, then wouldn't a list of the 25 best companies in that group be even better?

This experiment would be the same as selecting a Major League Baseball all-star team. What a collection of great players! Would you be willing to place all of your investment dollars in a select list of stocks like this? Of course! Why would you want to waste your money by owning the other 475? And why stop there? Shouldn't we take advantage of the expertise of these 10 prestigious stock pickers while we can and narrow it down further to the best 10 stocks or even the best 5? And let's go all the way—surely a distinguished, experienced panel such as this could finally agree on THE best stock out of all of them in which to place your hard-earned and hard-saved dollars, right?

If you are feeling a bit uncomfortable with this concept, you are not alone. When it really comes down to it, you know that no individual or team of experts—no matter how qualified they seem to be—can pick the best stock in any group of 500, even if they could reach a consensus (which with all those egos in the room would be nearly impossible). In fact, you know they cannot even pick the best 25 with any consistency. How do you know that? Because if they could, they would. And believe me, you would hear about it.

Only fools would risk their entire portfolio on 1, or 10, or 25, or even 50 stocks out of the S&P 500 Index—no matter how qualified the selection panel may appear to be. So why then do investors do the exact same thing when they hire an active mutual fund manager? There are approximately 8,000 stocks listed on U.S. exchanges.[20] The average U.S. actively managed stock fund holds 156 stocks. These fund managers are in effect saying that they have picked the top 2% of all stocks! That is the same as picking the top 10 out of the S&P 500. In addition, the average turnover in the entire mutual fund universe is over 85%.[21] So every year on average, professional money managers change their minds and trade away 133 of the 156 stocks they have already picked. For experts, they don't sound too sure of themselves, do they? It is no wonder that more than half of the 2007 *Wall Street Journal's* Best on the

Street Analysts Survey was composed of newcomers.[22] Those falling off the list either could not match their previous lucky streak performance or perhaps decided to retire in order to go out on top. Picking stocks, or even hiring someone else to do it for you, is an exercise in utter futility. There are no stock pickers good enough for your portfolio.

Time versus Money

"Time is money" is the old adage. One constant of Wall Street methodologies is to use performance numbers to turn the heads of investors. Have you ever put your money in a mutual fund with a great track record and then watched and waited . . . and waited . . . and waited for the return on which you based your investing decision, only to find that it never appears. One of our missions is to change that.

It is now possible to evaluate mutual fund families based on time and money. Morningstar, that online bastion of financial research, has committed to publishing a new way of measuring mutual fund returns called "dollar-weighted returns." Morningstar also includes a ratio that represents the percentage of the total return captured by the dollar-weighted number. So what does a dollar-weighted number mean exactly? And how, if at all, does it help investors?

In the past, published returns have been based on point-to-point time measurements. In other words, the returns are time weighted. This means that returns are calculated by comparing the price, say, on the day the fund began to the price on the present day, which results in a figure otherwise known as the "since inception" return.

Morningstar also measures time periods in such increments as 1, 3, 5, or 10 years.

This method is imperfect, however, in that it assumes investors bought on the first day of the time period being measured and held the investment until the last day of the time measurement period. Anyone familiar with investing understands that people don't move their money in and out of funds on these exact reporting dates. They may get in on June 12 of one year and then sell out on April 3 three years later. When you further consider the impatience of investors and managers alike, and the in-and-out nature of active trading, it becomes even more obvious that the point-to-point time measurement model is suspect when it comes to giving potential investors the best gauge of the return of a particular investment.

Dollar-weighted returns, on the other hand, are calculated by taking into consideration not only the performance over the life of the investment but also the cash flow in and out of the fund. Returns achieved when more money is in the fund carry more weight than returns achieved when fewer investor dollars are present. Losses are treated the same way, and they are weighted more heavily if more money is present.

So why is this different and important? Because measuring the cash flow in and out of a fund gives a better view of how the fund family performs when more (or fewer) investors are actually experiencing ownership of the fund in question.

Nearly all investors chase returns. Figures 3-3 and 3-4 are charts that I used to illustrate this in the past. As originally printed in my first book, *Wealth Without Worry*, the figure shows the cash flow in and out that is experienced when funds are doing well versus when they are not.[23] The fund track shown in Figure 3-3 uses return data

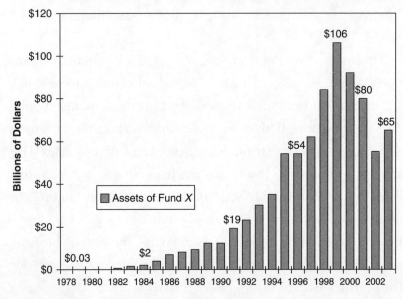

Figure 3-3 The Fidelity Investments Magellan Fund Performance versus Fund Size from 1978 through 2003
Source: James N. Whiddon with Lance Alston, *Wealth Without Worry: The Methods of Wall Street Exposed,* Brown Books, Dallas, 2005, p. 49.

equivalent to the returns of the Magellan Fund managed by Fidelity Investments, which we will call Fund X for the purpose of this illustration. The Magellan Fund, made famous by manager Peter Lynch, reigned as the largest fund in the world, peaking in assets managed at about $106 billion in 2000.[24]

Notice the big returns that came in the first several years. These early years saw very little money invested in the fund. Once the word got out about the above-average performance, return-chasing investors flocked to take advantage of the impressive track record. The fund was closed to new investors beginning October 1997 to prevent the fund from becoming too unwieldy to manage.[25]

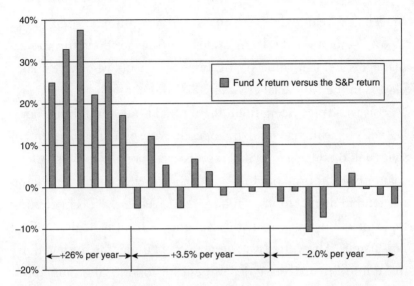

Figure 3-4 The Rate of Return for the Fidelity Investments Magellan Fund versus the S&P 500 Index
Source: James N. Whiddon with Lance Alston, *Wealth Without Worry: The Methods of Wall Street Exposed,* Brown Books, Dallas, 2005, p. 49.

Unfortunately, by the mid-1990s, the returns became average at best. From January 1, 2000, the average annual return of this fund was down 6.18% per year (through 2008), trailing the benchmark S&P 500 Index in six of nine years during that stretch.[26] Fidelity reopened the fund to new investors in January 2008 after a strong year in 2007 when the fund experienced a return of nearly 19%.[27] It seemed that the money managers were using the old trick to attract more return chasers. In spite of this move, net assets under management continued to fall after the reopening, and they have declined to be about one-third of the 2000 peak—approximately $35 billion as of September 30, 2008.[28] As shown in Figure 3-4,

Magellan's year-to-date return was down through September 45.6%.[29] Additionally, I am quite sure the positions the money managers held in some of the financial giants who were major players in the "financial crisis of 2008" did not help.[30]

This is a typical scenario in the mutual fund world. Fund families will create myriad funds in hopes that one or more management styles will produce a fund that reports exceptional numbers. After a year or two, they roll out the "winners." In other words, fund families tend to market funds that have done well early. It is interesting that you will never hear anything about the fund strategies that did not "hatch." Those funds are quickly swept under the rug and don't make it to the marketing department for rollout. Also, incredibly, the SEC does not require those failed funds' returns to be reported. Therefore, many of the good returns are experienced only by the few investors that started with the funds. The returns more often than not drop off over time for various reasons—not the least of which is that the manager's picking or timing luck runs out. Because of this return-chasing scenario, not surprisingly, dollar-weighted returns tend to be lower than time-weighted returns because most of the money arrives after the hype and after the returns that created that hype. With this said, Morningstar Managing Director Don Phillips believes that dollar-weighted return figures "come closer to capturing the cumulative investor experience."[31]

The differences between the conventional time-weighted returns and the new dollar-weighted returns are most evident in funds that use hedged strategies. As part of its research to determine the usefulness of using dollar weights as a reliable guide, Morningstar considered 80 such hedge funds. For the 10-year period ending December 31, 2005, the total annualized time-weighted return was 2.93% higher than the dollar-weighted return.[32] That's a huge difference in terms of what investors think they are getting versus what they probably are actually receiving. Could we say that the long-time reporting of time-weighted returns is just more Wall Street smoke and mirrors? Readers should consider this a rhetorical question.

What was really fascinating about this research is that Morningstar also applied its success ratio to several fund families. The highest percentage (109%) went to Dimensional Fund Advisors (DFA), a company whose dollar-weighted returns are actually—and amazingly—higher than its time-weighted returns.[33] They were the only family to exceed 100% in the study. This clearly indicates that Dimensional Fund Advisors' investors are very disciplined in applying a buy-and-hold strategy. Multiple studies have demonstrated that a buy-and-hold approach is likely to net a better long-term return than an active trading strategy. Other fund families didn't fare as well. For example, Dodge & Cox, Fidelity Investments, and Vanguard all scored above 85%, but other popular families like Putnam scored only 67% and Janus, only 25%.[34]

The dollar-weighted method of return evaluation is not likely to be the exposé that will end active management or the incubation process that Wall Street fund peddlers love so much. Their clever marketing of mutual funds that do well early in their history has been too lucrative to stop now. They depend on uninformed investors to make their fund selection decisions based on the more commonly tracked time-weighted (date-to-date) performance measurements. Unless you join our revolution and recommend this book to your friends and family, they are likely to never hear of this, and the misinformation campaign will continue for decades.

Also, don't expect your retail mutual fund hawkers to offer this information eagerly either—but for obvious reasons it is prudent (and might be kind of fun) for you to ask them about this topic.

Bottom Line

Wall Street depends on the enormous glut of information in our world to confuse you and to coax you into throwing up your hands and trusting them with your money. They tout their abilities to time and pick the markets, and yet we all know that telling the future eludes all mortals—including them.

They know that in the investing world, just as in any other walk of life, a lie told enough times will eventually be considered truth. So they bombard the airwaves and printed pages with their propaganda. Furthermore, by inducting very smart and highly educated men and women into their ranks, they maintain credibility with the masses. They have century-old war chests of cash and an army of lobbyists at their disposal, and they will not ever go quietly into the night. The limited and/or biased information that they provide to prospective investors is just enough to make them commit because they know not where else to turn.

That is why I am here leading *The Investing Revolution*. And like all other revolutions before us, this one will be won at the ground level—one investor at a time.

four

UNDERSTANDING MARKETS

Markets go up and markets go down.
—Ronald Reagan, October 19, 1987 (Black Monday)

One of the biggest traps individual investors fall victim to is what I call the *in-perpetuity bias*. That is the tendency of investors to feel, and thus internalize as a belief, that markets, once headed in a certain direction other than "sideways," will forever continue in that direction. It is always fascinating to observe investor attitudes and expressions of euphoria in bull markets or extreme anxiety in bear markets. They tend to act as though they have never seen economic changes before. Yet, as I tell listeners over and over again, the only constant we can depend on in life—or in the stock market—is change.

The following discussion is designed to give you a clear understanding of just how markets really react, what you can do to stay calm and reassured that free capital markets are the ticket to long-term wealth, and why you should continue to subject yourself to the continuous hills and valleys—sometimes even very deep valleys—of the global economy.

Possibility versus Probability

Aristotle said, "The probable is what usually happens."

I once heard a psychologist describe the difference between possibility and probability. "When you get on an airplane, you realize that there is a real possibility that it will not arrive safely at its destination. You have seen it happen. Planes do crash and people perish. But the fact is, your chances of dying in an airliner crash are only 1 in 11 million. Your chances of being killed in an automobile accident are 1 in 5,000.[1] One could argue that driving to the airport is riskier than getting on a plane. It is possible that one day the plane you are on—God forbid—goes down. However, it is not probable. If you thought it was probable that kind of tragedy would occur, you would certainly no longer fly on airplanes (some have taken this stance, I know). If we confuse these two concepts and live our lives where possibilities become probable and probabilities are considered only possible, we will really be in trouble. Our lives would be turned upside down."

Because of the conflicting advice proffered by the investing world, investors often confuse possibility with probability. Especially in difficult markets, investors may believe there is the probability that they will lose everything if they don't make some type of tactical move with their money. Wall Street firms foment this belief by broadcasting hyped messages through their marketing machine. This could be "the big one," they say. They seize the fear they helped create and communicate the idea that unless you rely on their expertise to time the market just right and pick the correct individual securities or industry sectors, you could experience devastating losses in your portfolio.

An example of this is a broker advising investors to "go to cash" with the promise that he will get them back in at just the right time after a market storm has passed. He indicates he has numerous experts in New York that will tell him when to tell you, and thus he will limit your losses and heighten your gains.

Or he may recommend certain products that "protect against the down side but give you all the upside." It sounds very appealing. (Never mind the fine print that limits the sharing in the upside or the surrender penalties that go on for more than a decade in some cases.) This type of advice can unwittingly commit investors to a long-term strategy in the name of "safety" that will be outdated as soon as the market turns positive again. These types of strategies are designed to reduce your fear of losing everything. But the cost is too high.

Sadly, when you succumb to irrational fear in a down market, you make long-term decisions based on short-term metrics that will hurt your chances of success well down the road. This all stems from confusing what is possible with what is probable.

The bullies of Wall Street are also experts at using greed. On the greed side of the equation, Wall Street capitalizes on your poor performance (or at least perceived poor performance) during bull markets. When things are going well in the stock market, as they usually are, Wall Street uses advertisements that play on your emotions and your fear of "missing out" on the big returns. It knows that you want to "keep up with the Joneses" or at least get your share of the proverbial pie. The comparisons that go on in your mind and the inevitable conversations that occur at dinner parties are part of Wall Street's plan. It knows how your brother-in-law is going to tell you only about his best investments, and not the stupid stock picks he made. This creates doubt in your mind that you aren't getting what you deserve.

Wall Street's financial marketing partners uptown on Madison Avenue are experts at their craft. They tout the spectacular return of the latest incubated fund. "Did you make 35% annualized return over the last three years? Well the Perfect Capital Growth Fund did. Where have you been? Fire your incompetent money manager and come to us. Our stock pickers are smarter than the broker you are using now. Stay where you are and you are sure to miss out." Wall Street is promoting the idea that it is possible to beat the market—but only if you use its methods.

Wall Street firms have clouded and purposely confused the realities of possibility and probability in the minds of investors in order to encourage dependence on them. I maintain that there is a possibility that markets can go down and stay down for a very long time. But this is not probable as witnessed by the fact that since the Great Depression, the S&P 500 Index has had only one time period when it declined for 3 calendar years in a row, and it has had positive annual returns for 52 out of the last 67 years (almost 80% of the time).

Conversely, I would offer that it is not just possible but it is probable that you will share in the gains of a bull market and avoid bigger losses in a bear market with minimal effort using a special technique of diversification. You should then enjoy an optimistic expectation in both up and down market cycles. You must be secure in knowing that your investment approach is solid in good times and bad. You must know the difference between possibility and probability in your portfolio, or it will drive you crazy.

How do you gain the proper understanding? Get the facts. If you can understand the historical truths of the free capital market, you will also be better equipped to recognize and debunk the myths proffered by the financial services world, the popular media, and the politicians. The following points will give you a good foundation of information to get you started on the path to understanding markets:

1. The stock market is in a bull market almost 80% of the time.[2]

2. Stocks are safer than bonds in preserving purchasing power—which is the only thing that really counts because it involves your principal plus inflation. The real return of stocks (after taxes based on 2008 tax rates) has averaged 6% more per year over bonds since 1926.

3. There have been seven recessions since 1960 lasting an average of only about nine months each.[3]

4. The stock market is resilient: The Dow Jones Industrial Average rebounded to its September 11, 2001, level just 59 days after the tragedy.[4]

5. Missing the best 25 days of the S&P 500 Index in 38 years (13,879 days) from January 1970 through December 2007 would have cost you 3.15% per year in annualized returns.[5]

Even with these facts absorbed on an intellectual level, let's ask the question, "How likely is a 1930s-style depression to occur, and what do we do to protect ourselves if it does happen?" After all, the events of 2008 warrant at least entertaining the possibility. The media has consistently offered their analysis of the similarities between the 1930s and 2008. But the real consideration should be the dissimilarities that exist.

For example, there was no FDIC insurance coverage for bank accounts and no SIPC coverage for brokerage (custodial) accounts during the Depression. In 1929 to 1930, over 1,300 banks closed, and their depositors lost everything. Second, unemployment approached 25% in the 1930s. Today we see the unemployment rate in the 7 to 8% range. Most economists would put "full" employment in the 4 to 5% range considering that there are about 1 to 2% of Americans in the unemployment rate who can work but do not care to be employed. The rate will almost certainly go higher before it comes down again, but it will likely never see the Depression era rates. Last, the GDP fell by one-third during the 1930s, but no such fall in GDP numbers is expected this time around.

Now let's answer the second part of the question. Let's say that the Chicken Littles are right and the "big one" occurs. World markets implode in a 1930s fashion. Then what? How can you protect yourself in the occurrence of a high-impact economic event? You can do so through what is called "insurance." We use auto and home insurance, health insurance, life insurance, personal liability insurance, and even lawsuit insurance. Insurance was invented for this very purpose—to protect against unlikely but devastating events in life.

Use the same prudent planning with your portfolio. With proper diversification, you are in effect buying insurance for the possibility that the free capital markets implode. Having literally 10,000 to

13,000 individual securities (stocks and bonds combined) in your portfolio will help mitigate and spread the risk. We call this type of risk reduction *superdiversification*.

Superdiversification in its current form was not available at the time, but it is important to note that in the five years (1931 through 1935) following the first full year of the Great Depression in 1930, every major asset class had a positive average annual return. Leading the way was small-cap U.S. growth companies with an annualized five-year return of 26.2%. Even in the biggest crisis ever faced by the U.S. economy, markets recovered. And the smaller companies, spurred on by the necessity of innovation, recovered the fastest.

It is not simply a possibility that you will succeed; it is relatively assured and a very high probability that you will succeed—if you are able to escape the ingenious and brilliant emotional marketing schemes of Wall Street and employ the simple strategy of superdiversification. I am pleased to inform you that the odds are overwhelmingly stacked in your favor if you superdiversify your portfolio. Just stay focused on the facts of the market and superdiversify, and success is your inalienable destiny. It will also help you maintain sanity concerning your money.

The Volatility of the Market

Market volatility is one area where listener questions related to anxiety are constant. I have devoted several programs to the topic, and many shows have involved discussion of the issue either directly or indirectly. The volatility of markets is a subject about which I believe there is a great deal of confusion and misplaced concern.

Because of this, I want to establish a clear understanding of what it means for markets to be volatile.

When markets trend downward in particular, there is always the observation by "expert" commentaries that volatility is very high and thus dangerous. *Volatility* connotes a somewhat pessimistic tone in our society as is clearly evidenced in the first meaning listed with the word in most dictionaries: unstable and potentially dangerous; apt to become suddenly violent or dangerous. But I believe that in the context of investing, the word *volatility*, like the word *risk*, is a neutral word—not a negative one. In fact, a better term to use in its place is *variability*. Variability of returns is important for investors to have in their portfolio as economies and markets move to and fro. It is a natural part of how markets work and ultimately grow.

The data will help prove this point, but I want to remind you of three basic, but important points concerning markets:

1. *Free markets work.* The efficient market hypothesis supports the idea that the price of a security is correct in that it is based on the fact that all the information about it is available to the public at any point in time.[6] The market is the best way of organizing the millions of agents (investors, brokers, and so on) and their billions of transactions that take place each day. This system provides the best estimation of current market value.

2. *Risk and return are related.* Simply put, without risk, there is no return. Your investment strategies must be guided by research and models that recognize the proper relationship between risk and reward.

3. *Diversification is essential.* You must have exposure to all asset classes and not be concerned with market momentum, individual securities, or stock market index sectors. Portfolios must be structured to provide comprehensive asset class allocation and international exposure using literally thousands of individual securities—not just hundreds or dozens.

Is the market in fact more unstable during some periods than it is in others? Is it more unpredictable—and thus riskier—in down markets than it is in bull markets? Figure 4-1 shows monthly S&P 500 Index returns for the years 1990 through 2008. The gray shaded areas in the figure are months in which returns rose 6% or more or declined 6% or more. While there were 20 months that showed a gain of 6% or more and 17 months that showed declines of 6% or more, the interesting point is that from May 2003 through December 2007 (52 months), no shaded areas appear.[7]

During this almost five-year stretch, some financial headlines and many financial product peddlers still proclaimed the volatility of stocks; but in fact, it was a rather tame period in terms of volatility. Remember, Wall Street loves to talk about volatility and will seize upon any opportunity to do so because it wants you to be fearful and trading. And the financial media love to talk about volatility because they also want you to be fearful and buying from their advertisers. Wall Street and the mainstream media are highly motivated to disseminate the volatility storyline ("unstable and potentially dangerous") even when markets are relatively stable. When was the last time you heard a financial firm hawking "stable"

Year	Annual Return, %	Jan, %	Feb, %	Mar, %	Apr, %	May, %	June, %	July, %	Aug, %	Sept, %	Oct, %	Nov, %	Dec, %
1990	-3.1	-6.70	1.30	2.70	-2.50	9.80	-0.70	-0.30	-9.00	-4.90	-0.10	6.50	2.80
1991	30.5	4.40	7.20	2.40	0.20	4.30	-4.60	4.70	2.40	-1.70	1.30	4.00	11.40
1992	7.6	-1.90	1.30	-1.90	2.90	0.50	-1.50	4.10	-2.00	1.20	0.30	3.40	1.20
1993	10.1	0.80	1.40	2.10	-2.40	2.70	0.30	-0.40	3.80	-0.80	2.10	-1.00	1.20
1994	1.3	3.40	-2.70	-4.40	1.30	1.60	-2.50	3.30	4.10	-2.40	2.20	-3.60	1.50
1995	37.6	2.60	3.90	3.00	2.90	4.00	2.30	3.30	0.30	4.20	-0.40	4.40	1.90
1996	23.0	3.40	0.90	1.00	1.50	2.60	0.40	-4.40	2.10	5.60	2.80	7.60	-2.00
1997	33.4	6.20	0.80	-4.10	6.00	6.10	4.50	8.00	-5.60	5.50	-3.30	4.60	1.70
1998	28.6	1.10	7.20	5.10	1.00	-1.70	4.10	-1.10	-14.50	6.40	8.10	6.10	5.80
1999	21.0	4.20	-3.10	4.00	3.90	-2.40	5.60	-3.10	-0.50	-2.70	6.30	2.00	5.90
2000	-9.1	-5.00	-1.90	9.80	-3.00	-2.10	2.50	-1.60	6.20	-5.30	-0.40	-7.90	0.50
2001	-11.9	3.50	-9.10	-6.30	7.80	0.70	-2.40	-1.00	-6.30	-8.10	1.90	7.70	0.90
2002	-22.1	-1.50	-1.90	3.80	-6.10	-0.70	-7.10	-7.80	0.70	-10.90	8.80	5.90	-5.90
2003	28.7	-2.60	-1.50	1.00	8.20	5.30	1.30	1.80	2.00	-1.10	5.70	0.90	5.20
2004	10.9	1.80	1.40	-1.50	-1.60	1.40	1.90	-3.30	0.40	1.10	1.50	4.00	3.40
2005	4.9	-2.40	2.10	-1.80	-1.90	3.20	0.10	3.70	-0.90	0.80	-1.70	3.80	0.00
2006	15.8	2.60	0.30	1.20	1.30	-2.90	0.10	0.60	2.40	2.60	3.30	1.90	1.40
2007	5.5	4.50	-2.00	1.10	4.40	3.50	-1.70	-3.10	1.50	3.70	1.60	-4.20	-0.70
2008	-37.0	-6.00	-3.25	-0.43	4.87	1.30	-8.43	-0.84	1.45	-8.91	-16.80	-7.18	1.06

Figure 4-1   Monthly S&P 500 Index Returns for January 1990 through December 2008
Note: Shaded areas indicate monthly returns higher than 6% or more (20 shaded areas) or lower than –6% or more (17 shaded areas).
Source: Adapted from Standard & Poor's, "Historical Returns, January 1, 1926, to December 31, 2007," S&P Compustat Point in Time Database, October 9, 2008. (Standard & Poor's is a division of the McGraw-Hill Companies, New York.)

products or the talking financial heads tell you not to worry about volatility?

You should not only expect volatility—that is, variability—but I would submit you should long for it. The fact is that you can have large down years with one great month. (In 2002, the S&P 500 had a return of −22% for the year, but in October alone it was up almost 9%.) Markets can also have big up years with down months (1998 had a return of +28% for the year, yet August's return was −14%). Risk drives expected returns, and as investors, we cannot enjoy rates of return (Treasury bills) that are above risk-free returns without taking on risk, or volatility. Returns are not a free-lunch story. There will be time periods—maybe extended time periods—when the in-perpetuity bias tempts you to give in and head to the cash hills. You must stay the course. The facts of the market demand this of you. The only way to ultimately fail at this thing called "investing" is to lose your faith in the free market, and the billions of free men and women who are engaged in it.

We want the markets to react to new information. Time and again markets have been unpredictable and have no expected patterns—except for a long-term trend upward. The monthly return tables reinforce this point. The 52-month period from 2003 through 2007 was unusually stable in terms of monthly returns, yet as I recall, there were still entities with a vested interest suggesting just the opposite. So clearly, they had a heyday in a year like 2008 when volatility and losses put doubt in the minds of people without the proper knowledge of how markets work.

The rewards for taking risks in any asset class can come very quickly. Investors cannot afford to be out of the market and miss these fleeting opportunities. Just one month of returns may drive the reward premium for many months. Learn to appreciate the necessity for variability—your new word for portfolio volatility.

Bursting the Bubble Mentality with Daniel Gross

Every generation has had its memorable economic downturns. Yet from the minute Alan Greenspan uttered the expression "irrational exuberance," it became the catch phrase of an over-priced stock market.[8] The thought of a bubble in the stock market provokes panic. Too many remember the dot-com crash that followed Greenspan's speech (although not for another four years or so) and how those extreme dot-com losses contributed to what could now be called "irrational expectations."[9]

There's constant talk in the media about possible market bubbles. The dot-com bubble was followed by a real estate boom and subsequent bust in 2008. We are always waiting to find out where the next overinflated area of the world economy is: China, oil, consumer debt? While it is true that markets historically roar back quickly after a downturn, the fact remains that 9 of the 10 biggest one-day percentage moves in the S&P 500 were down. These sudden negative moves make investors understandably nervous and leave them asking what they should do with their assets to avoid getting burned. Yet, when you take a closer look at those 9 down days, there is more to consider. On average, there were 148 days remaining in the calendar year after each down day. The average period return to the end of the year was a positive 7.5%. When the bubble fear creeps into your investment decisions, wrong moves in and out of the market can often have a very negative effect on your portfolio.

I interviewed Daniel Gross on *The Investing Revolution* to learn about his unusual perspective when it comes to market bubbles.[10] A columnist for *Newsweek* magazine, Gross is also a historian and the author of several books, including *Pop! Why Bubbles Are Great for the Economy.*[11] While Gross agrees that losing money in the market is not a pleasant experience, he pointed out several economic advantages to market ups and downs. One of the most notable concepts he introduces in his book is that for each bubble that inflates, there is both a physical and mental infrastructure built out and in place after the bubble has burst. Gross looks back to some of our country's earliest bubbles as evidence.

Gross began by explaining that in the mid-1800s, the telegraph began to take the country by storm. Never before had information traveled faster than human beings could physically carry it. The newfound technology excited investors, and they poured money into the idea. Meanwhile, emerging companies threw up wires on poles the way kids spray Silly String at birthday parties. It is notable that many entrepreneurs and companies eventually went bankrupt, but by then, they had successfully wired the entire country. A new physical infrastructure was developed through the risk investors who were willing to take in the ideas and innovations of the day. From that, we eventually saw companies such as Western Union and the Associated Press spring up as they took advantage of the existing hardware.

Gross further explained that while telegraph wires were being strung around the country, the railway system was getting attention as well. A boom resulted when people realized the potential for travel and the exchange of goods beyond their small radius of influence. In typical bubble fashion, investors rushed in, but the country couldn't support the sudden onslaught of new construction and companies. The railroad bubble left behind a new way of thinking. While businesses were accustomed to serving only those within a few miles of their store or home, they could now reach those within a few miles of any railroad stop across the country. The mental infrastructure moved from a local way of thinking to a national way of thinking. Possibilities were now as seemingly endless as the miles of railroad track.

The more recent tech bubble provides another easy illustration of both the physical and mental aspects of new infrastructure. While many companies and individuals went bankrupt during the bear market of 2000 to 2002, largely as a result of the tech sector plummet, the country now had new hardware in the form of fiber optic cable and new thinking. Our society embraced the Internet as a personal and business resource. That meant that even after the tech bubble burst, the stage was set for companies such as Google or Yahoo! to take advantage of what was left behind and become wildly successful. The busted bubble did not wipe out the infrastructure created by those failed companies.

Yes, economic bubbles can be devastating at times. But they also have their place in the economy. The key factor that keeps them from being completely destructive is the resilient nature of the free capital markets. Using a 100% equity asset class portfolio, Figure 4-2 illustrates this resilience as we consider the most recent example of a burst bubble and recovery during the time frame of 2000 through 2007.[12]

Note that after it ultimately dropped to a low of −14.8% from 2000 to 2002, it rebounded 110.4% over the next four years. You could certainly have avoided the negative returns brought on by the tech bubble bust if you had timed it just right. But when in

2000, %	2001, %	2002, %	2003, %	2004, %	2005, %	2006, %
−4.9	1.5	−14.8	50.1	23.9	11.7	24.7

Figure 4-2 100% Equity Asset Class Portfolio for 2000 through 2007
Source: Adapted from Dimensional Fund Advisors (DFA), "Balanced Strategy: Equity 100% Equity," Matrix Book 2007, DFA Securities Inc., c/o Dimensional Fund Advisors, 1299 Ocean Avenue, Santa Monica, Calif., 2008, p. 60.

2003 would you have returned to the market? Would you have had the nerve to get in at just the right time after such a loss in value? How much of the recovery would you have missed if you had hesitated? These are all difficult decisions you could have avoided by simply staying the course because you understood how market cycles work.

You must be sophisticated and informed enough to understand and embrace the advantages that accompany economic cycles, and thus bubbles. We are blessed with an economic structure that is like a centipede. It may stumble occasionally, but it is so diverse and has so many legs to stand on that it will not fall flat on its face. Market bubbles are a part of a typical and successful market cycle and a necessary part of growth and progress for domestic and global economies—and for the success of our own individual portfolios.

There will always be bubbles. That doesn't mean, however, that there should be fear and trepidation associated with them.

Robert Samuelson and the Recession Forest Fire

If headlines bearing news of an economic recession create jittery feelings from time to time, you are not alone. During difficult market periods investors often consider reallocating their assets to "safer" havens. This tendency is natural because we all want to avoid losses.

One way to think of a recession or down market period is to compare it to a forest fire. This may sound strange at first, but think about it. Do you remember the first time you ever drove through a forest? I would say it is a good bet that you did so in the family station wagon with the windows rolled down so you could feel the cool mountain air. I am sure you recall the numerous signs featuring our fire prevention friend Smokey the Bear. His message was always the same: "Only you can prevent forest fires." Preventing fires in national parks is the park ranger's number 1 priority. Yet, in an average year, over 100,000 wildfires burn over 4 million acres of land in the United States.[13] So no matter how hard we try, forest fires are going to occur. Furthermore, they have some very beneficial effects on the environment. Charcoal enriches the soil, and some plant species flourish in the wake of conflagrations. The cones of the jack pine tree, for instance, will not release their seeds unless exposed to intense heat. Some of the most beautiful and awesome trees such as the Sequoia and Douglas fir grow best in open sunlight areas, such as those cleared by fire.

It is the same situation with the economy. We do everything we can to prevent a recession. Curtailing a downturn is job number 1 for the Federal Reserve. The economy is always a political issue, and it receives the lion's share of the attention in most election cycles because politicians know that in the end, voters tend to vote their pocketbooks. Yet recessions inevitably occur. Like the occurrence of forest fires, there is no changing that fact. And as is true of forest fires, good things come out of economic downturns.

The key is to stay calm and disciplined, and all will likely turn out well as it has in the past time and again. Panic and react, and your hysteria could undoubtedly make a bad situation worse.

To back up this concept, in July 2007 I invited Robert Samuelson to join us on *The Investing Revolution*.[14] Samuelson is a contributing editor for *Newsweek* and the *Washington Post*. Harvard educated and from New York, one of the recurring topics in his writings is

Social Security and the unwillingness of politicians to deal with problems he and others believe it will have in the future. Samuelson also does not vote in any elections (be they national, state, or local) as he believes that voting interferes with his impartiality as a journalist. I admire his attempt to remain unaffected by biases, which is an uncommon stance these days. In the interview, we discussed a thought-provoking article he wrote for *Newsweek*, "The Upside of Recessions."[15]

Since my birthday was the week of the show, Lance Alston, my research guru and longtime cohost, surprised me with data concerning recessions in the United States since the year I was born—1960.[16] To set the stage before we brought on Samuelson, Lance told me and our audience that the Dow Jones Industrial Average closed at 593 that year; 47 years later it closed at 13,264.5. (Incredibly, if the Dow grows at the same rate of only 6.83% in the next 47 years, it will be at 295,975.) Lance also informed us that seven recessions have occurred since 1960 and that we have had only two recessions (1990 and 2001) since I graduated from college.[17] (For the record, in most economic circles, a *recession* is defined as two consecutive quarters of negative economic growth as generally measured by the GDP.)

Lance also enlightened us to the fact that these downturns had an average duration of only about nine months. That means we have been in a recession about 12 to 14% of my life.[18] (That is not much when you consider the percentage of the time that the media spends talking about bad economic news.) The fact that we are in a recession only about one out of seven or eight years is completely acceptable, especially since the economy naturally needs this regrouping time in order to move ever further ahead in the future. If success and prosperity are never threatened, complacency sets in. I would also remind you that the business cycle moves from peak through a contraction or recession, through the trough, and back to recovery and expansion as dependably as any other life cycle in nature.

Samuelson explained two reasons why occasional downturns in the economy are, on the whole, constructive. First, a downturn tends to reduce and keep inflation under control. Second, a recession will discipline businesses and investors, making known the risks inherent in the business enterprise. "If we promise people that there will never be another downturn—an impossible promise but one they might believe temporarily—they will make bad investment decisions. By that I mean that both corporations and individuals will make foolish investment decisions. So it is true that recessions have social costs—profits decline, unemployment goes up, income goes down. These are things that nobody likes. But we often think of them as having no benefit at all. But they actually do have some long-term benefits."

The equities markets tend to be a precursor to recessions, and those markets tend to start going downward about four to six months before the economy as a whole begins to slow. Each time the market has bottomed out, it has subsequently rebounded to eventually end up well ahead of where it was prior to the downturn. Another interesting fact is that the market rebound has usually occurred several months before the economy as a whole has recovered.

Figure 4-3 depicts a typical stock market cycle as represented by the S&P 500, laid beside a typical business cycle. As you can

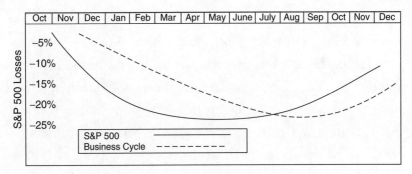

Figure 4-3 Recessions: A Historical Perspective, Hypothetical Recession Beginning on January 1
Note: Recessions average 10 months in length, during which the average S&P 500 Index losses are 20.21%. Typically there are huge market gains in the last 4 months of recessions while market fears rise during the first 4 months of recovery.

imagine, it would be particularly difficult to make portfolio moves based on macroeconomic data if the stock market were not on the same schedule. If you were using economic indicators to try to determine when to get back into the market, you would likely miss it. Investors nearly always sell lower and buy higher when they try to time the market. This is because even if you have accurate and timely data—which is unlikely—in order to time the market correctly, you have to be right twice. You must be right on the timing of the exit and right on the timing of the reentry. This imperfect methodology usually results in losses. Yes, getting out of the market does provide a few days of relief, at least psychologically, but this relief will be offset by the troubling question of when to jump back in and the disappointment of realizing that you missed out on the biggest gains of the year. The best time to get back in is always anybody's guess.

Figure 4-4 shows the incredible amount of growth that has occurred in the last four months of the recessions that have happened since 1973.[19] You can also see the results in the first four months after the recessions. The numbers speak for themselves. Given this data, we caution you to not make a mistake you will regret. Bailing out of the market when stocks take a dive—no matter how steep—is the last thing investors should do. Staying the course has always proven to be the winning strategy. When markets turn positive again, they do it very quickly. Often the biggest gains occur in only a few days. Investors like to think that the market climbs gradually over time, but history dictates that it actually has a tendency to spike upward when things turn for the better.

Recessions are good times to stop and reflect on why you invested in the market in the first place. You became a partial owner of firms all over the world that are doing nothing but striving vigorously to make a profit, regardless of the economic ebb and flow in

	Average Returns for Asset Classes, %		
	Large-Cap Stocks	Small-Cap Stocks	Micro-Cap Stocks
Last 4 months of recession	22.96	36.09	32.57
Last 4 months of recession through first 4 months of recovery	35.93	53.97	54.12

Figure 4-4 Stock Performance during the Last Four Months of the Recessions That Have Happened Since 1973
Source: Adapted from the National Bureau of Economic Research (NBER), *U.S. Business Cycle Expansions and Contractions,* NBER, 1050 Massachusetts Avenue, Cambridge, Mass.

the future. You must remember that difficult times call for innovation and creativity to solve problems. That is precisely what goes on in each company during a recession. Companies monitor their own results and make decisions to improve and take action to avoid the same difficulties moving forward. Ingenuity and a desire and plan to grow and improve products and services are required to survive. That is where new revenues and thus profits are derived. Having only success can spoil us and cause us to never seek better ways of doing things. In bad economies as difficulties are overcome, the collective growth potential of firms is enhanced. As sure as the spring will follow winter, and new growth follows a forest's destruction, prosperity and economic growth will follow a recession.

There is never going to be an economic fire that cannot be put out with innovation, perseverance, and an abiding confidence that free will and free enterprise reign. The Roman poet Horace once said, "Adversity reveals genius, prosperity conceals it." It is no surprise that he also coined the well-known and oft-used phrase "carpe diem."

The best time to seize the market is always — today.

Sell Low, Cry High

The winning streak continued for the equity markets both at home and abroad in 2007. Five years in a row, in fact. To hear the media drumbeat of gloom at the time, along with the subsequent 2008 market turmoil, you may not remember this free market accomplishment. Still worse, many individual investors missed out on the double-digit returns that many passive investors enjoyed during this five-year time frame. For the record, in 2007 U.S. equities as represented by the S&P 500 Index returned 5.49%, and the international markets as represented by the MSCI EAFE Index returned 11.63%.[20]

But what about the doom-and-gloomers? Five years of positive numbers was great, but they had a heyday when the difficulties of 2008 set in. One of my favorite poems of all time is "If" by Rudyard Kipling. You may remember the well-known opening and closing lines: "If you can keep your head when all about you are losing theirs / yours is the Earth and everything that is in it." In other words, you will be in control of your life. Investing is a part of our lives that oftentimes can give us a sense of being out of control. But as in many other areas of life, ignorance and misinformation breed fear. So permit me to provide a bit of perspective to bolster your confidence that more winning months and years are ahead in the capital markets for decades to come.

If you listen to our radio program for any length of time at all, you will notice that I sometimes say, "Let's pray for a bad year." I say this partly tongue in cheek—but then again I understand market cycles. Data show that after down periods in the market— even severe drops—a bull market is virtually inevitable. There have not been four consecutive down years for the S&P 500 Index since the Great Depression.[21]

If you are like most American investors, you are very impatient. You probably get nervous when you begin to see your monthly statements decline two, three, or four months in a row. So even though the data are clear on the brevity of market downturns in terms of years, I wanted to see if this brevity of downturns applied to monthly time frames as well.

My analysis focused on monthly returns from 1990 to December 2007 in three areas:

- The S&P 500 Index[22]
- The Vanguard Small Cap Index Fund[23]
- The 80% stock asset class portfolio (ACP) model[24]

The S&P 500 had only four negative years during this 18-year time frame. When individual months were observed, there were some fascinating results as well. For example, the S&P 500 Index lost a whopping 20.8% in October 2008. Can you imagine seeing that kind of value disappear in 30 days from your own portfolio? Would you have jumped ship? Well, if your nerves could not take it and you had sold the stocks on September 1, not only would you have lost the 14.5 % but you would also have then lost the 26.4% these stocks gained in the last four months of the year. Ouch! That means when you sold, you suffered a real loss plus an opportunity loss for a net total loss of more than 20%. That is a huge short-term thrashing made worse because of a lack of patience and perspective concerning market volatility. I refer to this as the "sell-low, cry-high scenario." You must avoid the "seller's remorse" that comes from dumping your stocks at a discount and reentering the market after its inevitable rise.

The findings were similar with the Vanguard Small Cap Index, which represents small-cap U.S. stocks. As recently as 2006—a great year by all accounts for the markets in general—this index fell 8.05% from April through June of that year. It then rose 11.44% in the next four months. Again, if you had sold out on August 1 because you just could not take it anymore, a double-digit loss was your fate.

Finally, I took a look at the effect of superdiversification in the 80% stock portfolio model. Superdiversification is something I preach all day, every day. It is an important precept of *The Investing Revolution*. Not surprisingly, the 80% model was considerably less volatile month to month in this lower-risk portfolio. In fact, in only 3% of the months analyzed between 1995 and 2007 was there a loss of 5% or more (the ACP model was created in 1995).

In comparison, the S&P 500 Index had 7% of the months with 5% or greater losses, and the Vanguard Small Cap Index had approximately 12% of the months with 5% or greater losses. Those statistics alone speak to portfolio stability with proper diversification. But again, if you wanted to panic, then August 1998 figures would have been your cue even with a superdiversified asset class strategy with 80% equities. That month experienced a 12.8% loss . . . followed by a 15.9% gain from September through December 31.

One additional piece of interesting data appeared from the analysis. When looking at all the months during the 18-year period, there was only one instance of five months in a row of negative returns in the S&P 500 Index. It lost 15.3% during this streak (June through October 1990). Furthermore, there were no instances of six months in a row of negative returns. And that five-month losing streak in 1990 was followed by a positive return of 23.3% over the next five months (November 1990 through March 1991).

I know when you are in the midst of a market storm, it is hard to accept this fact, but the reality is that the stock market simply does not have a tendency to go down and stay down for extended periods of time. Whether you are considering decades, years, or even

monthly time frames, micro- and macroeconomic cycles ultimately bring favorable results to faithful free market disciples.

Today's Crisis: A Blip on the Radar

In the spring of 2008, I received a call from a reporter with a
national media outlet just after the big Federal Reserve weekend
meeting following the Bear Stearns collapse. The conversation
lasted for a good 15 to 20 minutes, which is unusually long for that
type of interview. I was asked if we had noticed a greater uneasi-
ness among investors given the unusual circumstances of the
weekend's events. I indicated that there had been no unusual activity, and toward the end of the conversation I tried to sum up my
thoughts by saying, "I feel that this episode is simply representative
of an old storied firm making a bad decision [to offer subprime
mortgages] and paying the price for it. It is no different from any
other industry when company executives make bad decisions."

In the weeks following the Bear Stearns collapse, additional
major financial firm difficulties arose: Fannie Mae and Freddie
Mac were taken over by the government, the venerable longtime
firm of Lehman Brothers declared bankruptcy, Wall Street giant
Merrill Lynch sold itself to Bank of America, Washington Mutual
was absorbed by JPMorgan Chase, and the American International
Group (AIG)—the nation's largest insurer—was bailed out with
a plan to give an 80% stake to the U.S. government; only to be
followed by the auto bailout and the ultimate dismantling of Citi-
group Corporation. In all, the taxpayer bailout as of the date this
book went to press was expected to approach more than a trillion
dollars.

Jeremy Siegel said it well in an article entitled "The Resilience of American Finance," which he wrote for the *Wall Street Journal* in mid-September 2008: "It is shocking that firms that withstood the Great Depression are now failing in what economists might not even call a recession.[25] But their failure was not caused by lack of demand for their services. It was caused by management's unwillingness to understand and face the risks of the investments they made. The names of the players will change, but the future growth of the financial services industry is assured."

I saw the Bear Stearns and the other situations as I see all market events—as simply, change—the only constant in life. How can you gain confidence that change will usually be a positive experience, even one as unsettling as seeing the world's oldest and most notable financial institutions vanish from the map overnight? My mom used to say that "worry gives a small thing a big shadow." The key to alleviating stress over events of this nature is to understand and stay focused on the positive effects that time always has on money invested in free markets.

For example, if you were to look closely at the S&P 500 Index over the last 82 years, you could easily see how time in the market mitigates negative downturns and has proven positive the overwhelming majority of the time.[26] In other words, over the long haul, it continues an upward trend. As seen in Figure 4-5, when any calendar 5-year rolling time period is examined, positive returns occur nearly 86% of the time. When 10-year or 15-year rolling time periods are observed, positive returns occur 95 to 100% of the time.[27] Furthermore, since the Great Depression (1929 to 1932), the S&P 500 Index has never had a 4-year period of time when it lost ground each year.[28] The most recent 3-year

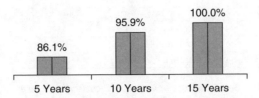

Figure 4-5 S&P 500 Index, 1926 through 2007, Rolling Time Periods
Source: Adapted from Standard & Poor's, "Historical Returns, January 1, 1926, to December 31, 2007," S&P Compustat Point in Time Database, October 9, 2008. (Standard & Poor's is a division of the McGraw-Hill Companies, New York.)

losing streak was from 2000 through 2002.[29] However, just like clockwork, in 2003 the market came roaring back, growing a healthy 28.7%, followed by 4 more positive years from 2004 through 2007.[30]

With this incredible track record in mind, consider all of the events that have occurred since the 1920s: World War II, the Korean War, Sputnik, the Cuban missile crisis, the assassination of President Kennedy, the Vietnam War, President Nixon's resignation, hyperinflation, Iran hostages, oil embargoes, Black Monday, the Persian Gulf War, the impeachment of President Clinton, the terrorist attacks of 9/11, and the Iraq War.

Furthermore, consider the fact that three of these events in particular had an especially sudden and shocking impact on the psyche of the American people and on the securities markets. The surprise attack on Pearl Harbor was instigated by a rogue nation in search of global dominance. The Kennedy assassination was carried out by a supposed lone gunman of counterpolitical persuasion. The 9/11 attacks in New York and Washington were perpetrated by terrorist groups not affiliated with any single sovereign government.

Tragedy	Date	DJIA Closing	Days to Recover
Pearl Harbor	December 7, 1941	112.52	334
Kennedy Assassination	November 22, 1963	711.49	4
9/11	September 11, 2001	8,920.70	59

Figure 4-6 Dow Jones Industrial Average Recovery to Pretragedy Levels
Source: Adapted from the Dow Jones Indexes, "The Performance of the Dow Jones Industrial Average after Major World Events," Dow Jones & Company, New York, October 7, 2008, www.djindexes.com/mdsidx/index.cfm?event=showavgevents.

While all of these events were different, all threatened the very fabric of our society and in the case of Pearl Harbor, even the existence of our society. These events had negative impacts on the stock markets. Figure 4-6 shows the number of days it took the Dow Jones Industrial Average to recover to pretragedy levels.[31] We can see that the recovery from these horrific events was relatively short as the billions of daily economic factors took control and overcame the negative effects. Capital markets are resilient even in the very worst of circumstances.

Next time the sky-is-falling news is released, compare it to the horrifying days of the past and ask yourself, "Is this news worse than any of these terrible events?" And even, may God forbid, you answer yes to that question, we know and have ample evidence that free markets have always risen to the occasion and moved past today's blip on the radar.

Bottom Line

Sir John Templeton, the investment pioneer and philanthropist, once said, "The four most dangerous words in investing are 'This time is different.'" He was right. The mechanism for changes in the market may not be the same as before—maybe it is subprime mortgages instead of war, or the failure of a major bank or the health of the president—but the ultimate results are the same. Free markets the world over are expanding, and there is no stopping them. Bubbles blow up and burst, and recessions come but then the economy thrives because of innovation. There will always be crises in progress somewhere in the world, and some of them—like 9/11 or the financial crisis of 2008—will shake us to our very core. Through it all, when you are able to look at the 30,000-foot view of our great free market miracle known as capitalism, you will see with optimism that success, and even greatness, is always on the horizon for investors who really understand markets.

five

KNOWING THE INVESTING WORLD

It is a sign of strength, not weakness to admit that
you don't know all the answers.
—John Loughrane

I learned at an early age that everyone is ignorant—just on different topics. For more than a decade, I too adhered to the investing principles I learned from the Wall Street operatives at large brokerage houses. It seemed reasonable that economic forecasting was legitimate and important. Picking stocks and timing the market were what brokers did, right? Bond speculating and making bets on certain sectors of the economy or going to cash or precious metals during a recession were the prevailing "textbook answers." I have also lived enough years to know that the more I learn, the less I know. This is humbling and yet exciting. If we really could know everything (like we did when we were 18), what purpose would our lives have after that? This chapter contains several subjects that I know you will enjoy and I hope will maybe even give you an ah-ha moment or two.

Why Stocks Are Still Safer Than Bonds

One of the great thinkers in the financial services world is Nick Murray. His brilliant articles and his book entitled *Simple Wealth, Inevitable Wealth* shape the way I believe all investors should think about money and investing. One of the simple yet most profound principles Murray advocates is that the long-term goal of investors should be to protect their purchasing power, and not focus on protecting their principal as they are prone to do.[1]

Stocks are by far the most effective and efficient tools to use to overcome the insidious effects of inflation. Figure 5-1 shows the

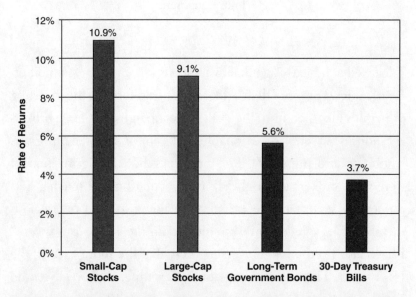

Figure 5-1 Average Annualized Returns for the Period of 1926 through 2008
Source: Adapted from the Center for Research in Security Prices (CRSP), "Annualized Returns 1926 to 2007: Small Cap, Large Cap, Long Term, 30-Day, January 1, 1926, to December 31, 2007," CRSP Custom Data Set, Center for Research in Security Prices, Chicago Graduate School of Business (GSB), University of Chicago, 105 West Adams Street, Chicago, Ill.

annual compound rate of return for some general asset classes over the last 83 years. The graph shows the average annualized return of bonds to be generally a little more than half that of stocks. The owners of stocks have clearly had the advantage.[2]

When inflation is taken into consideration, the gap widens even further. This is known as the *real rate of return*. With inflation averaging approximately 3.1% during this time frame, the real return multiple for stocks changes from about twice as much to three or even four times as much as bonds, as seen in Figure 5-2.[3]

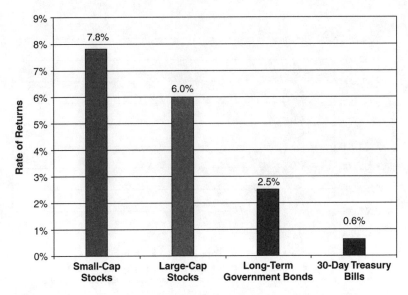

Figure 5-2 Average Annualized Real Returns for the Period of 1926 through 2008

Source: Adapted from the Center for Research in Security Prices (CRSP), "Annualized Returns 1926 to 2007: Small Cap, Large Cap, Long Term, 30-Day, January 1, 1926, to December 31, 2007," CRSP Custom Data Set, Center for Research in Security Prices, Chicago Graduate School of Business (GSB), University of Chicago, 105 West Adams Street, Chicago, Ill.

Finally, think about the effect that taxes have on the stock-bond comparison. When considering the higher marginal tax rates of bond interest (potentially 35%) versus the capital gains and dividend treatment available in equities (15% or even 5% at lower income levels), we have the makings of a huge gap. The results in Figure 5-3 show a definite advantage to holding stocks versus bonds when the effects of inflation and taxes are brought to bear on a long-term portfolio. (Income tax rates have fluctuated over the last eight decades; 2008 rates were used for this comparison.) Take a look at the difference in actual dollars when comparing small-cap stocks to Treasury bills over this 83-year span.

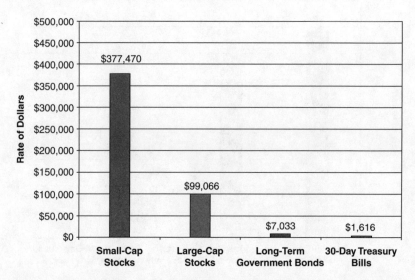

Figure 5-3 Average Annualized Real After-Tax Returns on $1,000 Invested for the Period of 1926 through 2008
Source: Adapted from the Center for Research in Security Prices (CRSP), "Annualized Returns 1926 to 2007: Small Cap, Large Cap, Long Term, 30-Day, January 1, 1926, to December 31, 2007," CRSP Custom Data Set, Center for Research in Security Prices, Chicago Graduate School of Business (GSB), University of Chicago, 105 West Adams Street, Chicago, Ill.

Even after seeing these numbers, many will say, "Stocks are still too risky for me." This sentiment is widely held—especially among investors nearing retirement—but it's simply not valid.

This fear of stocks is born out of two misperceptions:

- Investors do not understand the meaning of "long term."

- Investors do not really understand true portfolio risk.

A "long-term investment horizon" is defined as five years or longer. Money that is needed within a five-year period should be invested in less volatile instruments—mostly short-term bond funds or money market funds. It is interesting to consider that almost all portfolios (with just a few exceptions) are set up to be long-term propositions. Exceptions would include portfolios designed to save for a down payment on a house, to pay off short-term business debt, or to save for a college education. In all of those cases, the money has an end point when it will be used for a specific expenditure in a given time frame. Even at that, a college education portfolio can and should be invested for capital appreciation—especially early in a child's life.

If a nest egg is needed for any type of income generation, it should be considered a long-term investment. With retirees' living longer, this income may be needed for 30 or 40 years after retirement. You may be tempted as you near retirement to go to a large bond or cash equivalent position to protect your portfolio and get "yield." Yet, as you have just witnessed, the total return for stocks versus bonds is not even close—especially when inflation and taxes are considered. Even money that you may set aside for family or charities should be positioned to grow and benefit those for whom it is intended.

Whether you are in preretirement, retirement, or a stage of life when you want to leave a legacy for loved ones or a cause in which you deeply believe, you should manage your portfolio in such a way as to achieve real growth. That means planning for the long term and using equities, not bonds.

With long-term thinking established, I turn your attention now to the second misperception concerning a fear of stocks—the true meaning of *portfolio risk*. The first definition of *risk* in most dictionaries is the possibility of suffering harm or loss. This is the definition that comes to mind for most investors who are afraid of losing their money, their principal. However, in a proper investing context, you cannot be content with protecting only your principal. Rather, you must protect your purchasing power, which encompasses the principal and its future growth and income (that is, its total return).

As you learned earlier, the word *variability* is another way to express risk or volatility. It is a word that connotes good—not bad—to investors who are seeking market return. Remember, *variability* means the quality, state, or degree of being variable or changeable.

If you are like most people, you generally dislike change and often assign a negative connotation to it. However, when something is changeable, the potential to become better also exists. *Change* does not inherently imply a negative. When we invest, we want changes. Why? Because most of the time, change in a securities market is a positive experience, not negative. Therefore, if you can embrace the power of change and realize through a study of ample data that free markets must grow over time, then you can have confidence that taking on the risk of the market as a whole means you have a greater opportunity for positive change. Ironically, and not intuitively, herein lies the basis for genuine portfolio protection, and the case for holding stocks is made even stronger.

The year 2003 is a case in point. By all accounts, 2003 was a unique year in the stock market.[4] How could anyone have ever predicted what would transpire? Consider the following: The S&P 500 Index had just experienced its worst 3-year run since the Great Depression—losing almost half of its value. There was the threat of the SARS epidemic from Asia, the start of the Iraq War, the plunging of the U.S. dollar, the mutual funds scandal, malfeasance fallout in major corporations such as Enron and WorldCom, and reports of an overall weak economy with slow job growth ahead. Yet in the midst of all of this, as a stock investor, you would have had to be completely unlucky to earn less than 25%. The large-cap U.S. stock asset class had its best year in the last 5, large international stocks had their best in the last 17, and micro-cap stocks had their best year in 36 years.[5]

The Dow Jones Industrial Average (DJIA) hit its low on March 11 at 7,524 and then proceeded to climb almost 3,000 points by the end of the year.[6] Investors were naturally nervous early in the year due to all the bad news. Many stayed on the sidelines watching as the bad news continued and the stock market climbed. The lesson was the same then as it is now and forever: Get in and stay in. Bad news and events will have an effect on the markets, but they will recover.

No other nation or economic system has ever existed like the one we are blessed to be a part of now. In light of this phenomenon we call "capitalism," optimism is the only logical reality. Fear of loss should be replaced by hope of change. Hence, you can now see market fluctuations in a whole new light. You should no longer mistake variability for loss, and you should desire to have market returns through positive market change. Given this paradigm, you can now know that stocks are actually safer than bonds when your objective is to protect your long-term purchasing power.

Jeremy Siegel and the Pessimist's Favorite Investment

Talk radio is one of my favorite pastimes. One day, I was listening to my favorite station, and I heard an advertisement for gold as "the best investment out there." It was in early 2008 when markets were a bit choppy and listeners were obviously ripe to hear this message—at least that is what the purveyors of such a message clearly hoped. The statement in the radio spot that struck me as both very funny and incredibly pessimistic was the claim that "gold has never gone to zero." Can you imagine any enlightened capital market investor falling for such a pessimistic tagline? Yet that "hook" likely worked, and the company selling the gold coins or bars or statuettes profited during that ad campaign.

Investors are suckers for safe harbors when they believe Chicken Little may be on to something. Like Wall Street, gold peddlers are brilliant at marketing fear, at just the right time. As an example of this gullibility, Figure 5-4 shows the gyrations in the American Eagle gold coin demand from January 2007 through April 2008.[7]

Notice the level of sales of gold coins from February through October 2007. Stock markets were doing quite well during this time frame. The Dow Jones Industrial Average was up 12.1% during this nine-month period.[8] Then from November 2007

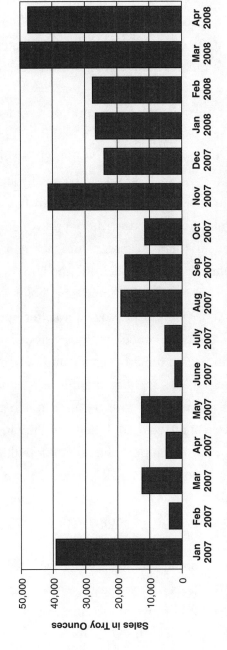

Figure 5-4 American Eagle Gold Coin Monthly Sales from January 2007 through April 2008

Source: Adapted from Carolyn Cui, "Precious-Coin Market May Lose Its Luster," *Wall Street Journal*, May 4, 2008, p. B1.

through March 2008, stock markets headed downward. The DJIA declined to −11.0% in just five months.[9] Headlines about the mortgage crisis, oil prices, and a weak dollar dominated the media landscape. Gold purchases soared in an obvious reaction of panic for many investors.

Gold and other precious coins are commonly touted as "investments," and never more so since the price of gold traded above $1,000 an ounce for the first time in March 2008.[10] Dealers will claim gold coins are an excellent way to balance your investment portfolio and reduce risk. They claim that with the security and profitability of gold, you can own the world's oldest and most trusted asset. They sell them as "safe, secure, and convenient."

Using these concepts of safety, security, and convenience is tantamount to politicians who proclaim that they "believe in America, want to fight for your rights, and provide a better future for your children." Who doesn't want to believe those canned promises?

Let's say you fall prey to the propaganda and want to own some gold coins. First of all, as a practical matter, it is quite expensive when you consider transaction costs (often as much as a 5% premium over the price of the gold) and then add shipping costs. The next consideration is the cumbersome task to store the silly things in a secure location. Do you get a half-ton safe to put in your closet next to your sneakers? Or do you take them to a safety deposit box at your local bank with the additional rental cost and inconvenience associated with bank hours?

Perhaps gold coins aren't your forte. Maybe you feel that a more sensible way to buy gold is via a gold exchange-traded fund (ETF). You can buy and sell ETFs instantaneously with hardly any transaction costs. Some gold investors fear the use of ETFs because they think that the financial system could totally collapse and their shares in the ETF will become worthless. (There's that rosy economic outlook again.) Why is it assumed that gold would be worth anything under those circumstances? There are certainly no guarantees. Nonsubscribers to ETFs claim that gold coins can be hidden in the event of a monetary system collapse—when the government massively expropriates wealth. Ownership of an ETF, they claim, cannot be hidden. But the truth is that both gold ETFs and gold coins are bad for your portfolio. The reasons hinge on something much more important than cost or simple inconvenience.

Jeremy Siegel is a professor of finance at the renowned Wharton School at the University of Pennsylvania. If I could have only one book in my business library, Siegel's *Stocks for the Long Run* would have to be it, and I consider him a legend in the investing arena.[11] No doubt you have probably seen Professor Siegel regularly on networks like CNN, CNBC, and NPR, and he writes regular columns for *Kiplinger's Personal Finance* magazine and Yahoo! In March 2008, I invited him on the program to discuss the timeless investing concepts in his classic book.[12] It's now in its fourth edition, and it was named one of the 10 best investment books of all time by the *Washington Post*.

The question that I felt needed most to be asked was simply, "Are stocks still the best vehicle for the long term for wealth creation?" Professor Siegel responded, "Yes. In fact, we know that, after a correction or bear market, where I guess we're just on the border now, actually that's when stocks are best for the long term. Only when it's right at the peak do people usually not get good returns going forward. So the fact that we are down from the peak, you know, nearly 20%, I think offers excellent opportunities going forward. And the valuation of the market today is also extremely reasonable relative to our normal metrics. What I have found, surprisingly enough, is that the returns on stocks in the nineteenth century were just as good as those in the twentieth. In fact, the long-term average return on equities is 6.5 to 7% after inflation, and that's a real return, and it's been remarkably persistent over these many, many decades. That doesn't mean every decade you're going to get that, but over the two centuries. So it gives me more confidence that that's the long-term normal. And in fact, international studies that have been completed within the last four or five years confirm that long-term equity returns in virtually every country in the world have also been excellent."

After establishing Professor Siegel's unwavering confidence in stocks, I brought up gold as an alternative in difficult stock market periods. He responded, "I looked at gold as one of the major assets going all the way back to 1802, the beginning of the nineteenth century. Let me just mention the following fact. If you put a dollar in the stock market back then and reinvested the dividends, after inflation you would have over three-quarters of a million dollars accumulated today. If you put a dollar in gold, after inflation, [and] took it out to sell it, even at today's market, you'd have $2.55.

"I mean, gold may be a wonderful short-term asset, and certainly the people in the short run have done well, I will admit. But as a long-term investment, it pales. It even underperforms fixed income assets, Treasury bills, bonds, munies [municipal bonds], and virtually any financial asset. It's really a short-term asset. It takes care of fear, anxiety, and a number of things if you're a good market timer, which most people aren't. But if they are, they could profit. But as a long-term holder, it just drags down the returns in your portfolio."

I was astounded by his answer concerning the value of gold over time. I had always known that it was only a short-term pacifier for jittery investors. But the extreme underperformance of gold was surprising. You would have made a buck and a half in two centuries? Certainly no pesky inheritance tax would have come into play, and you would have had about 1.70 euros now if you were also trying to hedge currencies. Not much of a return on your money. So, which is really "safe, secure, and convenient"? I say you can buy a great deal of convenience with an extra $749,997.45, which you would now have using Siegel's historical recommendation.

The truth is that gold may offer some good short-term returns in volatile monetary or equity markets, and it has the added characteristic of being shiny and nice to look at. But when scrutinized properly, it doesn't hold up. While it is often romanticized as the monetary vehicle used for over 5,000 years in all cultures, what real value can it provide for your portfolio in the future?

The important issue to understand concerning gold and other commodities is that they are really not investments. They are speculations. A gold coin does not produce anything. It cannot really be "profitable" when it creates no profits. As Gene Fama Jr., a regular on our program, once put it, it is somewhat like collecting comic books: "You buy Action Comic No. 1 and hope some rich guy who is a bigger sucker than you will eventually show up on your doorstep to buy it from you for more than you paid for it."[13]

Stocks, on the other hand, represent companies that can produce something—a product or service. This allows them to have future earnings potential, and the sky is then the limit for value in that company. Is the sky the limit for gold or other precious metals or commodities? Even though the price seems very high at $1,000, it was at $850 an ounce 29 years ago (January 21, 1980), and it was trading in the $850 to $900 range in the midst of the financial crisis of late 2008.[14] Will gold ever go to $2,000 an ounce? If it were to double in value, assuming a current value of $1,000, in just 10 years, this would represent an annualized return of only 7.2%. A well-diversified asset class portfolio of 100% stocks returned 15.9% annualized since 1980 (January 1980 through December 2007).[15] Reality numbers check: $850 invested in stocks in a retirement account in January 1980 was worth $45,674 on October 31, 2007.[16] The same $850 invested in gold was worth about what you originally invested. However, as promised, it did not "go to zero."

Buy gold and bet on a worldwide collapse of world financial markets if you wish. You will be counted as a genius by all your family, friends, and associates if the "end" does come. But be forewarned, they will also likely look to you for a loan. (As the saying goes, "Always borrow money from a pessimist; he doesn't expect to get paid back.") But for as long as free capital markets have been around, the pessimist has always eventually been proven wrong and has ended up much poorer.

Economic Forecasting: Cash Only

George H. Walper, Jr., is president of Spectrem Group, a research and consulting firm that specializes in the affluent and retirement markets. Spectrem is publisher of the monthly Spectrem Affluent

Investor Index (SAII) and Spectrem Millionaire Investor Index (SMII).Walper is also coauthor with Spectrem's managing director Catherine S. McBreen of the book *Get Rich, Stay Rich, Pass It On: The Wealth-Accumulation Secrets of America's Richest Families.*[17]

During a visit on the radio program with Walper concerning his book, it came to light that an important characteristic shared by the financially successful is a tendency to have what he calls a "perpetual wealth personality."[18] Associated with this personality type is the inclination to be "optimistic and willing to take a relatively large degree of risk." It sounds pretty straightforward. But when considering this concept further, an interesting thought occurred to me: It is also that person who can ignore the pessimism that pervades our society who makes it to the top financially and in every other walk of life, for that matter. It made perfect sense. Who takes risks? The proverbial "eternal optimist." So, is there a better place on earth or time in history to be optimistic than here, in the mainstay of free capital markets: the United States of America? We don't have an emigration problem; we have an immigration problem (many of you probably had forgotten that the other spelling of the word even existed). The perpetually successful have never forgotten that America is the Land of Opportunity.

If you can follow the lead of the optimists' mindset, then you can begin to understand their thinking when it comes to investing. Consider the definition of "long-term money." As you have learned, *long term* in the investing world should be defined as a time period of five years or longer. Any money that needs to be used in five years or sooner should simply not be invested in financial instruments that fluctuate in value with the securities markets. Short-term money should be invested in cash or cash equivalents such as short-term bonds, money market funds, or certificates of deposit. If you can use these simple rules of thumb, you can think like the perpetually wealthy and create an incredible liberation from the myriad economic indicators and forecasts that surround us in our media-crazed world.

Imagine having such an outlook about money that enables you to completely ignore the endless reports on earnings, unemployment, dividends, interest rates, the trade deficit, durable goods, consumer spending, the CPI, GDP, and so on. So how can all this valuable information about finances be disregarded and pushed aside when there are so many intelligent, well-educated people working diligently to bring you this news?

Think about this: How far out are economic forecasts typically projected? They are usually tied to the current quarter, perhaps the next quarter, right? On rare occasions a financial talking head will really go out on a limb and forecast the next 18 months. No one ever talks about what the economy is going to be doing in five years. They don't even know what will happen tomorrow afternoon truthfully. Yet, if we are using the five-year long-term money rule, is there any reason whatsoever to care about what will happen in the next month, quarter, or even 18 months?

Here is the secret (whisper it for effect, if you wish): Economic forecasts really only affect your cash. And what possible calamity can befall cash? "Cash is king," right? Oh sure, I know that the interest rates on cash accounts fluctuate with all the short-term economic data. That is because cash and cash equivalents are by nature, short-term investments. But remember, fixed income — into which cash falls as a category — has only two purposes: reduce short-term volatility and provide cash flow. The vast majority of your growth comes from equities. So even if your money market account or certificates of deposit earn 2% instead of 4% because of short-range economic factors, that has very little effect on your overall portfolio if it is properly allocated.

Uninformed, pessimistic investors "go to cash" when they perceive that there is an economic difficulty in the short term. The only problem is that the in-perpetuity bias lulls them into thinking that short-term forecasts are really for the long term. But in a free capital market, the forecasts never are. Forecasts inherently are short term in nature. And even those are often inaccurate.

So what effect will this concept have on your attention span for economic forecasts if you realize they affect only your short-term cash and fixed income investments? You'll stop listening and watching. You'll gain optimism and peace of mind.

Now you may be asking the legitimate question, "Yeah, but what if there is an economic issue or condition that arises that affects my long-term, five-year-plus investments? Shouldn't I be concerned then?" Well, first of all, it is possible that markets can turn downward and stay there for extended periods of time—even longer than five years. However, it is not probable.

Herein lies the other side of the secret that optimistic, perpetually wealthy Americans know (again in a low voice): Risk in free capital markets is not all that risky when time is factored in. In fact, going back to 1927, I could not find a single asset class that has gone down for five or more years in a row. The Standard & Poor's 500 Index was down four straight years during the Great Depression (1929 through 1932) and down three years in a row on two occasions since then (1939 through 1941 and 2000 through 2002).

The S&P 500 also has been considered to be in a "bull market" 80% of the time and in a "bear market" only 20% of the time since 1926.[19] Furthermore, after downturns, markets come roaring back with phenomenal speed and growth. After each of the aforementioned three- and four-year slides, the S&P gained an average of 23.9% per year (including dividends) over the next four-year period.[20]

The eighteenth-century Anglican bishop Beilby Porteous said, "He who foresees calamities suffers them twice over." Isn't that the curse of the pessimist? There is no surer way to become pessimistic than to pore over financial forecasts. No matter how good the economic metrics look, the media will always find the negative to report. Walper talks about how to develop the "perpetual wealth personality" by adopting these two simple and effective governing precepts: (1) Ignore the short-term economic forecasts and the meaningless news that they offer, and (2) invest your long-term dollars with confidence and optimism in free capital markets.

Why Asset Classes and Not Sectors?

Another topic that comes up often with our listeners concerns the confusion between sector investing and asset class investing. Research has indicated that the largest determinant of portfolio performance is asset allocation. In other words, how the portfolio is divided among different asset classes. Each asset class is made up of a particular type or category of stock. Examples of asset classes are large U.S. value, small international growth, emerging markets, and long-term bonds. Note that asset classes are not the same as sectors. Sectors are made up largely of particular industries or segments of the economy. Some examples of economic sectors are utilities, financial services, and biomedical technologies.

You may believe that you need to be aware of the sectors where you are invested because the financial media often talk about sectors such as oil and gas or information technology in a way that is recommending (or not) those areas of our economy for your portfolio. Choosing sectors for your portfolio traps you into playing the same old timing-and-picking game that is a recipe for portfolio inefficiency. Exchange-traded funds (ETFs) have also been creating clever advertisements for sector funds for several years in an effort to garner a portion of your investment dollars.

In an effort to illustrate the difficulty in choosing sectors for investment purposes, I offer Figure 5-5, which shows the S&P 500 Index sector returns for the calendar year 2007:[21] You can see that energy, materials, utilities, and consumer stables were big winners. On the other hand, if you or your money manager bet on financials or real estate, then you found hard times. It looks so obvious

Consumer discretionary	−14.30%
Consumer staples	11.60%
Energy	32.40%
Financials	−20.80%
Health care	5.40%
Industrials	9.80%
Information technology	15.50%
Real estate	−17.40%
Materials	20.00%
Telecommunications	8.50%
Utilities	15.80%

Figure 5-5   The S&P 500 Index Sector Returns for 2007
Source: Adapted from Standard & Poor's, "Sector Returns 2007," S&P Compustat Point in Time Database, October 9, 2008. (Standard & Poor's is a division of the McGraw-Hill Companies, New York.)

now in hindsight. But if it were that easy to pick the best sectors in which to invest, the reward for risk—the long-term market return—would not be present.

Wall Street likes to draw your attention to sectors more than asset classes because sectors are easier to explain and advertise; and admittedly they are more interesting to investors. This is problematic because money managers change their fund asset class percentages and sector weightings over time. They often change their composition by moving from growth to value, or small to large, or energy to financials, or even stocks to bonds. In addition, they are prone to increasing or decreasing their fund cash balances based on cash flow requirements and market situations. These ad hoc allocation adjustments contribute to a phenomenon known as "fund drift." *Fund drift* refers to a fund's security positions moving or drifting away from their original or stated investment objectives. This action creates portfolio inefficiencies and can significantly change the composition of a portfolio over time. It also means that the portfolio allocation first determined in a written financial plan can become superseded by the manager without the investor's approval.

Efficient asset allocation is accomplished when the mutual funds in your portfolio maintain their asset class allocation integrity. This is accomplished by rebalancing the asset classes periodically. I recommend an annual assessment of a portfolio to facilitate this rebalancing. The rebalancing process will increase the chances of selling high and buying low as those asset classes that have grown the most during the year will be pared back automatically through the rebalancing process, and any laggards will then be purchased. It is not intuitive for most investors to sell a fund that has done well and then buy one that has done poorly. But since you know that markets run in cycles, you do not have to be concerned about buying asset classes at a low point. In fact, now that you understand the surety associated with market cycles, you can shift your thinking to a "the market is on sale" mentality and reap the rewards that elude most investors because of their unfounded fear of market cycles. You have, in effect, learned one of the most important secrets of free capital market success.

When it comes to investing in sectors, there is far less research available to establish meaningful correlations. When you employ a process that properly allocates your investment portfolio in all asset classes based on your individual goals, needs, and tolerances for risk, you will automatically receive weightings in all of the sectors in the economy. This reduces the worry of being improperly diversified and also tends to eliminate the gamble inherent with any sector bets you may be tempted to place.

Jane Bryant Quinn's Bad Investment Rule of Thumb

"Never buy anything whose price you can't follow in the newspapers. Even when the price is published in the newspaper or online, don't buy anything too complex to explain to the average 12-year-old." So reads what Jane Bryant Quinn calls her "First Law of Investing and Its First Corollary."[22]

Quinn is a financial revolutionary whose pedigree precedes her. In addition to her current regular columns in *Newsweek* and at Bloomberg.com, her history includes a stint at *CBS News*, first on *The CBS Morning News*, then on *The Evening News with*

Dan Rather. She has appeared regularly on ABC's *The Home Show,* and she has made frequent guest appearances on *Good Morning America, Nightline,* and many other programs. The *World Almanac* named her as one of the 25 most influential women in America. I was honored to have her join us on *The Investing Revolution* to discuss her books *Making the Most of Your Money* and *Smart and Simple Financial Strategies for Busy People.* [23]

Her First Law of Investing is her advice to those investors who want to believe that the complicated products are the sophisticated ones. They are lured by complex formulas and limited availability, not realizing that those are the very things that should raise the red flag. The best investments, she believes, are the clean and simple. Well-diversified mutual funds will make you rich. Complicated products will not. And yet that doesn't stop Wall Street from offering them because there are always those who believe that when it comes to investments, the road less traveled is the road to riches.

Quinn says the competition is stiff, but there are a few investment vehicles that she considers to be the worst offenders.[24]

At the top of her list are tax-deferred variable annuities (VAs). These are essentially mutual funds inside an insurance wrapper. They're sold as ways of growing your money tax deferred and providing yourself with a lifetime retirement income. What are the problems?

First, they're often sold as investments for individual retirement accounts (IRAs). That's a waste. These are tax-deferred investments. You don't have to put them into another tax-deferred plan. Brokers sell them for IRAs because that may be the only pool of investment money the customer has. Second, the fees are huge and not at all clear. When you add them all up, you may be paying more than 3% a year (including a hidden commission). With costs like that, your investment won't go anywhere fast. Third, the broker will show you how your withdrawals can increase in the future, giving you a rising retirement income. Trouble is, your checks are highly unlikely to go up. Let's say that in retirement, you're taking 5% of your original investment each year. Your remaining investments have to rise by an average of more than 8% a year (covering the 5% withdrawal plus 3% in fees) for you to have even a hope of a rising check in the years ahead. Fourth, the money you take out is taxed as ordinary income. If you'd bought regular mutual funds, your profits would be taxed at the lower capital gains rate. Fifth, this money is taxable when left to heirs. Any gains in your regular mutual funds can be left to heirs tax free.

Next on her list are auction rate securities—mercifully not sold anymore. These were marketed by investment advisors as something similar to money market mutual funds, places to put cash that paid 5%, instead of perhaps 3%. The problem was that the investment was based on auction rate securities. Quinn describes these as "perpetual investments with no fixed maturities but with short-term renewal dates, often once a week." Once the renewal date arrived, the shares were put up for auction. You could rebid for your shares or offer them up to other investors and take the cash. These sounded appealing not just for their higher dividend rates but because they seemed to lock up cash only a week at a time. In truth, you could cash out your shares only if other investors were bidding on them. Sometimes they were not bidding, which meant that those holding shares were stuck in the investment. While they may have earned that extra 2% in dividends, the money wasn't available to them and may not have been for months or even years.

This market has largely shut down, but it's an object lesson for liquid savings. Don't fall for investments that mysteriously pay more than money market rates. There's always a hitch.

Third on Quinn's hit list is the unit trust, which is a fixed port-folio of securities, often municipal bonds.[25] Shares in the package are sold, and it sits unchanged for a period of time, sometimes up to 30 years. Those with shares are sent a pro rata share of the interest and dividend payments at certain intervals (every quarter, for instance) and then a pro rata share of the proceeds when the port-folio reaches maturity. The problem is that there's no tracking done to see if the unit trusts actually earn what they promise. In addition, there's risk of losing money if the trust doesn't reach maturity. Also, the stream of interest and dividend income may not remain steady because the makeup of the portfolio can change in various ways, such as through the sale of certain securities.

Penny stocks are fourth on the list for their shady marketing tac-tics.[26] These stocks, which glean their name from their price tag of $5 or less per share, are from questionable companies with little or no track record. These stocks are typically sold over the phone as part of schemes that manipulate the stock prices in order to keep money flowing in. Once enough money has been invested, the truth about the stock price is revealed. Prices drop, and when the investors move to sell, they realize the orders often aren't processed unless the "profits" are used to purchase other stocks. Often the process continues until the investors are wiped out. In another ver-sion of the hustle, the stocks are sold in empty businesses that then take the invested money and buy small, private companies, some legitimate, some not.

The list could go on, and does in Quinn's books. She offers a few general guidelines on how to spot a bad investment, including anything touted as "safe" with a higher-than-normal yield, any mutual fund with the word "plus" in the title, anything complicated, and anything hyped on a television infomercial or sold over the phone in a cold call. When in doubt, hearken back to Quinn's First Law. Is it something I can track in the newspaper or online? Could I explain it to a 12-year-old? If the answer to either of those is no, then look for other investments that are clean and simple: well-diversified mutual funds. Investing shouldn't be complicated. If it is, you're doing something wrong.

Bottom Line

Former Chairman of the Joint Chiefs of Staff Admiral Arthur Radford once said, "A decision is an action you must take when you have information so incomplete that the answer does not suggest itself." In many areas in life, things are not always what they seem to be. Unfortunately, it is that way in the financial services world. That makes decisions tougher to make. My duty in this chapter was to clarify some big-picture truths and encourage you to examine fully the investment options you are presented from time to time. We all have paradigms that need shifting. I hope you have been in some way enlightened to the degree that you will make better decisions with your money now that you know more about the investing world.

THE GLOBAL
CONNECTION

Freedom is what America means to the world.
—Audie Murphy

George Washington said, "A people . . . who are possessed of the spirit of commerce, who see and who will pursue their advantages, may achieve almost anything." I would submit that he meant any people—not only his beloved fellow citizens associated with the fledgling American economy. I believe we are among the most blessed in history as we live during a time when the world has seen the light. Capitalism is expanding around the world at a tremendous pace. You are a part of the greatest economic transformation the world has ever known. May you remember and ponder this fact as you read and learn more about global free enterprise.

Bob Litan on Good Capitalism, Bad Capitalism, and Emerging Markets

In July 1987, Ronald Reagan stood at the Brandenburg Gate in West Berlin, Germany, and urged Mikhail Gorbachev to tear down the Berlin Wall.[1] The wall had become a primary symbol of the Cold War, standing as a visual representation of the barrier that existed between capitalist and communist societies. Two and a half years later, the wall did fall, and capitalism was declared the economic winner. However, after 20 years, there are still significant differences among global economies. There are European and Asian societies that quite obviously have not matched the economic growth found in the United States.

Consider that just one century ago, the purchasing power of one person in the United States was one-tenth of what it is today. In the five years ending 2007, the American economy grew 3.5% each year, a rate that will double an economy in just over two decades.[2]

I had the privilege to visit with economist Robert Litan, coauthor of *Good Capitalism, Bad Capitalism, and the Economics of Growth and Prosperity,* on this very topic.[3] Litan has had a distinguished career serving on the staff of the Council of Economic Advisers (1977 to 1979). He has also served as deputy assistant attorney general in the Antitrust Division of the Justice Department (1993 to 1995) and as associate director of the Office of Management and Budget (1995 to 1996). He is vice president of research and policy at the Kauffman Foundation, and he has been affiliated with the Brookings Institution for nearly 20 years where he leads a team of economists monitoring the global economy and seeking answers to economic policy issues in the United States and around the world.

In the first chapter of his book, he states the following: "The most astonishing thing about the extraordinary outpouring of growth and innovation that the U.S. and other economies have achieved over the past two centuries is that it does not astonish us."[4] I asked the professor to comment.

"We take growth for granted. If we [were] living in the eighteenth century, our lives generally speaking would not be that much different from people's lives a thousand years before. Put another way, there was virtually no economic growth throughout the world in most places until about 1800. Then starting with the Industrial Revolution and continuing to the present day, economies in what we now call the 'developed world' started to take off. The developing world now is catching up. But by and large since then, we've had growth anywhere from 2 to 3% a year, which doesn't sound like much except when you realize that at that rate you can double your living standards every generation. And so each generation has gotten used to the fact that they're going to live better than their parents. This is now taken for granted, and this is something that would not have been taken for granted throughout most of human history."

One of the most interesting assertions in Litan's book is that capitalist systems are not all alike. He categorizes four types of capital market systems and provides an example of each.[5]

"Well, let's take us back to the date when the Berlin Wall fell in 1989. After that happened, there was a lot of 'triumphalism' that capitalism had won and communism had lost, and the implicit notion behind that was that capitalism was some monolithic system that celebrated the ownership of private property and enabled people who started businesses and who owned shares to get the profits from their businesses essentially unregulated. [It also held that] people would have very strong incentives, in other words, to invent and develop new companies. Well, it turns out that if you look around the world, all countries could be called 'capitalist' with the exception of perhaps Cuba and North Korea. Even China now is probably 30 to 40% capitalist, on its way to being substantially capitalist. And if you look around the world, though, at the roughly 190 countries, you'll quickly realize that the capitalism in Europe, let's say, differs from the way it's practiced in Latin America, from Africa, the Middle East, and so forth. Countries are all different. What I do in this book is, rather than specifying 188 or 190 different kinds of capitalism, reduce them to four. And the four have common features within each group.

"The first group is what we called 'state owned' or 'state directed capitalism.' Those are societies where private property is still allowed as it is in all forms of capitalism. But in a state directed society, the state uses a combination of ownership of the banking system or other incentives to direct resources in one particular industry or in several. So you can think of Asia, parts of India, parts of China, of course, as being examples of state directed capitalism.

"The second kind of capitalism is 'oligarchic capitalism,' and by that we mean systems where power and money are concentrated with the elite. You'll see such systems in Latin America, the Middle East, in many nations in Africa. What makes oligarchic capitalistic societies different from state directed and the other two is that when you have power concentrated among a few, they tend not to care about what happens to the rest of society. They're interested mostly in whatever will maximize their own welfare, not the average welfare of other citizens. And so they're the only form of capitalist society that doesn't elevate growth to be the number 1 economic objective.

"The third kind of capitalism is what we call 'bureaucratic' or 'big-firm capitalism.' Again, it means what it says. There are economies that are dominated by large firms, typically well established. You think of Japan and Europe, or at least Western Europe. Big firms are great for achieving economies of scale, for being quite efficient, and for coming up with incremental innovation. But they're not great for doing something really radical—introducing such things as the personal computer revolution or being at the forefront of the Internet revolution. You don't see the breakout kinds of really radical new companies in big-firm societies, and that's why in recent decades they've run into trouble. Even though as late as the 1980s many people thought that Japan and Europe were going to overtake us here in the United States, that turned out not to be true.

"So that leaves the fourth category, which is what we call 'entrepreneurial capitalism.' Again, it means what it says. Those are societies where the energy in the economy is driven by new firms. They're the ones that are most likely to do radical innovation. The ideal form of capitalism is a mix between big-firm and entrepreneurship or entrepreneurial capitalism. You need that healthy component of new firms to keep your economy fresh and new, and at the same time you need some big firms to mass-produce and provide incremental innovation for the innovations that are developed by the new firms. And we think that over the long sweep of history, if economies want to grow, they've got to move toward some component of entrepreneurial capitalism. Otherwise, they're slated to fall behind."

Litan talks in his book about the fact that the interest groups can actually ossify an economy. I asked him how worried we should be about this American way of doing business.

"The growth of interest groups can lead to gridlock. Actually the economist who is most identified with making that argument is the late Manser Olson from the University of Maryland who wrote a book I think called *The Rise and Fall of Nations* in the 1980s. [It is] a terrific book which argued that if you get too many interest groups, especially that compete against each other, they essentially buy off favors from the government, and in effect they ossify a country. There was a journalist named Jonathan Rash who also made the same kind of argument in a political career. Now, how do you prevent ossification if you've got so many interest groups? Think about K Street in Washington full of all those lobbyists, and by the way, if you count the number of lobbyists in Washington, there are far many more today than there were 30 years ago, so you have to worry about interest groups.

"The way you break the power of interest groups is in a peaceful fashion, because obviously we don't want war. You get new technologies that are disruptive, that sort of shake up everything, and they shake the barnacles of all the interest groups of the society off the ship so to speak. You get new interest groups that are formed, and hopefully by the time or before they ossify, you'll get a new technological change. So you can think of in the last 30, 40 years in the United States, you think of the transistor, which led to the PC, which led to the Internet, and now biotech and now technology. We're getting a series of major breakthroughs in technology that reshuffled the investor landscape, and that's the one great virtue of our system. As long as we get those changes, we won't fall victim to ossification."

We are pleased whenever we see nations aspire toward any type of free capital market system. State directed or oligarchic systems are a start, but history has shown, as Litan outlines, that if economies want to thrive, they must move toward a more entrepreneurial structure. While a bit of big-firm capitalism can ultimately help advance the products and ideas that grow from an entrepreneurial society, it is that healthy entrepreneurial component—the reliance on new firms, products, and ideas—that will do more for economic growth than will any other reform. Litan points out the example of Ireland, whose economic development has grown annually by more than 7.5% between 1997 and 2007.[6] (By the way, this tremendous economic transformation was spawned by a dramatic lowering of income taxes in Ireland. Politicians, take note.)

While the global economy is a long way from the ideal form of capitalism as a whole, progress continues. Litan's book points out that one thing to consider is that the economies of emerging markets are influenced by geography and culture. Geographic factors, such as access to water and overall climate, and cultural factors, such as the support of entrepreneurship, can hinder the evolution of capitalism. However, they can be overcome (and have been in many countries). Building roads to the sea is certainly easier than enacting government policy, but neither geography nor culture should be considered a permanent barrier. Indeed, only when there is progress to be made can a growth rate beneficial to investors be experienced. Underdeveloped economies have a lot more potential for growth. This simple fact is essential to consider.

Emerging markets are perhaps the least refined, and as a result they have the most potential for growth. Imagine living in an economic culture where opportunities are something you only read about in a book. Then along comes a time and a cultural change that allows the freedoms of owning property. The rule of law, rather than the rule of human beings, is instituted, and a chance of owning your own business or studying to enter any career that you wish becomes a new reality. Imagine the excitement and enthusiasm with which you would pursue your dreams. That is the society we live in, but for most of the world, this is still a relatively distant concept. As you consider emerging markets around the globe, it is these opportunities that provide growth and signal a healthy economy and increasing wealth in a society. Fortunately, the economic climate that is dominating around the world is based on freedom in some form.

The world is not controlled by a centralized government. That has been tried, and it has failed. There is even a growing list of millionaires and even billionaires in China, of all places.

As emerging markets progress worldwide, the truth is that bad capitalism occurs when the economic wealth is not shared across a population. All too often, the benefits of capitalism are not realized, as seen in countries like Venezuela, which is currently limiting individual freedoms. Cuba and North Korea remain the only two stalwart holdouts, and one never knows—even with them, it may only be a matter of time.

Emerging markets are essential to a properly diversified investment portfolio. As market systems around the globe continue to evolve, investors see that progress reflected in investment returns. Over the five years ending in 2008, emerging markets as measured by the MSCI Emerging Markets Index returned 9.02% annualized, compared to losses of 1.38% from the S&P 500 Index over the same time period.[7]

Your investments in emerging markets should be made in limited amounts (no more than 8 to 10% in a 100% equity portfolio) and should be spread globally across all emerging economies.

The emerging market asset class should be considered a requirement for your portfolio. We know that economic progress, however slow and painful, leads to new freedoms. As President Reagan said on that day in 1987, "There stands before the entire world one great and inescapable conclusion: Freedom leads to prosperity."

Global Diversification

Investors often ignore international markets because they regard them as too risky. This is a mistake. Investors also tend to believe that if they own domestic companies that sell products or services overseas, they are investing internationally. Research indicates that stock prices of companies tend to follow the trends of their domiciled country even if a majority of their business comes from foreign markets.[8]

International markets tend to move in different directions from domestic markets. "Different" may mean that they are both going up or down but each at a different pace. Figure 6-1 demonstrates how U.S. and international markets outperformed each other during certain time periods. The case of foreign markets being led by Japan in the mid- to late 1980s was a good example of times when international markets have outperformed U.S. markets by a wide margin.[9] Additionally, even during the bull market run seen in the United States from 2003 to 2007, international markets were the winners. Diversification into foreign markets during these and other time frames has preserved capital for many investors.

Invest internationally has become pretty standard advice from most advisors. But the next question becomes, which countries or regions should be included in your portfolio? The Heritage Foundation, in conjunction with the *Wall Street Journal*, has created the annual Index of Economic Freedom. For the last 14 years, the

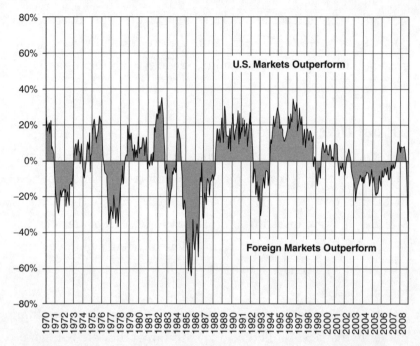

Figure 6-1 U.S. and Foreign Markets Perform Differently from January 1970 through December 2008
Source: Adapted from Kim R. Holmes, Edwin J. Feulner, and Mary Anastasia O'Grady, "2008 Index of Economic Freedom," Heritage Foundation and Dow Jones & Company, Inc., Washington, D.C., 2008, www.heritage.org.

index has documented the link between economic opportunity and prosperity. It is based on 10 indicators in these areas: business, trade, fiscal, government size, monetary, investment, financial, property rights, freedom from corruption, and labor. While some of these category descriptions may sound very similar at first look, there are nuances in the meanings of the indicators such that they provide valuable information.

The list of the top 10 countries in the 2008 index gives some perspective on how the data are compiled and used.[10] As you consider the information in Figure 6-2, you should reflect on the gains your portfolio could make if you diversified your portfolio into the economic systems (countries) that are the most free and are therefore the most likely to grow and prosper.

Former British colonies in Asia lead the world in economic freedom. Hong Kong has never relinquished the number 1 spot in 14 years. With Singapore and Australia also near the top, the Asia-Pacific region has 3 of the top 5 freest economies in the world. Europe has 3 of the top 10 freest economies and 10 of the top 20.

Ireland may be a surprise to you, along with Chile. These are both notable for different reasons. Ireland implemented a much lower income tax several years back, which has caused the boom in that small island nation of approximately 4 million citizens. As for Chile, it is cited as one of the few nations that have privatized their social security system. Not only that, it also uses a passive asset class approach with a large percentage of the assets in its system. Do you think the U.S. government (ranked number 5 in the index) might be able to learn a thing or two from these "upstart" free economies? Probably not. But that doesn't mean that you as an individual investor cannot learn some valuable lessons.

Some other notable rankings in the index from which you can perhaps garner a lesson include the following.

Venezuela: As President Hugo Chávez takes a more antidemocratic and anti–free market position, his country's index ranking at number 148 (tenth from the bottom) continues to decline. This is in spite of the tremendous natural resource wealth—particularly oil—contained within Venezuela's borders.

Cuba: To no one's surprise, Cuba (number 156) is followed only by North Korea (number 157), dead last on the list.

Country	Overall Score	Business Freedom	Trade Freedom	Fiscal Freedom	Government Size	Monetary Freedom	Investment Freedom	Financial Freedom	Property Rights	Freedom from Corruption	Labor Freedom
Hong Kong	90.25	88.18	95	92.8	93.07	87.21	90	90	90	83	93.3
Singapore	87.38	97.79	90	90.3	93.87	88.86	80	50	90	94	99
Ireland	82.35	92.22	86	71.5	64.5	84.91	90	90	90	74	80.4
Australia	82	89.32	83.8	59.2	62.83	83.68	80	90	90	87	94.2
United States	80.56	91.69	86.8	68.3	59.81	83.67	80	80	90	73	92.3
New Zealand	80.25	99.9	80.8	60.5	55.99	83.67	70	80	90	96	85.5
Canada	80.18	96.74	87	75.5	53.67	80.98	70	80	90	85	82.9
Chile	79.79	67.48	82.2	78.1	88.24	78.82	80	70	90	73	90
Switzerland	79.72	83.89	87.2	68	61.55	83.57	70	80	90	91	82
United Kingdom	79.55	90.79	86	61.2	40.06	80.75	90	90	90	86	80.7

Figure 6-2 2008 Index of Economic Freedom

Source: Adapted from Kim R. Holmes, Edwin J. Feulner, and Mary Anastasia O'Grady, "2008 Index of Economic Freedom," Heritage Foundation and Dow Jones & Company, Inc., Washington, D.C., 2008, www.heritage.org.

And finally of note are the former Soviet bloc nations, which are doing quite well, thank you. They include Estonia at 12, Lithuania at 26, and Armenia at number 28. (For anyone that might doubt that there is no link between economic freedom and all other freedoms, I would have them explain this.)

What does all this mean to your investment portfolio? First of all, think in terms of regions, not individual countries. This will prevent you from getting into a country "picking game." The Pacific Rim region with its high-ranking countries is an obvious choice. The second that I would recommend weighting heavily within your international allocation is Europe. If you use the Index of Economic Freedom (IEF) to compile five regions—Europe, Asia-Pacific, the Americas, sub-Sahara Africa, and the Middle East and North Africa—a majority of the freest economies are in Europe. Given this fact, the solution is to use passive international funds that focus on a collection of countries similar to the MSCI EAFE Index, which tracks companies in Europe, Australasia, and the Far East.

Morgan Stanley Capital International developed the MSCI EAFE Index over 20 years ago.[11] It incorporates the countries of Australia, Austria, Belgium, Denmark, Finland, France, Germany, Greece, Hong Kong, Ireland, Italy, Japan, The Netherlands, New Zealand, Norway, Portugal, Singapore, Spain, Sweden, Switzerland, and the United Kingdom. The average Economic Freedom Index ranking of these 21 countries is 23.9.[12] This puts this collection of countries as a group in the top 15% of the world in economic freedom. Ideally, you would want to invest in all of these while also including Canada, which is ranked number 7 in the IEF. This would bring the average ranking up just a bit further to 23 and add another strong free economy to the mix.

As I mentioned, international markets tend to move in different directions from the U.S. market. To drill down a bit further on this point, Figure 6-3 outlines the returns of who "wins" each year. We went back to 1970 to compare the MSCI EAFE Index with the Standard & Poor's 500 Index—a proxy for the U.S. market.[13]

As you can see, there is no definitive pattern. The better returns in a given year are random and cyclical. One never knows which markets will turn out best in a given time frame. You may be surprised to see that the MSCI EAFE Index had higher returns in almost twice as many years as the S&P 500 (25 versus 14). The annualized return for the EAFE was 8.97% for the 39-year period while the annualized return for the S&P 500 was 9.47%. A very close race to be sure. The EAFE had a negative annual return 11 times, or about once every 4 years, and the S&P had negative returns 12 times, or about 1 out of every 3 years. There were also notable runs in each index. For example, after a downturn of −36.3% in 1973 and 1974, the EAFE then ran off 6 straight positive return years and had an average return of 22.3% over the next 15 years. A second streak of 5 years with a total return of 112.4% took place from 2003 through 2007 after a fall of −50.9% occurred during the 3-year time frame of 2000 through 2002. Likewise, the S&P has had its own share of streaks—overwhelmingly positive on the whole.

When I looked at the two indexes individually, I noted that the EAFE gained or lost more than 10% in 31 of the 39 calendar years. The S&P 500 returned ±10% in 27 years. This weakens the argument that foreign markets are much more volatile than U.S. markets. The most astonishing fact of this analysis is the annual average differential in returns (the average amount of difference in returns of the indexes compared to each other in single years)

	1970	1971	1972	1973	1974	1975	1976	1977	1978	1979	1980	1981	1982
S&P 500	−1.4	10.6	15.0	−21.6	−34.5	28.2	18.2	−13.1	−2.3	4.5	17.8	−12.7	16.9
MSCI EAFE	−10.5	31.2	37.6	−14.2	−22.1	37.1	3.7	19.4	34.3	6.2	24.4	−1.0	−0.9

	1983	1984	1986	1986	1987	1988	1989	1990	1991	1992	1993	1994	1995
S&P 500	18.0	2.2	27.4	17.1	0.8	11.9	25.7	−8.7	26.6	4.5	7.1	−1.3	34.0
MSCI EAFE	24.6	7.9	56.7	69.9	24.9	28.6	10.8	−23.2	12.5	−11.8	32.9	8.1	11.6

	1996	1997	1998	1999	2000	2001	2002	2003	2004	2005	2006	2007	2008
S&P 500	19.0	31.1	26.6	17.9	−12.1	−13.2	−23.9	26.3	7.4	1.4	12.9	1.4	−37.0
MSCI EAFE	6.4	2.1	20.3	27.3	−14.0	−21.2	−15.7	39.2	20.7	14.0	26.9	11.6	−43.0

Figure 6-3 Performance of the MSCI EAFE Index versus the S&P 500 Index from 1970 through 2008
Source: MSCI Barra, *Emerging Markets: A 20-Year Perspective,* New York, September 17, 2008,
www.mscibarra.com/products/indices/em_20/.

between the MSCI EAFE and the S&P 500: a whopping 14.2% per year. So in the long run, the average return was about equal. Yet the differential each year was nearly 15%.[14] This is a testament to how diversifying into international markets reduces volatility.

I recommend maintaining at least 30% of the equity portion of your portfolio in international asset classes, and 50% is certainly not out of the question. With nearly 60% of the total capitalization (total of all companies' values added together) now residing outside the United States, it only makes sense to take advantage of the growth that free economies at all stages of development will experience at some point. This includes diversifying across large and small categories and emerging markets.

The notion and practical application of capitalism is expanding, not contracting, around the world. Global diversification is of extreme importance in a properly allocated portfolio. It allows you as an investor the avenue to share in the prosperity that free markets bring—even at times when the U.S. economy may be lagging.

Where in the World Should You Invest?

Of the approximately $37.4 trillion in world market capitalization on December 31, 2007, the United States held $15.7 trillion, or 41% of the total.[15] Obviously this means that international markets hold the other 59% and long ago surpassed the size of domestic markets. To put that in perspective, in 1970, the U.S. markets held about 60% of world market capitalization.[16] So there has been a shift globally even though the U.S. economy has been quite healthy on the whole over the last four decades. If you wanted to mirror the market exactly, this would direct you to maintain international holdings that would make up more than half of a portfolio.

Consider also the ratio of developed countries to emerging markets. Developed countries make up 88% of world market capitalization. Emerging markets account for 10% with 2% not invested. This amount invested in emerging markets is comparable to just over triple the market share of Microsoft, General Electric, and Exxon Mobil combined.[17]

While we hear much about it on the news, as it works to develop its market system, China's market capitalization in 2006 was comparable to that of two Microsofts.[18] Perhaps this should give some perspective and dampen the fervor with which some investors are rushing into China funds.

Given this information, should you emulate the world capitalization exactly in your portfolio? Once you eliminate under-developed markets (about $2 trillion), the math indicates a 50/50 mix, which is actually a suitable ratio. I recommend that at least 30% of the equity portion of your portfolio be invested in international markets, including emerging market asset classes. Then perhaps over time the amount can be increased to as much as 50%. This strategy provides substantial and meaningful exposure to the economies overseas that will inevitably outperform U.S. markets during certain economic cycles.

It is worth noting that studies show individual investors all over the world are much more comfortable investing in companies domiciled within their own borders. Americans like American companies, Germans like German companies, and so on. This seems to be a natural phenomenon based largely on familiarity.

But you should not let this emotional aspect distract you from the facts that point to a global approach to managing your money.

World markets are a vital part of investing money prudently. If investors have the proper perspective concerning the rest of the financial globe, then they can reap rewards and avoid the inefficiencies that accompany myopic attitudes about investing.

What about China? There has been a recent surge in news coverage over China and its strengthening economy (see Figure 6-4). Much of that reporting has been spurred by and has focused on two things. The first is that the Chinese economy, as measured by its gross domestic product (GDP), has grown, according to the World Bank's quarterly report, an average of 9% over the past several years (versus about 3 to 4% in the United States). In addition, it was announced in July 2005 that China was revaluing its currency. The yuan, its value long tied to the U.S. dollar on a fixed exchange rate, is now measured against a basket of world

$6,991,000,000,000	GDP
$1,217,000,000,000	Exports
$901,300,000,000	Imports
1,330,044,605	Population
803,300,000	Labor force
313,321,639	Military manpower
5,963,274	Area (square miles)
467	Airports
73	Life expectancy
33	Median age

Figure 6-4 China by the Numbers
Source: Adapted from Kim R. Holmes, Edwin J. Feulner, and Mary Anastasia O'Grady, "2008 Index of Economic Freedom," Heritage Foundation and Dow Jones & Company, Inc., Washington, D.C., 2008, www.heritage.org.

currencies, which, in addition to the dollar, includes the euro, Japanese yen, and, to a smaller extent, the British pound.[19]

The media coverage concerning China has created speculation over whether or not the country is a good place for your investment dollars. The important thing to keep in mind, however, is that while the country may be a good economic story, it's not necessarily a good investment story.

Kenneth Lieberthal, author of *Governing China: From Revolution Through Reform* and former National Security Council senior director for Asia, discussed with us the numerous challenges the country faces that not only will make it a potentially higher risk investment but will also gradually slow its growth rate.[20]

One of those challenges is the population migration from rural to urban areas, Lieberthal informed us. Since the early 1990s, roughly 150 million people have left the rural areas—where they contribute nothing to the country's GDP—for the city, where they boost the GDP but also require the government to provide additional schools, housing, health care, and roads in order to maintain social stability. It's estimated that another 100 million will have made that move by 2010, and an additional 100 to 150 million by 2050. "We are witnessing the largest-scale migration from rural to urban areas in human history," says Lieberthal.

Another, and perhaps the largest, challenge China faces over the next 10 to 15 years is the availability of clean usable water. Northern China, where nearly half of the population lives, has seen its water table (the distance drilling must occur to reach water) fall by three feet every year since 1960.[21] Water that is available tends to be polluted and will require a large investment in order to resolve the problem.

In light of the country's societal and environmental issues, China will, over the coming years, see its economic growth slow down, either voluntarily or involuntarily. "They have effectively set up a government that is a growth machine," says Lieberthal. "At every level of the national hierarchy—from the center in Beijing, through 31 provinces, through 600 cities, through more than 2,000 counties to 50,000 townships—there are enormous incentives to make their local economies grow. So when the government wants to slow down growth, it really has to hit the brakes pretty hard."

Many experts have monitored developments in China since its movement toward being a more capitalistic society in the last two decades. In recent years, reforms have eased the concerns about investor-related issues such as accounting standards, banking regulations, property rights, bankruptcy procedures, and foreign exchange transactions. As a result, many have concluded that China now meets the proper criteria for investing.[22]

Many investment managers invest in Chinese mainland companies through the Hong Kong exchange. This universe of mainland stocks is large enough to be divided into diversified strategies with distinctive large-cap, small-cap, and value characteristics, consistent with the asset class approach in other markets.

China will most likely turn out to be one of the larger markets in the emerging markets strategies. As of September 2008, it was the third-largest country in the MSCI Emerging Markets Index, after South Korea and Taiwan.[23] As with any investment, China is not the place to be just because it's making headlines. You should always guard against the temptation to pick individual securities or individual countries in overseas markets—even one that represents one-fifth of the world's population and has such a booming economy. Rapid development does not always lead to shareholder returns—whether in a country or a company. It is one of those nagging counterintuitive truths about investing. Always remember that if you want to be a prudent investor, you must superdiversify into multiple asset classes rather than focus on particular countries or sectors, however appealing they may seem.

T. Boone Pickens on Energy Independence

There perhaps is no economic issue of our time that is more important than energy. We have dedicated entire radio programs to the subject several times over the last five years. Let's face it: Petroleum is not just the fuel of our automobiles. It is the fuel of free capital markets. Oil is a global issue. It is the proverbial riddle, wrapped in a paradox, topped off by a conundrum. And there are widely differing opinions and sound bites: "Drill here, drill now, pay less." "The government has already allowed huge amounts of land for oil exploration that are not even being used." "What about our carbon footprint?" "The Alaska National Wildlife Refuge (ANWR) is in the frozen tundra. Let's use it to rid ourselves of overseas oil dependence." "It would take 10 years to get more oil even if we started now." "Cutting demand is the only way to bring down the price of gasoline." "The demand in China and India is driving up prices." "Speculators are causing all the problem." "We need more nuclear power plants." "We must build more refineries." The arguments are endless.

It is noteworthy that almost anyone who owns a mutual fund or has a pension owns part of an oil company. That includes the majority of Americans. We are literally all in this together. So what should you believe? And what can you do about it?

In mid-September 2008, we invited the irrepressible T. Boone Pickens to join us on *The Investing Revolution*.[24] The 80-year-old Pickens had been barnstorming his energy policy across the airwaves for several months, and we were excited to have him enlighten us with his west Texas wit and knowledge on the subject. In researching Pickens's background, I was surprised to learn that he and I had quite a bit in common. We went to the same high school in Amarillo, and we both played varsity basketball there. He also attended my college alma mater, Texas A&M, for a brief time on a basketball scholarship, before ending up at Oklahoma State University. Pickens is the founder and chairman of BP Capital, and his latest book, *The First Billion Is the Hardest*, is a riveting account of a life spent pulling off improbable triumphs.[25]

In my first question, I reminded him that he had accurately predicted that oil would go to $150 a barrel before it actually did in July 2008. Most consumers thought it would never stop going up; yet at interview time, it had actually fallen below $100 a barrel. My question to Pickens was simple. What's going on with the price of oil?

"Well, you've got a recession here in the United States, and you've got a recession that's going to show up in Europe very shortly, and the Japanese have struggled. So you've got problems around the world, and with that, you have less demand for crude. But don't worry; it will be back up to $150 by this time next year."

I found his declarative tone on this point not very reassuring.

Pickens had been working hard to get the word out on his "10-year energy plan," as he calls it, to reduce our dependency on foreign oil. I asked him to share a few of the plan's main points with our listeners that weren't quite as familiar with it.

"We will get the energy problems for America straightened out. I fully intend to do that. To date we have not had an energy plan for America in over 40 years, and we can't go any further because we're importing now almost 70% of the crude oil we use. That comes [with] a price of $600 to $700 billion, and we can't stand that either. If you do a fast forward for 10 years and we don't do anything more than we've done in the last 10 years, we will then be importing 75% of our oil, and the cost will be over a trillion dollars a year. So all this is going to bring us down to being a second-rate country if we don't do something about it.

"And so I've analyzed the problem, and I have a solution, and the solution is that we use resources in America and quit buying foreign oil. One of those resources is that our power generation [can] be done with wind and solar, and when you do that, you release natural gas from the power generation sector and use it for transportation fuel, and that is cheaper. It's cleaner, it's abundant, and it's ours. So then you have the perfect solution because every time you buy a gallon of natural gas for your car instead of a gallon of diesel or gasoline, you're going to reduce the cost of foreign oil directly. So the only way you can reduce the foreign oil bill is with another resource in America, and the only resource you have in America that can do that in large quantities is natural gas."

When investors watch the stock market they anchor on the trend, they have in-perpetuity bias. If the market is going up, then investors get the feeling that it will always go up. When the market is in a bear mode, investors are influenced by the media and begin to get the uneasy feeling that the market will never turn positive again. But it has always come back because freedom reigns.

The same situation exists in the oil market. Consumers see the price go up for weeks or months, and it appears to them as though nothing will ever stop it. But it will. It must. It always has. The free market will eventually correct the problem—if the government will allow it to do so. I asked Pickens to comment on this risk of consumers' being lulled again into a sense of complacency during time periods when the price eases a bit.

"Well, I think that that is a fear that I have, yes, and that's what's happened to us in the past when the price of oil went up back in the 1970s, the 1980s. We would then start to think about alternatives, and then the price would come down. You know, if you look at the problem and how did it all come about, all of us are somewhat to blame. But really, the reason we got ourselves in this predicament is because we didn't have the leadership in Washington. And the second thing, which is a contributing factor, of course, is that we had cheap oil. And so we just said, 'Send us the oil. Never mind the price.' And then one day the price got too high, and gasoline at $4 a gallon started to wake people up. And they said, 'Well, is this what we're headed for?'

"When you look at the OPEC countries five years ago, their revenues were $250 billion. This year their revenues will be $1.25 trillion—five times as much as it was five years ago. Why do you think that trend is going to change? It isn't going to change. You're going to pay more and more for oil if you don't do something about your problem."

To wrap up our conversation concerning energy policy, I asked him what would be the most important advice he would give to the next president. In true form, his answer was on point.

"Show some leadership. [And] that a problem well analyzed is a problem half solved. So get your problems analyzed well, and go to work on them and get them solved. But get something done before you go out of office, and good luck."

I know I am biased with Pickens's being a good old fella from the Texas panhandle like me, but I must say, I was taken by his kind and sincere demeanor. I have a feeling if given the chance, T. Boone Pickens will indeed help us "get the energy problems for America straightened out."

Marvin Zonis on the Global Political Economy

Marvin Zonis is a global political economist and professor emeritus at the Graduate School of Business at the University of Chicago, where he teaches courses on international political economy, leadership, and business strategy in the era of e-commerce.[26] He is one of the original experts on the top-rated ABC television show *Nightline*, and his perspective on the global economy is unmatched. He joined us on *The Investing Revolution* in April 2007 to share his comments on various aspects of the global political economy.[27] In the limited time we had to visit, I wanted to get an overview of geopolitical regions of the globe that held a special interest from an individual investor's standpoint.

As I recalled, Professor Zonis came to prominence as a guest expert on ABC television during the Iran hostage crisis. Naturally, I started off with that subject given Iran's recent saber rattling. Professor Zonis said, "There's no question that the situation in Iran is grim for the people who live in Iran, and it's grim for the rest of us. They are not only aggressive across the Middle East but they are also certainly proceeding to master nuclear technology. Now whether that means they're actually going to develop a bomb or not, I'm doubtful about it. But it's certainly suggested they're going to get a screwdriver twist away from having a bomb if they want to get one. President Reagan sent then Secretary of Defense Donald Rumsfeld to Baghdad in 1982 because the United States understood that Saddam's army was the wall that kept the Iranians out of the Middle East. So in April 2003 when we overthrew Saddam, that wall was gone, and the Iranians and the Shiites energized revolution across the region."

I don't think I have ever considered that Saudi Arabia could be unstable. In fact, I had always thought that it was one of the steadier nations in the Middle East. However, true to form, Professor Zonis was able to offer another insight on that vital region of the world. "Right now, it's very stable because high oil prices allow the regime to spread the money around the kingdom. But if you look over the long-term fate of the kingdom, I think there's no question that it's highly unstable. Not to suggest anything's going to happen in the near term, but about 20 percent of the population of Saudi Arabia is totally poverty stricken and living in absolute misery, a very large percentage of the population is illiterate, and the women of Saudi Arabia are denied participation. That's not going to continue indefinitely."

Shifting focus to China, Professor Zonis offered the following insight concerning the short-term outlook versus the intermediate- or longer-term vision: "That's the key issue: 5 to 10 years is much better than 2, 3, 4 years. I think in the immediate future, China is going to be able to continue this world-record-breaking growth, and it will become a much more powerful force in the economy, really in the world, but certainly in East Asia.

"There are two big dates [for] China. One is August 2008, that's the Beijing Summer Olympics. The other is June 2010 when Shanghai plays host to a world's fair. The government of China sees these two great events as focusing world attention on the emergence of China as a global independent superpower—not necessarily to challenge the United States but to be seen as a country that is economically, politically, militarily, technologically of superpower status. I believe that while they'll keep it going through those dates—because it's so important to their sense of the way China will be perceived in the world—after those dates, this is a situation that is not likely to be able to be sustained.

"The basic reason is because China's economic growth continues to come out of capital investment—that is, building factories, building plants, building roads, building dams—and not out of the consumption of the Chinese people. They've got to switch from capital investment to personal consumption because they're just going to run out of their ability to produce factories, and the world will not buy their stuff, and making that switch is going to be real tough."

Even though our interview was prior to Medvedev, concerning Russia as a political powerhouse, he had this to say: "There is the question as to whether or not Russia can form an anti-American bloc. There's no question that Putin would like to do that, and he's kind of making overtures to the Chinese as to whether they would like to form with Russia a group to try to stand up to the American superpower that Putin has criticized again and again. My bet is China won't do that. The West, America, is too important to

China and its economy. But what it does suggest is that Russia will not be an easy country to deal with for the foreseeable future. Because it's got so much oil, so much gas, so many raw materials, Russia will be able to generate huge amounts of revenue and use that revenue to swing its weight around in the world. And it's going to swing its weight contrary to the interest of the United States and not compatibly with us." Again, his insight has turned out to be right on as we saw Russia flexing its muscles in the Caucus region in August 2008.

One of Professor Zonis's most interesting answers came when I asked him about the Cold War. Are we better off now than when we were in a standoff with the Soviet Union? "I think its [relationship with Russia] is less stable because when the United States and the Soviet Union were squaring off with nuclear weapons and presenting a meaningful, serious risk of global conflict, each of the superpowers kept its allies, its underlings, its subordinates in line. They did so because the fear was that if some minor power in Africa, or wherever, were to get into a squabble with a different country that was really a subordinate of the other superpower, it might draw the superpowers in. So the United States and the Soviet Union sat on everybody to prevent this danger from arising. Now the system is broken open, and every country is more or less free to take the risks it wants to take, and we see that in the tremendous number of local wars and more recently in the rise of terrorism, which was less of a threat 25 years ago."

In my final question, I asked the professor where the potential risks were moving forward. "[We need to] think about the countries whose economies might be devastated by a significant terrorist attack. That's one of the reasons we're so concerned, for example, about recent terrorist attacks in Morocco. That was a country making some real progress—it had a free trade agreement with the European Union, it was seen as politically stable, and it was attracting foreign investment capital. If that should come to an end because of terrorism, that's a country that could suffer. On the other hand, in the United States, it's very difficult to imagine a terrorist attack of the magnitude that would really disrupt the American economy. For example, the September 11 attacks, however horrible they were and however many lives were lost, did not end up disrupting the economy. What governments have to do is be aware of their relative stability and attractiveness in terms of foreign investments and work hard with the global community to get after potential terrorists."

It is interesting to note that Professor Zonis said that the September 11 tragedy "did not end up disrupting" the U.S. economy. If you are like most Americans, this assessment gives you pause at least—or you may just not agree. But there is, and will always be, a political and economic ebb and flow of events around the world. These events and the decisions made by the leaders of sovereign nations affect us. They affect our economy and our own national policies. This element of change is a constant. Constant too are the principles and values of free markets. Capitalism perseveres through good times and bad.

Mohamed El-Erian on What Happens When Markets Collide

Mohamed El-Erian is the CEO of PIMCO, one of the largest investment management companies in the world. He formerly served as president and CEO of the Harvard Management Company. Of course, that's the fund that manages the university's $35 billion endowment. He also spent 15 years at the International Monetary Fund working on policy issues. El-Erian has been featured by *Bloomberg, Forbes*, the *Financial Times, Latin Finance*, CNBC, the *New York Times*, and the *Wall Street Journal*. His new book, *When Markets Collide*, is a bestseller, and I wanted to get his insight on just how the world economy is changing and interacting.[28]

One of the interesting points that El-Erian makes in his book is that it's no longer sufficient to understand only the United States, Japan, and Europe if you're trying to understand the global economy. Today the list of countries that investors need to understand has expanded considerably. On the show I asked El-Erian why understanding other parts of the world is so much more important now.[29]

"Because the world is changing, and it's changing very rapidly. If you want to understand what's driving world growth, you also have to look at countries like China, India, Brazil. If you want to understand what's happening to inflation, you have to ask the question, how are those countries doing on the production and consumption side? And finally, wealth is flowing away from the traditional powers to these new countries. So whatever aspect you look at, you have to include these emerging economies."

As a follow-up, he discussed the increasingly influential role of pools of capital such as the sovereign wealth funds and how they are changing the dynamics of global economics.

"We went on a binge in the United States of consuming far ahead of our income using our houses as ATMs, and we incurred significant debt. In the process, the rest of the world in countries like China, the Middle East, and Russia accumulated larger and larger wealth. And now like anybody who's gotten wealthier, they're starting to ask the question, how should we invest [our profits]? Because they don't have a history of being wealthy, their behavior is very different from traditional holders of wealth. So any investors trying to understand price behavior have to factor in the behavior of these newly wealthy countries, and that's a critical issue in explaining some of the conundrums that we've seen over the last couple of years.

"China is expanding rapidly in Africa, but the industrial countries will remain the main destination for its capital. I think it's not a question as to whether China is willing to invest in the west. It's very willing. The question is, are they able? And in particular, there's understandable sensitivity when such investment goes into strategic areas."

I then moved on to the economic changes that happened in 2007 because of the subprime debt market. Are the financial institutions, and the innovations that they're coming up with, affecting the way people invest their money?

"Oh, absolutely. In fact, we're going through a major dislocation that reflects the fact that rather than interpret these changes as something that is permanent, people in 2006 and 2007 largely ignored it. And the resulting destruction has been [exacerbated] by the fact that we had a significant innovation in international finance. [We used] structured products, the ability of derivatives to create exotic mortgages — subprime mortgages that enabled people who couldn't otherwise afford a home, afford a home. In addition to these fundamental economic changes, we also had innovation.

And like other innovations in the history of humankind, there was a phase of initial overproduction and overconsumption. And now the system is trying to clean up these excesses, and it's not easy because it's coming at the same time that the global economy is changing."

The concept of "stable disequilibrium" is one that El-Erian's company has researched regularly. He discussed what it means and what it translates into concerning investors' behavior.

"For a long time the world seemed very calm, and in fact the word 'Goldilocks'—it's not too hot, it's not too cold—and the phrase 'great moderation' started to enter the language. As a result we had a tremendous amount of complacency in the marketplace. We said be careful. We called it a 'stable disequilibrium.' By that we meant for now it's stable, but it is fundamentally disequilibrium, which means it cannot be sustained. Therefore, rather than betting on a great moderation and betting on Goldilocks, it's important for investors to prepare themselves for when this stable disequilibrium will become unstable. And that's why we turned negative so early on the housing market, and of course, starting from last year, the stable disequilibrium gave way to an unstable disequilibrium. We have to go through that until we come to a new equilibrium."

I then asked El-Erian about an excerpt from his book dealing with the equity risk premium. There is a group within the investment community that maintains that the reward for holding stocks is either vanishing or at least being reduced by the new global economy. I wanted to get his thoughts on this important concept.

"I think there is an equity risk premium out there. I don't think it's as stable and predictable as we'd like it to be, and it's certainly not as stable and predictable as the modelers would like it to be, which means an investor should be exposed to equities but should be exposed to equities that are internationally diversified and that are only part of a comprehensive portfolio. So the one trap not to fall into, and unfortunately, some do, is to say, 'Well, there must be an equity premium, and therefore, I'm going to be heavily invested in just U.S. stocks.' That's not how to do it. It is more that 'There is an equity premium, and I can capture it through diversified exposure.'"

Bottom Line

As President Ronald Reagan so eloquently stated in his second inaugural address, "There are no limits to growth and human progress when men and women are free to follow their dreams."[30] Whether it is freedom of religion, assembly, speech, or any other choices we are at will to make, the ability to pursue and conduct free commerce is the catalyst and engine that drives all other liberties. Forget what you see on the evening news. Trouble spots around the globe will never all go away. But free markets are expanding, and you must set aside any fears you have concerning them. People in every nation want to succeed. Our Creator instilled this desire within us. We want and need to always do better. Newfound freedoms are giving that opportunity to many people who did not have it before. For this, we should be thankful, and you should remain optimistic because—eventually—the optimist is always right. I hope I have allowed you to gain a little clearer understanding of just how valuable capitalism is and that you can harness the market's strengths and perceived weaknesses to improve your investing experience.

seven

INVESTOR BEHAVIORS

If everyone is thinking alike, then someone isn't thinking.
—General George Patton

Amerian poet Edwin Markham once said, "Choices are the hinges of destiny." In this chapter, I will try to get inside your head. Not in a bad way but in a revealing way. I want to help you understand how and why you think the way you do about money and investing. What causes your choices about money to be as they are? Why are you tempted to follow the herd? Why do losses hurt so much more than the joy that gains provide? And why do you tend to ignore the opportunity cost in a financial situation and make poor choices when faced with several options that vary greatly? All this and more will unfold as I examine your investing behaviors.

Barry Schwartz Offers a Paradox: Why Less Is More

Dr. Barry Schwartz is a professor of social theory and social action at Swarthmore College. He joined *The Investing Revolution* to discuss his fascinating bestselling book *The Paradox of Choice.*[1] The illustration that opens the book finds the professor shopping to replace a pair of jeans. He gives the salesperson his size and is immediately peppered with questions: Slim fit, easy fit, or relaxed fit? Stonewashed or distressed? Button-fly or zipper? Faded or regular? His response to the salesperson is, "I just want regular jeans. You know, the kind that used to be the only kind." The salesperson has no idea what he is talking about.

The story ends with Schwartz's leaving the store with the best-fitting jeans he has ever had, but feeling worse. The reason, he says, is that when our choices increase, so too do our standards. In the past, we may have been satisfied with a pair of jeans that fit just OK (since they were the only pair available), but now we expect the perfect fit and the perfect look, all at the perfect price.

This wide array of options is found in so many aspects of our lives. When faced with overwhelming choices, Schwartz says we fall into two separate personality types.

"A *maximizer* is somebody who is out to get the best: the best chocolate chip cookie, the best restaurant, the best jeans, the best investment, the best job, the best anything. A *satisficer* is somebody who is looking for a good enough chocolate chip cookie, pair of jeans, investment. Good enough can be very good. You can have high standards, but you don't need the best.

"If you're out to find the best, there's only one way to get the best, and that's to examine all the options. If you don't examine all the options, how do you know that the one you didn't examine wouldn't turn out to be the best? If that's your goal, in a world with the kind of choices we have, life becomes a nightmare.

"On the other hand, if your goal is simply to find something that's good enough, you can look at your cookies or your jeans or your investments one at a time, and as soon as you find one that meets your standards, you choose it and you don't worry about what else is out there. The distinction between looking for good enough and looking for the best is not a terribly important one in a world of limited choices, but in the world we live in, it becomes increasingly important, and people who are out for the best are, by almost everything we can measure, pretty miserable."

Schwartz uses the example of finding 285 different kinds of cookies at the grocery store. A daunting choice, no doubt. But what about the decision involved when you consider choices in the investing realm? How do you adequately examine the thousands upon thousands of individual securities and mutual funds available to individual investors?

Schwartz includes in *The Paradox of Choice* a case study involving participants in 401(k) plans.[2] Of the 1 million people across 1,500 companies researched, there was a striking correlation between how many people participated in a plan and how many investing options were available. For every 10 additional options, participation decreased by 2%. In some cases, Schwartz reports, employees were passing up as much as $5,000 in matching money from the employer, all because they couldn't figure out how to decide, so they just didn't. People fail to realize that in so many situations, any decision is better than no decision.

The key to overcoming "paralysis by analysis" is to work your way out of the maximizing state of mind. "It's maximizers," Schwartz says, "who suffer most. It's maximizers who have expectations that can't be met, . . . who worry most about regret, missed opportunities, social comparisons, . . . who are most disappointed when the results of decisions are not as good as they expected."

While maximizers by their very nature aren't content to settle on a decision when a better one might be available, the trick is to embrace and appreciate satisficing rather than being resigned to it. All maximizers have had occasions when they've been satisficers simply because maximizing every decision would be impossible. Maximizers should consider those times in their lives, however trivial they may seem, when satisficing has been comfortable. Then, for decisions they're facing, they should develop standards for what is good enough. Boil the decisions down to their absolute minimum requirements.

This is actually easier in the investing realm than you might think. A maximizer is going to play Wall Street's games—picking stocks, timing the market, and chasing returns—all in the interest of beating the market. A satisficer, however, knows that there's really only one decision to be made: owning the market. Once that decision is made and the satisficer investor holds a superdiversified portfolio, the work is largely done.

"Becoming a conscious, intentional satisficer," Schwartz says, "makes comparisons with how other people are doing less important. It makes regret less likely. In the complex, choice-saturated world we live in, it makes peace of mind possible."

Whether we like it or not, irreversible decisions in our lives have to be made with incomplete information. Given that we live in such an information-laden world, with so much immediate access to data, this decision dilemma is both ironic and axiomatic. The good news here, however, is that the satisficing investing decision—to own the entire market—isn't just the "good enough" Schwartz alludes to. It's also the best. So, in a beautiful turn of irony, choosing the satisficing route—not to choose from the thousands of options Wall Street has laid on the table—the satisficer has chosen the option the maximizer wants but will never get.

Jason Zweig Explains the Brain: How Do We Decide?

You see it all the time: the investors who believe that, through careful analysis, extensive research, and tedious calculation, they, and they alone, have discovered the secret to beating the market. They're often seen hunched over laptops toggling between spreadsheets that calculate numbers based on complex formulas. They're dedicated and determined. When I had a conversation with Jason Zweig, *Wall Street Journal* columnist and author of *Your Money and Your Brain*, he informed our listeners that they're also half out of their minds, literally.[3]

Zweig's book explores the area of neuroeconomics, which he describes as being a mix of neuroscience and economics, with a lot of psychology thrown in.[4] It's an area of study that explores what's happening in the brain as financial decisions are made.

There are two aspects of the brain that Zweig says are often engaged in a mental tug-of-war: the reflexive brain (the intuitive side) and the reflective brain (the analytical side).

Researchers refer to the reflexive brain as "system 1." It's the system that engages and responds quickly—so quickly at times that the rest of the brain tends to catch up later. It's the reflexive brain that will swerve to miss something in the street or pull away when something hot is touched. Zweig quotes Matthew Lieberman from UCLA as saying that the reflexive system gets "first crack at making most judgments and decisions."[5] Our intuition first screens issues in order to conserve the rest of our mental energy.

The other part of the brain is the reflective system. It serves as the backup system to intuition and tackles more complex problems. If asked to alphabetize the 50 states, intuition would stall. When it does, the reflective brain leads to a conscious consideration of the issue.

But what does all of this have to do with investing? By recognizing and understanding the two very different ways of thinking, you can avoid problems that arise when you lean too heavily on one side or the other. Let's take a closer look.

If the reflexive brain were the only thing you used to make investing decisions, intuition would have you responding emotionally. A drop in the Dow or a surge in a stock's price can both get your heart racing and your palms sweating. You may respond by wanting to pull out of the market quickly or buy up one of its "rising stars," but those reactions are intuitive ones. The reflective side of the brain needs to be engaged to put it all in perspective.

On the other side of the coin, if you use only your reflective brain to sort and analyze and compute, you drown yourself in all the data and numbers available on various investments and thereby squelch your intuition that would tell you there's nothing new to be found. As Zweig says, you "end up losing the forest for the trees—and your shirts as well." That is what has happened often to the investors with the "secret formulas" and extensive spreadsheets.

Zweig demonstrates the fallibility of our reflective brains with this illustration. Imagine yourself pushing a cart full of groceries up to the checkout lane, wondering how much it's all going to cost you. Your reflexive (intuitive) side gets a ballpark figure by doing a quick estimate on the amount of groceries and assigning a cost based on past experience. Your reflective (analytical) side adds up the exact price of each item and keeps a running tally in the brain. "Chances are," Zweig says, "after the exacting effort of adding up barely a handful of individual prices, you will lose track and give up."

The reflective system, according to computational neuroscientists who use the principles of computer design to study the human brain, makes decisions by what's called a "tree-search" method. It's a method named for a standard decision tree. With each decision made, a whole new set of choices opens up. Your reflective brain sorts through experiences, predictions, and consequences methodically to make each decision. Zweig compares it to an ant "moving up and down, back and forth, along the branches and twigs of a tree to find what it wants." The problem with this methodology is that it's limited by your own mind and the problem's complexity.

Many investors work hard to engage their reflective brains when making investment choices, trusting their analysis over their intuition. And, in part, that's the right choice. However, it's possible to tip the scale too far in the other direction and become a victim of your own limitations. It's the reflexive side of the brain that intuitively tells you many of those efforts are in vain. When that intuition is stifled, you become like that ant, scurrying along the branches and leaves of a tree. You can busy yourself with a tedious search for the answer, but have you considered that the answer may be much simpler and more obvious than you let yourself believe?

If you haven't figured it out yet, Wall Street loves your reflexive brain mostly because it causes you to make investment decisions quickly and emotionally. Advertisements that tout the speed with which trades can be made are clearly targeting your reflexive brain. Other approaches that tug at your heart strings or play on fear or greed (depending on which way the market is headed) are attempts to influence your reflexive brain and thus emotional actions.

They don't stop there, however. If you are of the more reflective (or analytical) ilk, Wall Street is ready for you too. It continually rolls out complicated computer programs and products that feed upon this desire to analyze your investment options ad infinitum until you feel that you have done adequate due diligence or you just get tired of the process and pull the trigger. The more complex a strategy looks to you as a reflective investor, the more credibility it has with you. Insidiously, Wall Street knows this, and it markets to it brilliantly.

Finding the happy medium, a brain balance if you will, is the key to success. Both your reflexive and reflective brains were bestowed upon you by our benevolent Creator for a reason. Use them both, and employ a passive investment strategy that uses modern portfolio theory and superdiversification. That way, via owning all free capital markets in your portfolio, you have used a sophisticated approach that satisfies your need to be analytical and a system that gives you the confidence that you have done the right thing by placing your faith in capitalism, which thus fulfills your intuitive tendency as well.

Peter DeMarzo's Five Characteristics of the Herd Mentality

Charles Mackay observed in his classic nineteenth-century book about bubbles, *Extraordinary Popular Delusions and the Madness of Crowds,* "It will be seen that they go mad in herds, while they only recover their senses slowly, and one by one."[6]

According to Peter DeMarzo of the Stanford School of Business, "It isn't the risk of losing per se but the risk of doing poorly relative to their peers that investors fear the most."[7] Dr. DeMarzo visited with us on *The Investing Revolution* and told us how the "keeping up with the Joneses" school of investing demonstrates yet again how investors quickly fall prey to an active management trap.[8] I think the following list gleaned from my discussion with Dr. DeMarzo is a good litmus test of five characteristics you can use to determine if you have grazed off the path of investment success by following the herd.

1. Herd investors fear being poor while everyone around them is getting rich. This fear causes investors to question discipline and saving techniques. They become very impatient with markets, and they may buy overpriced assets simply for the hope of a big gain. This short attention span can easily lead to long-term disappointment.

2. To avoid being left behind, herd investors choose portfolios that look like everyone else's rather than creating a financial plan that is specific to their individual needs. Just as none of us lives in a house with exactly the same floor plan as anyone else's, everyone needs to have his or her own financial blueprint. Picking an investment allocation based only on what others are doing is not a path to a secure financial future.

3. Investors who have a herd mentality feel a kinship during losses—after all, they share the same misery, and that

provides some consolation. This consolation is misleading, however. They are caught up in the old misery-loves-company syndrome.

4. Herd investors cluster around the pie-in-the-sky opportunity to catch the "next big thing." This attitude lends itself to either investing long after the big money in any venture has been made or throwing money at lame ideas and concepts that likely will not produce revenue or profits. Dot-coms, real estate, and gold come to mind here.

5. Herd investors fear the "herd" knows something they don't, and they automatically assume the grass is greener on the other side of the fence. But globally diversified portfolios put investors on both sides of the fence to always enjoy the green lush grass somewhere.

Following the herd virtually assures buying overpriced assets and experiencing mediocre returns. Free capital markets are truly a field ready for harvesting. But you must be prudent and be willing to take the road less traveled—the road Wall Street, and its crowd, does not want you to take.

Peter Bernstein Explains Why Losses Hurt So Much

In the summer of 2006, I conducted the first of two inspiring interviews with Peter L. Bernstein, author of nine books including the worldwide bestseller *Against the Gods: The Remarkable Story of Risk*.[9] This fascinating book brought to light for me so many things concerning risk and reward in not just the securities markets but in other walks of life as well. It is a truly captivating read, and I was thrilled to have Bernstein as a guest.

In *Against the Gods*, Bernstein tells about the work of Daniel Bernoulli in St. Petersburg in the early 1700s.[10] He explains that Bernoulli attributed differing values to differing risks with the idea, as Bernoulli put it, "[that the] utility resulting from any small increase in wealth will be inversely proportionate to the quantity of goods previously possessed." The idea that there is maintained an inverse relationship between what you already have and what you next obtain—or lose—was a revolutionary concept.

In economic theory, utility is the amount of satisfaction or pleasure that somebody derives from consuming a commodity, product, or service.[11] The concept of declining utility is a way of explaining why investors, in particular, strive to avoid pain much more than they try to bring about gain.

As Bernstein explained, "Utility means what is something worth to me. All of us have different kinds of utility structures. A hamburger may mean more to you than it does to me, and good pasta may mean more to me than it does to you. So we each have a different set of values. As you get wealthier, the next additional unit of wealth doesn't mean quite as much as the first one. If you have $5,000 and you get to $10,000, that is fantastic. If you get to $15,000, that is also great, but it isn't quite the thrill of going from $5,000 to $10,000, and from $15,000 to $20,000, and so on. As the additions come in, they have less value than the original ones. As you have more capital, you should be willing to take less risk and pay more attention to preservation."

Another example shows the concept clearly. An investor with $100,000 that gains 10% in her portfolio as she might reasonably expect (the S&P 500 Index has averaged 10.8% over the last 41 years) is generally content and happy.[12] No expectations have been exceeded, but all is well. If the same investor loses 10% of $100,000, her portfolio balance falls to $90,000.

At this point, several psychological things seem to occur. For most investors, there is often no real expectation of losing money—any time. Even though the S&P 500 has had a negative return in 9 of the last 41 years, which is still only 22% of the time,[13] investors often ignore the fact that markets go down. Also, in order to get back to "even," the portfolio that goes down 10% must then earn 11.1% the next year. The feeling of playing catch-up enters the picture. Not only that, but the opportunity cost of not earning the 10% they expected begins to weigh in during the second year. Now that difference must be made up as well. So opportunity costs are going to be piled onto the losses. In order to make things right, the 10% loss plus the opportunity cost means earning over 22% the next year.

You can begin to see the stress that is created when money loses value versus the limited satisfaction that occurs when things go the way you expect with your portfolio (earning 10% in this example). Not only that, but as humans—and especially Americans—we all get spoiled. We earn 10%, and then we expect 11%. We earn positive returns for 8 or 9 years in succession and feel like we'll never see another down year. We tend to assimilate pleasure but not pain. But the fact is that returns usually do not occur within a convenient narrow margin every year. In fact, if you consider the S&P 500 Index, in the 39 years from 1969 through 2007, only 3 of those years saw the return fall within a range of 8 to 12%.[14]

Perhaps the ancient Greek philosopher Epicurus summed it up best over 23 centuries ago when he wrote, "Riches do not exhilarate us so much with their possession as they torment us with their loss." Hopefully you now have more insight into your own feelings about losses and you realize that those feelings are common. However, there is more good news. Those feelings are not necessary once you have a proper understanding of common investor behaviors.

Opportunities Lost: The Fear Tax

Life is full of decisions. There are advantages and disadvantages of choosing a certain alternative. You can take an umbrella to work in case it rains, but then there is something extra to carry to the office and back home. Exercise during lunch, or eat your lunch with a friend or coworker. Relax and watch your favorite television program, or spend some quality time with the kids. We all make choices, great and small.

Some decisions, however, including those involving your investments and portfolio, have long-lasting effects. For example, there's the fundamental decision as to whether to put your money in the stock market or not. If you decide to enter the market, the next question becomes, when? While there is potential to make money as the markets move forward, there is also potential to lose money as the markets retreat.

General concepts about the market are understandable, but there are a number of unknown variables. No one knows by how much or when the market will move in any particular direction. Faced with that decision, you may choose to take the "safe" route and keep your money in bonds, in bank CDs, or under the mattress. This decision doesn't take into account the opportunity cost. I sometimes call this the "fear tax." As defined by economists, the opportunity cost is the cost of something in terms of an opportunity forgone (and the benefits that could be received from that alternative). To calculate the opportunity cost, when you make a decision, you need to consider not only the opportunity you are passing up but also what you could have gained from that opportunity.

To calculate the opportunity costs involved when considering the stock market dilemma, you must take into account how markets generally move and what you would be giving up by keeping money outside the market.

An example of the application of this concept lies in the bear market of March 2000 to October 2002 and the subsequent bull market.[15] That bear market commonly brought losses for investors in the 10 to 40% range (for some, much more), but it was followed by bull market gains of 149% (January 1, 2003, through October 31, 2007).[16]

To fully appreciate the opportunity cost of this situation, let's suppose you rode out the bear market, but in October 2002, you decided you'd had enough. You withdrew your money, and you had yet to get back in the market. Not only did you suffer the losses of the bear market but you also didn't get the advantage of the 149% gain that followed. The initial losses were exacerbated by the opportunity cost. That is significant. While it was not actually played out in dollars and cents in the portfolio, the realization of the benefits of the missed opportunity were nearly just as painful. The gains were there for the taking if only you had persevered.

In fact, if you were to receive a W-2 after each bear market for the fear tax you paid due to the lost opportunity costs, it would quickly get your attention and get you fully invested in the market at all times forevermore (Figure 7-1).

Whether it's making the routine decisions on a daily basis or putting money in the stock market, you must consider opportunity costs to understand the full advantage (or disadvantage) of any decision you make. Once again, if you can understand how markets work, the fear tax is one tax you should never have to pay.

Richard Thaler's Deal or No Deal

One of the most intriguing game shows to come to prime time television has been NBC's *Deal or No Deal*, hosted by Howie Mandel.[17] The premise of the show is that a contestant has 26 briefcases from which to choose. Inside those briefcases are dollar amounts ranging from 1 cent to $1 million (sometimes more during sweeps week). One briefcase is chosen at the beginning of the show as the contestant's winnings, but it is not opened. The remaining briefcases are then opened one at a time, leading to a process of elimination to determine which amount the prize-winning briefcase holds. Along the way, a "banker" will try to lure a player away with tantalizing offers to quit the game. Statistics at work, the offers increase or decrease based on which cases have been eliminated. Once an offer is made, the player then determines if it's a "deal or no deal." If a player passes up the deal, he or she keeps playing and eliminating cases.

We visited on *The Investing Revolution* with Richard Thaler, Ph.D., professor of economics and behavioral science at the

PAYER'S name, street address, city, state, ZIP code, and telephone no.		Payer's RTN (optional)	OMB No. 1234-5678	**Copy B**
The Bull Market			**2003-07**	**For Recipient**
			Form **1099-FEAR**	This important hypothetical information illustrates the amount of gain shown by the JWA MRB from 01/01/03 to 10/31/07. Were you invested properly?
PAYER'S Federal ID number	RECIPIENT'S ID number	1 Interest income not included in box 3 income $	3 Starting portfolio value on 01/01/03 $ 1,000,000.00	
RECIPIENT'S name Chicken L. Investor		2 Early withdrawal penalty $	5 Fear tax as of 10/31/07 if not invested $ 1,591,186.00	
Street address (including apt. no.) 123 Elm Street		4 Federal income tax withheld $		
City, state, and ZIP code Anytown, USA 12345		6 Foreign tax paid $	7 Foreign country or U.S. possession	
Account number (see instructions)				

Form **1099-FEAR**   (this is NOT an official tax form)   JWA Financial Group, Inc.

Figure 7-1 Hypothetical W-2

Graduate School of Business, University of Chicago.[18] Thaler is considered by many to be one of the originators of the field of behavioral economics, which integrated psychological research with economic theory. Professor Thaler's book *Nudge: Improving Decisions about Health, Wealth, and Happiness* aims to demonstrate that business and public policy can be designed to make it more likely for people to act in their own interests.[19]

He also was intrigued with the *Deal or No Deal* concept, and with three other Dutch economists, he cowrote a research paper entitled "Deal or No Deal? Decision Making under Risk in a Large-Payoff Game Show."[20] Professor Thaler gave his explanation of this concept in our interview. "Well, you know, that show presents a great opportunity to see how people make decisions under very high stakes, so people often have decisions that have hundreds of thousands of dollars at stake. And what we found to be the most interesting finding on that show was that people behave very differently depending on how the show evolved. If they were playing for very high stakes and then got unlucky, they are very risk seeking. And that's something that we also see in the stock market, that when prices fall, people are reluctant to take their losses and get out."

Deal or No Deal is the perfect microcosm of what most investors do when it comes to making decisions about their securities portfolios. I decided to take a look at some of the similarities and offered this synopsis of the game show and the stock market for our listeners.

- *The maddening crowd.* The *Deal or No Deal* studio often takes on the atmosphere of a Roman coliseum. The audience, entertained by the contestants' quandary, encourages them to keep going with shouts of "No deal! No deal!" It's the same mantra Wall Street, in much subtler form, repeats to investors: "Keep going! Keep going! You can win big!" Those chants tend to entice you the same way the rallying cries of the audience influence the show's contestants. But like Wall Street, the audience is not risking its money—only yours.

- *The emotion.* After one round of play, the contestant's family is brought onstage to offer advice. While the contestant wrestles with his or her decision, the spouse or parent or child of the player offers his or her opinion. You are certainly not exempt from the influence of emotion when you make investing decisions (like your brother-in-law's stock tip at Thanksgiving that puts pressure on you). When your family's future is on the line, there's more of an interest in how it's handled. Some play it safe, some take risks, but none are exempt from their own opinions. When those opinions differ, as they sometimes do, emotions ride high.

- *The guilt and speculation.* One *Deal or No Deal* contestant played the game long enough to end up with a $701,000 offer, which she gladly accepted.[21] After deals are taken, show host Howie Mandel walks the contestants through what presumably would have been their next few moves. In this woman's case, she would have ended up with an even larger offer from the banker. In the end, the briefcase she set aside at the beginning of the show actually held $1 million. The $701,000 she walked away with wasn't a bad day's work, especially when she started with nothing and played the game with house money. However, after she accepted the offer and the rest of the game was prospectively played out in front of her, there were visible signs of disappointment and regret (not to mention the audience's groans). Investors react the same way when they sell a stock and make a positive return—they continue to experience regret and defeat as they watch it rise even higher.

There are, however, some good lessons contained in the program's methodology. The program's host says the key to success is to come in with a plan and stick with it. Players get into trouble when they come to the game with a plan—"Get to $100,000," say—and then, being wooed by the lights and the crowd, change their strategy midgame. "You need to stick with the plan," Mandel says. "You can't get emotionally involved."

The game, just like the markets, can work in your favor, but you must go in with a plan. "A plan" does not mean a hope of timing or picking correctly. It means having a written financial plan that takes into consideration your unique situation: assets, liabilities, risk tolerance, and goals.

If you want to see a microcosmic display of what investing is for most people, you should watch *Deal or No Deal*. In the meantime, when the proverbial lights and crowds of Wall Street threaten to lure you away from your goals, remember those two words: "No deal."

Ori Brafman on What Sways You

In August 2008, we invited author Ori Brafman to join us to talk about his latest book, a *New York Times* bestseller, *SWAY: The Irresistible Pull of Irrational Behavior*.[22] When Brafman is not writing, he lectures internationally in front of Fortune 500, government, and military audiences. He holds an MBA from the Stanford Graduate School of Business, and he is also the coauthor of another highly successful book, *The Starfish and the Spider*.[23]

If we ever decide to change the format of our show, I think it would be to discuss sports, politics, or psychology. The psychology area always intrigues me. Brafman has looked at plummeting stocks and doomed relationships—and many other subjects in between—in search of an explanation of how intuitive judgment plays such a critical role in our behavior. He spoke about his research and what "sway" really is.

"I wrote this book with my brother, who is a psychologist, because we used to have these long conversations about why perfectly rational people—executives, airline pilots, judges—make irrational decisions. And what it comes down to is that we all know that there's rational decision making and that there's emotional decision making when you're feeling excited about something or sad or happy about something. Then there's really a third category of what we call 'sway,' and it's the psychological undercurrents that trigger irrational behavior without our realizing it, and that's what was so interesting for us. We all make irrational decisions without knowing that we're doing something irrational at the moment."

One of the more fascinating aspects of his book dealt with monetary incentives and how they are a lot trickier than they first appear. He explained this to our listeners.

"This is really kind of intuitive because you think that in order to motivate employees [for example], the best thing to do is pay them more money. There's a study in Israel where they had students take the GMAT, which is the SAT for business school, and they said, 'Please do your best, and it will help us a lot if you take this test.' And they scored 40 students.

"Then they brought in a second group of students, and they gave them the exact same spiel about doing their best, but they also said, 'For every correct answer we'll give you two and a half cents.' And you think that these students would have even more motivation to do better, but the opposite thing happened. The students who were paid actually performed much worse on the test than the students who were not paid. And the reason for that is that we have two parts of our brain. There's the social or altruism center, which is the friend that wants you to help him move and he or she is not going to pay you anything. And then there's another part of our brain called the 'pleasure center.' It's kind of the Las Vegas center, right—it's sex, drugs, and rock and roll. Monetary incentives actually get processed in that part of the brain. So whenever you introduce money into the equation, you erase altruism and have some counterintuitive results."

Another of the interesting concepts Brafman discussed was value attribution—something that is a very important marketing technique employed by Wall Street. He gave us a description of the "Nathan's Famous Hot Dogs" example he used in his book.

"Once you assign a value to a person or a thing, that value tends to stick. Back in the early twentieth century, there was this guy Nathan who had a great recipe, his wife's recipe, for hot dogs. And not only did he find a really tasty recipe but he also found a way of selling his hot dogs for about half the price of what was the competition in New York. And he opened up his shop, and he expected everyone to come because they were better hot dogs for a lower price. But lo and behold, no one showed up.

"The reason for that was that people thought his hot dogs were actually cheapo hot dogs. You think, 'Well, you know, it's half the price. How good can it be?' And what he had to do was pay his friends to wear a doctor's outfit and stand by his hot dog stand and eat those hot dogs. Only then did people actually start coming, and only then did he become 'Nathan's Famous Hot Dogs' because people attributed, 'Well, if it's a doctor eating it, then it must be a quality hot dog. Therefore, I'll buy it as well.' But before that happened, it was this cheapo half price. So again, if you think that you're going to cut the price in half and beat the competition, some irrational psychology starts happening, and people view your items as cheap. So sometimes your best bet is actually to raise the prices rather than cut them."

Lastly, I asked Brafman about his research into *Who Wants to Be a Millionaire* as that game show is aired in Russia and France. The responses of the Russian and French audiences in those TV studios were a study in the cultural interpretations of fairness concerning issues of finance. As the world economy becomes more global, the morays of differing cultures will become much more important.

"In America one of your best options if you're on *Who Wants to Be a Millionaire* is to poll the audience. And a lot of the times, the audience is right on the dot in terms of your getting to benefit from a lot of people's opinions. But when they tried to do the same thing in Russia, the Russians would actually purposely give the wrong answer to the contestant. And it happened so often, in fact, that they actually stopped offering the poll-the-audience option. The reason for that [behavior] is that in Russia, the idea of one person's excelling over the group was actually really frowned upon. 'Why is it that this guy should win when I don't get anything in return?'

So people should be really mindful of the fact that fairness plays such a strong role—not only in decision making but also in whether people think that their voices are heard.

"It turns out that it's not just Russians and Americans that have different perceptions of fairness. It's also venture capitalists who measured the success of the companies that they were funding not necessarily based on how much money they were making but on how often the CEO of the company would call them. The CEOs who called very often would be perceived by the venture capitalists as being very successful CEOs because people feel it's so important for them to have their voices heard."

It is easy to see from Brafman's research why many investors are "swayed" into imprudent money decisions. The key for you is to understand these behaviors—and by understanding, avoid them as well.

Gary Becker on Human Capital

In December 2007, we had the opportunity to visit with another Nobel Laureate on *The Investing Revolution*.[24] Professor Gary Becker won the Nobel Prize in Economic Sciences in 1992.[25] He's also a senior fellow at the Hoover Institution, a professor of economics and sociology at the University of Chicago, and the author of *Social Economics*. Professor Becker is recognized for his expertise in human capital, the economics of the family, and economic analysis of crime, discrimination, and population.

The subject of human capital and how it relates to our everyday decisions is an intriguing one. Professor Becker had this to say to open our discussion of the topic:

"Human capital is very important in everyday life because it refers to the knowledge, the information, the skill, [and] the learning that people have. In the modern world, knowledge and information are the main currencies of choice, wealth, income, earnings, and all the other things that people are interested in, including health. So it's very closely related to people's daily decisions of all types."

He also quoted George Bernard Shaw when he said, "'Economy is the art of making the most of our life.' . . . The idea of economics is it helps people make choices, and these choices are not just restricted—although they're important—to the dollars-and-cents aspects of their lives but also to choices in all dimensions. I have studied questions like marriage and divorce and having children and crime and addictions that people have."

Professor Becker has looked at a concept called "social capital." He gave our audience an explanation of how social capital relates to human capital and how they are different.

"I like to think of [social capital] as a special aspect of human capital or special version of human capital where what's involved is not simply the learning and skills of a person, and maybe the relation of those skills to the economy, but the closer relation between the behavior and skills and knowledge of one person and that of other people. So it's that linkage between different people's behaviors. That is what we usually mean by 'social capital.' So, for example, one frequently cited aspect of social capital would be if I have good relations with my neighbors and they see some people sort of working on my front door trying to get in that they don't recognize and they call the police—that's an aspect of social capital, that they're concerned about my well-being, and as a result of that, they're helping me out."[26]

In his book *Social Economics*, Becker extends the standard utility function for individuals to include more than just goods and services.[27] He includes the environment that affects someone's choices and his or her behaviors. I asked him why it is important to extend the conventional framework to include the environment and if it can teach us more about ourselves. His answer supported Hemingway's famous refrain of "no man is an island."

"We as individuals do not function in isolation. Much of traditional economics was developed under the assumption that in some fundamental sense, we were in isolation. Sure, we had markets where we worked and we bought goods, but we didn't directly link up with other individuals. And what we know about modern life, the modern economy, is that we're closely related to the environment in different dimensions and other individuals who we may directly interact with—such as our spouse, our children, our neighbors, our employees—and who matter to us in [different] ways. [Take] fellow employees. They will matter to us not just because of the fact that we're simply working at the same type of company or same type of job but also because we have a relationship with them as well."

We often talk about "reversion to the mean" as it relates to the stock market; we use this term to express the notion that over time, markets will return to an expected average return. It was interesting to consider that reversion to the mean also occurs in other areas. Becker explained.

"Some things, some annoyances that people have, pain that occurs, not continuously, you may never get used to. A child dies.

I don't think people ever really get used to that. The pain may decrease, so there is some reversion, but it's never complete. While other things—the size of your house, that kind of goes away completely, and that's why people are continuing, as they get more income, to expand the size of the house, the type of view. So it does differ for different items, and there's very little in some, but there's a lot in much of what we do."

This concept that we see again and again indicates that pain—in whatever walk of life, including investing—is not easily assimilated. Pain does not go away quickly or easily.

Pleasure, or success, on the other hand, is absorbed quickly and all too easily. We experience triumph or accomplishment in an endeavor, and then we look for more and better to follow.

I believe our challenge is to find contentment in our circumstances and strive for excellence in all that we do—with all our might. This will bring a satisfaction and sense of joy to our lives. We are blessed to live in a nation and a time that avails us such an opportunity.

Tim Harford Looking Undercover at Economics

In September 2008, Tim Harford of the *Financial Times* joined *The Investing Revolution* for a second tour from London.[28] He calls himself "The Undercover Economist," and he wrote a book with that same title.[29] I like to call Harford the "James Bond of Economics" even though economics—known as the dull science—is hardly thought of in exciting spy thriller terms. But what is interesting about Harford's work is the perspective he offers on the economics that surrounds us on a daily basis.

He explained, "I would just wander into Starbucks or branches of Whole Foods, or basically just do what anybody would do, go about my everyday life, and I would be watching the world around me, what other people were doing, what these companies were doing, and spotting economics in all of it. And I used to get so excited [and] bore my friends about it all the time. I said, 'I'm going to write about all this hidden economics in everyday life.' That's how it started."

Harford's newest book is called *The Logic of Life: The Rational Economics of an Irrational World*.[30] One endorsement of the book said it "illuminates the hidden social order behind everything from sex, Las Vegas, divorce, and your boss." It doesn't sound like economics, so I asked Harford to tell us where those things fit in.

He explained how we are all unconsciously always weighing out costs and benefits—and this isn't just the costs and benefits of getting a pension or the costs and benefits of buying coffee at this store versus another. "Getting married, dating, sex, going to Las Vegas, our behavior in the office, crime, even addictions—they all have costs and benefits. Not financial costs, but other costs—health costs, status costs, the fact that we find something frightening or we find something fun."

The argument in *The Logic of Life* is that we are weighing these costs and benefits, but we're not aware of it. When you look closely using the data and work of an economist, you can reveal the way in which people are making these trade-offs that are weighing off these costs and benefits, even though they don't realize it.

Harford offered some of the classic experiments of behavioral economics that are challenging the traditional assumptions about economics that we've made all along. He told our audience about some economists that took some students, and they performed this little experiment on them. They asked the students to fill in a questionnaire, but the questionnaire was just a decoy. When they had finished filling in the questionnaire, the students were told, "Thanks very much for helping us out with our research, and as a gesture of gratitude we're going to give you a snack. What would you like? Would you like a piece of fruit, or would you like some chocolate candy?" The students almost always chose the candy bar rather than the fruit. They then varied the experiment at random with some other students. Again, the students filled in the survey, and then the researchers offered them a slightly different choice. They said, "Well, thanks a lot. We're going to offer you this token of our appreciation, and we're going to give it to you next week. What would you like next week? Would you like fruit, or would you like a chocolate?" And when the choice was postponed from that moment to the following week, students chose to have a nutritious apple rather than a candy bar.

Harford explained: "They changed their behavior because the moment of pain when you give up the sweets and you have to eat the healthy food is pushed a week in the future. And then when the experiment is [conducted] in a week's time and the researchers say, 'Well, we brought you your apple, but if you'd like, we can swap it for a chocolate bar,' the students would then immediately swap. So the students were making these inconsistent choices. That sort of research is making economists think differently about how we respond to short-term and long-term decisions."

As Harford was telling this research story, my mind immediately wandered to the way investors make the same types of irrational decisions with their nest eggs. They tend to be fairly rational when thinking out into the future, but they tend to be irrational in the moment. In other words, they can see the logic of long-term planning and how markets recover from downturns over time, but they get emotional when they see market drops in the here and now. It was a fascinating comparison.

Naturally, economists have a bit of jargon for everything. They call this behavior "hyperbolic discounting." All that really means is if you're making a decision immediately, you grab immediate benefits and you avoid immediate pain, even if the opposite action is actually better for you in the long run. As Harford explained, "When you're considering the same decision but the decision is postponed a week or a month or a year, you make a different choice. So if you are asked to exercise right now, you can't be bothered, but if you are asked 'Would you like to exercise a month from now?' you would say, 'Oh, yeah, I mean, I know it will be painful, but it will be good for me.' And then the closer you get to that moment where you have to actually go through the pain, then suddenly your mind changes."

As an investor, you must learn the importance of separating short-term and long-term decisions. And know that essentially all portfolio decisions are long term in nature. Adopting this attitude alone can mean the difference between great success with less worry versus mediocrity or even failure.

Bottom Line

The information I discussed in this chapter has hopefully allowed you to learn more about your own tendencies as you learned more about others through the research we have studied. My father told me when I was a youngster, "Son, learn from the mistakes of others because you have neither the time nor the money to make them all yourself."

A compelling argument can be made that we are often our own worst enemies. In my 23 years of experience working with investors, I have definitely seen this to be the case when it comes to money. I believe one effective way to combat "ourselves" is to seek professional help to create a written financial plan. This simple step will provide you with the discipline you need to eliminate the ad hoc, emotional decisions that all of us are so often tempted to make. There is always something magical that happens between the pen and the paper. It is one thing to shake hands with yourself and make a resolution to do better—but when you put things in writing, they tend to come true.

eight

WHAT'S IN IT FOR ME?

He that fears not the future may enjoy the present.
—Thomas Fuller

B enjamin Franklin once said, "By failing to prepare, you are preparing to fail." Within this chapter you will find several additional ideas or confirmations that will lead you to a clearer personal view of the world of financial planning and investing. My hope is that these concluding concepts will help you focus on the important aspects of your financial life and, as an old preacher exhorted, cause you to "stop majoring in minors, and minoring in majors."

The Million-Dollar Myth

When Regis Philbin first appeared on television sets asking "Who wants to be a millionaire?" his show was an instant success not only because few, if any, would answer "Not me" but also because the program made it seem possible.

One million dollars has long been the monetary holy grail, the financial finish line that many believe will provide a long-awaited financial sigh of relief. However, as with anything sacred, $1 million has plenty of myth and mystery surrounding it.

The good news is that $1 million is an obtainable goal. More people are reaching the $1 million mark than ever before. There are now, according to the *Wall Street Journal*, over 10 million millionaires worldwide with a collective net worth of almost $40 trillion.[1] About 30% of that wealth resides in the United States, with more than 3 million millionaires holding assets valued at around $11 trillion. While that's encouraging news, it must be considered that at the same time, those in America's wealthiest age group, those 55 to 64 years old (and now knocking at the door of retirement), have a median household net worth, including home equity, of less than $250,000.[2]

Only 2% of retirees will enter the retirement phase of life with $1 million to their name.

The question then becomes, if it's possible to reach $1 million, and more are doing it than ever before, why are so many still waiting for their $1 million ship to come in? Quite likely it's because, while $1 million is possible, the money is not going to show up as easily as we've been led to believe. There's more to reaching any financial goal than appearing on television to outlast the other survivors on a desert island or picking the right suitcase under a banker's watchful eye. While many laugh off Hollywood's get-rich-quick offerings as sheer fantasy, too many easily fall for the same illusions when offered by Wall Street. Contrary to what countless investors have been led to believe, $1 million is rarely found through a hot stock tip or by giving up lattes and saving your spare change.

Research continues to show that the vast majority of millionaires have earned their money by working hard at something they enjoy. In truth, however, the best ally available in the quest for $1 million is the stock market. Consider this: If, in the midst of the bear market in January 1973, you began investing in the market every month with the goal of reaching $1 million by the end of 2007, it would have required an investment of only $82.56 each month.[3] At an annual rate of market return (actual return for the time period) of 14.8%, it would have been obtainable through a superdiversified asset class 100% stock portfolio. The miracle of free markets and compound interest would have propelled you to your goal.

The other reality of the million-dollar myth, however it may be obtained, is that it's not what it used to be. *Investing Revolution* radio guest and columnist Jonathan Clements reported in the *Wall Street Journal* that the last 20 years of inflation have left $1 million today with just 54% of the purchasing power of $1 million in 1987.[4] Here's a practical illustration. If, at age 55, you find yourself with $1 million in a taxable account, wanting to quit work and simply spend your money down until age 95, your annual after-tax allowance from the portfolio would be $49,105.[5] This assumes an annual investment return of 8% and an average income tax rate of only 10%. It does not factor in the eroding effect that inflation will have over the four decades or the likelihood that income tax rates will be higher. This income figure is probably far less than those aiming for a cool million might expect.

The key to retirement planning success is not an amount but a percentage—not a percentage of return on your portfolio but rather a percentage on you in your personal written financial plan. Through the exploration of your individual financial resources, goals, habits, needs, and risk tolerance, the right retirement formula and personal plan percentage (PPP) will emerge. A percentage number of 100% or greater is an indication that you have enough financial resources to meet your outlined goals and maintain the lifestyle you require until age 95 (the default age used in most plans). If after you have had your financial numbers analyzed, your plan percentage is, say, 125%, then even better! That means you currently have 25% more than you need to live comfortably for the rest of your life. You may be in a position to upgrade your retirement lifestyle or give away more to loved ones or charity before and at death. If on the other hand, your plan percentage is only 85%, then you have some work to do. That does not mean it is time to panic; it simply means that you now know the facts and should make adjustments and improvements as soon as possible.

Each time you review your personal plan percentage, it will most likely change. Markets go up and down, and unexpected expenses and windfalls occur. Sometimes you change your mind about certain expenditures or you have a career move in the offing. You should consider all these factors periodically—preferably on an annual basis—so you can assess your progress and maintain a good handle on your financial status.

Whether you want to aspire to a $1 million portfolio and beyond, or simply want to keep the one you have built, you need a solid written financial plan in place. The number you end up with in your retirement nest egg depends on hard work, prudent investing, and above all, good planning.

Socially Responsible Investing (SRI)

Hopefully, there are very few in our country who would answer no to the question, "Do you think it is important to be a good citizen?" We all want to be socially responsible. We all want what is best for our families and communities and environment. Another term I often use in this regard is *stewardship*—we all want to take good care of what has been handed down to us by previous generations, our parents, and our Creator.

But how does this relate to the investing world? How can our values and sense of social responsibility be translated to our investment portfolios? Henry David Thoreau said, "Goodness is the only investment that never fails." Where can we find goodness in our investments? Many believe the answer lies in a popular trend in the investing world known as *socially responsible investing* (SRI).

According to the Social Investment Forum, over $2.71 trillion—approximately 1 in 9 investment dollars currently under professional management in the United States—is invested using some form of socially responsible principle.[6] Within this large category of socially responsible investing, other similar methods have emerged. Some associate "socially responsible" with the political left and therefore have increasingly sought alternative SRI mutual funds that use the nomenclature of "morally responsible" or even "Biblically responsible." All told, these categories of investments grew from $500 million in 1997 to over $17 billion in 2007 according to Morningstar.[7] Has this all occurred primarily because of a raised awareness of issues that affect our planet or a desire by many Americans to integrate their beliefs into all aspects of their lives? Is the momentum of SRI influenced by shrewd marketing techniques used by the masters of manipulation that reside on Wall Street? A closer look at this subject is warranted.

It is a fact that 51 of the 100 largest economies in the world are now corporations, not nations.[8] The 100 largest multinational corporations now control about 20% of global foreign assets.[9] These top 100 are household names. As much as 40% of world trade now occurs within these companies. Should we be concerned about how these companies-economies run their businesses? Absolutely.

Author Bruce Piasecki, in his book *World, Inc.*, says, "As power moves increasingly into the hands of business, the world is looking to corporations instead of governments to solve its problems."[10] The questions I want answered, whether we want to be "socially," "morally," or "Biblically" responsible investors, revolve around the feasibility and practicality of this type of investing from a financial standpoint, as well as how to support the values we each want to maintain in our lives. This is not an easy balance.

Let's take the financial aspect first. For the purposes of this discussion, I will lump together all three types of investing I have mentioned under the SRI heading. When it comes to SRI, the first consideration is the screens to be used that will best fit your personal values agenda. Is it climate, defense contracting, and diversity? Or is it Catholic values, pro life, and tobacco? Do you prefer screens for energy, environment, and executive compensation, or alcohol, charitable giving, and gambling?

As you can begin to see, the combinations of both positive and negative screens can be arithmetically interminable. Finding the fund or fund family that coincides with your values can be daunting and I would submit even impossible. It is unlikely that any two people on earth will have the same definition of "socially responsible" because like beauty, it is in the eye of the beholder. (One of the most unusual SRI concepts we have seen is the Blue Fund managed by Blue Investment Management.[11] The fund's criterion is based on the financial contributions made to the Democratic Party by any company and its top three senior executives. Of course all companies hedge their election bets by giving to both major political parties. Not exactly a pure strategy.)

If you do eventually decide that there are funds that are "close enough" to your values, then the cost becomes a factor. The average expense ratio of SRI funds according to Morningstar is 1.35%.[12] For the record, that is more than four times higher than what I would like to see in this category of expenses. Then of course what about return? Are there SRI funds that have randomly outperformed the general stock market? Yes, there are, but at what price?

CNNMoney.com reported on this issue in the spring of 2007. The editors looked at, for example, the $1.6 billion Domini Social Index (DSEFX) and found that it had underperformed other index funds in recent years.[13] This could have been due to its very high index fund expense ratio of 0.95%. The fund has since switched to an active stock picking strategy to "improve performance." It also changed the name to Domini Social Equity and hired active managers that took the expense ratio up to 1.15%. This change to active management will likely result in even lower performance over the long run, but at least it "justifies" the fund's higher expenses (stock pickers and market timers cost money, you know).

Other so-called SRI funds have decided to change or redefine their principles to give themselves more investment flexibility. The Pax World Balanced Fund (PAXWX) now allows alcohol and gambling stocks after its rules required the sale of Starbucks stocks, which licensed coffee liquor, and Yahoo!, which presented online gambling directories.[14] Similarly, the Calvert Group—another big SRI player—is reconsidering its prohibition on nuclear power stocks since nuclear reactor technology may eventually be useful in reducing greenhouse gases.[15]

These midstream changes in fund philosophies and objectives could be quite annoying to the avid SRI investor. Can SRI become so broadly defined as to be meaningless? Or must it become so narrowly defined eventually that the investment returns are greatly diminished? Don't look for help from the Securities and Exchange Commission in this area. If a fund you are holding is planning to change its strategy, SEC rules require it to notify you and send you an updated prospectus, but that is it. There is no mandate that the fund adhere to any SRI set of rules. So you may be pleased that you finally have a fund that is aligned with your values, but then, without your input, the fund managers may change their internal rules. Then you are faced with selling it and possibly incurring taxes and making another decision on where to put your money.

One other major problem: It is exceedingly difficult, if not impossible, to build a properly diversified portfolio with SRI funds alone because most hold only large-cap U.S. companies. So you are likely to have to invest the rest in non-SRI funds anyway if you wish to properly allocate risk.

Another consideration is the makeup of the investment portfolios of the companies in the mutual fund that you bought. You thought it was pure, but some of those companies in your fund are themselves investing in other companies or even countries that are involved in activities that go against the grain of your values.

For example, Disney may provide a great environment for families at their theme parks, but some may feel that their movie studios have created vulgar movies that would make Walt turn over in his grave. (The Gates Foundation has at least $224 million invested in companies involved in the gambling business and it screens only for tobacco. Yet according to the *Los Angeles Times*, as of December 2005, it held at least $43 million worth of investments in companies tied directly to tobacco profits.[16])

The motives for SRI funds are mostly pure, and I am as in favor of setting high standards and values in our lives as anyone. In general, we should all advocate good corporate governance and corporate responsibility as core values, and I believe these factors are important in promoting healthy and efficient capital markets, while also carrying broader social benefits. But there is a strong possibility that focusing on issues globally can create the classic "we can't see the forest for the trees" scenario.

It is important that your money and time be used for causes that are important to you in the forms of volunteerism and charitable giving. Former Speaker of the House Tip O'Neill once said that "all politics is local." Could we also apply that principle to social responsibility? After all, if we would get involved locally in good works, the global problems would also fade. Here are some alternatives to SRI investing that may achieve even more of what you desire in this regard.

First of all, understand the extreme difficulty in outlining your own socially responsible investing plan in today's world. Companies and their business transactions are complex and intertwined. How can you monitor all of the dealings and transactions of every company and every chief executive in a particular fund to make sure that they are in compliance with your values? Then what about the ad hoc changes the fund managers make that derail your wishes? In a black-and-white world, we should all strive to invest in SRI vehicles. The problem is, like it or not, the world is quite gray. If the chance of achieving social purity in your portfolio is next to impossible, why pay the high price to try?

Second, we would make a case that the returns obtained with an SRI strategy will almost surely lag behind a superdiversified asset class approach. When five-year returns for the 278 SRI stock funds available for analysis in Morningstar in late 2007 were analyzed, over half of them were performing in the bottom 25% of funds among large U.S. company stock funds.[17] I also discovered that the average turnover ratio was about 57%, indicating that a great deal of picking and timing was taking place (25% turnover is a good standard).[18] But even if that is not the case and we can call it a tie on the performance issue, the cost over 20 years of paying the higher expense ratio of approximately 1.35% versus 0.40% (where it should be) is huge.[19] That 0.95% difference compounded on $1 million would be $208,166 over 20 years. That is a great deal of additional investment money that you could use in more direct ways to positively affect your own community, cause, charity, or loved ones.

I could never do anything but encourage our readers and listeners to do good and not evil all the days of their lives. Help wherever you possibly can. Be good stewards of all you have been blessed with—from the planet to your home and communities to your favorite foundation or charity. Seize control of your dollars that can "make a difference," and don't leave them to the impulse of any fund manager no matter how noble the cause may sound or how well the sales pitch is given. Together, taking individual responsibility, we can make our world better for those that come after us.

How Charity and a Legacy Are More Than Money

With the baby-boom generation now reaching retirement age, the United States is on the verge of one of the largest transfers of wealth—as much as $41 trillion to $44 trillion, by some estimates.[20] While the desire to care for future generations is a noble one, the process of passing money between generations is often fraught with problems. Consider this: Studies now show that in 65 to 70% of the cases, inherited money is gone by the end of the second generation.[21] Go one generation further and 90% of the money is gone. Leaving money is one thing, but keeping that money in the family seems to be another thing altogether.

The problem, according to Rod Zeeb, cofounder of the Heritage Institute and author of *Beating the Midas Curse*, is that when families leave money to the children and grandchildren, that's often all they leave. Zeeb told our listeners on *The Investing Revolution* that the key is to pass along the heritage, the values, and the work ethic that earned that money in the first place.[22] Through his work with the Heritage Institute, Zeeb interviews countless families. He begins by asking what the most important thing in their lives is. "The answer is never money," Zeeb says. "It's always something about family or values. That's what's going to last through the second or third generation."

So how can you transfer your values along with your money? The first thing you can do is talk. Tell stories about your past and the things that are important to you. Demonstrate your beliefs in a way that clearly shows where your priorities lie. These are things, unfortunately, that many families realize too late they should have been doing. Zeeb suggests families with older children invite a facilitator and talk adult to adult about those things that matter most.

You can also set up situations in which children and grandchildren are given money or other assets and asked to handle them now. If future generations can learn and make mistakes under the watchful eye of their parents or grandparents, there may still be time for learning.

Reap the rewards of giving during your lifetime. Don't rob yourself of the joys and satisfactions that accompany the act of charity. Additionally, leaving an inheritance is often a difficult decision, and it's one that should be made with careful thought and consideration. When the time comes, help ensure that the money will be around for generations to come by passing along not just your valuables but your values as well. Managing your money properly is of utmost importance. But the real measure of your wealth is how much you would be worth if you lost all your money.

Changing Lives in One Minute with Ken Blanchard

I have been a fan of Ken Blanchard since I read his supersuccessful book *The One Minute Manager*. In fact, all new hires in my firm are given a copy as a gift on their first day.

The show theme when we interviewed Dr. Blanchard in June 2008 was simplification.[23] That theme is exactly what Ken Blanchard and Spencer Johnson addressed when they wrote

The One Minute Manager.[24] Few people have impacted the day-to-day management of people and companies more than Blanchard. More than 18 million copies of *The One Minute Manager* have been sold worldwide, and all of his books, including his more recent ones, still regularly appear on the bestseller lists. Blanchard has authored or coauthored more than 40 books; his latest is *The One Minute Entrepreneur*.[25]

Like any great teacher, Dr. Blanchard takes otherwise complex concepts and converts them into understandable pieces for the layperson. He is a master at simplification. Einstein once said, "Make things as simple as possible, but not simpler." And if ever there was a time in history when simplification is needed, it is now, in the information age.

I asked Dr. Blanchard about delegation and personal responsibility in light of *The One Minute Manager* and about how investors might use the tools that he developed to guide their investment decisions. He answered, "I think that investors need to know the difference between delegation and abdication. I think you delegate to professionals to do some research for you and take a look at where the market's going and all that, but don't abdicate and just turn your back on it. Later on if things [are not] working [you say], 'How could you do that to me? I gave you my money.' I think you ought to be a partner with your investment counselors. But let them run where they're good, and let them come back to give you some suggestions and educate you. So . . . delegate. But you have some personal responsibility, and don't blame them completely when things don't go completely right because there are variables that are out of everybody's control. But be part of the action."

Dr. Blanchard had recently talked to *Inc.* magazine and was quoted as saying, "The problem with American business today is that Wall Street demands short-term thinking, which means businesspeople focus on results and forget about the important people part of their jobs."[26] I asked him if he thought those Wall Street business emotions can sometimes leak into work and other family decisions, not just investing decisions.

"Yes. I think what happens is that if you start thinking that who you are determines the results you get—your performance and the opinion of others—you're really in a tough spot because those things will fluctuate on a day-to-day basis. We're not always on the top of our game. But if you think that's who you are, you start to become a human doing rather than a human being. You start forgetting what's really important in your life, which I think is your faith, your family, and your friends, and then work.

"I'll never forget the time I was on a program years ago with Tom Landry, the great Dallas Cowboys coach, who always was so calm in the midst of this crazy game. And people said, 'How do you do that?' He said, 'It's easy. I get my priorities in order. First comes my Lord, second comes my wife, third comes my kids, and fourth comes my job. So if I lose on Sunday, I've got a lot left over.' I think that's what you've got to do to keep things in perspective, to make sure you don't confuse your results with who you are."

USA Today has called Dr. Blanchard's latest book offering, *The One Minute Entrepreneur*, "bite-sized words of wisdom."[27] To write the new book, Dr. Blanchard gathered advice from several renowned business leaders. I asked him what his favorite insight was among them.

"My favorite insight was, 'Profit is the applause you get for taking care of your customers and creating a motivating environment for your people.' That's what needs to be taken into consideration, so you don't overemphasize results. The profit, which is really important, is also a function of taking care of two groups of people: your customers and your people. The second insight I just love was from Charlie Tremendous Jones: 'You'll be the same year after year except for the people you meet and the books you read.' That's a powerful thing because you always want to be open to learning. Otherwise, you'll become stale, and you might as well lie down and let them throw the dirt over you, because you're heading south."

Finally, I asked Dr. Blanchard if he could give us an idea or two that a reader might find in a book called "The One Minute Investor." His answer was classic and inspiring.

"One chapter I would put in is the 'Test of Perpetual Prosperity.' The Test of Perpetual Prosperity says that you're never going to become very wealthy if you're not serving and helping other people. If it's just about you and making money, it's eventually going to come back and bite you. But if it's to make money because you have an opportunity to serve others and help make a difference, that's important. I'd love to have a whole chapter on that.

"A second chapter I'd love to put into 'The One Minute Investor' book would be 'The Generosity Factor.' A lot of times people evaluate their success in life on how much money they make. I think you miss the whole purpose of life when you do that. . . . There's nothing wrong with making good money, but the big question is: What do you do with your money? 'The Generosity Factor' would talk about how generous you are with your time, your talent, and also your treasure. I would want to put investment in perspective because I think we've gotten a little too greedy."

I found Ken Blanchard to be about as genuine as they come. You could tell he was very comfortable in his own skin and was in the midst of a life well lived. He is the kind of guy that causes you to hang onto his words because you know you're going to get some nuggets. His thoughts on goals, expectations, and investing were right on target. His optimism was obvious, and I suppose that is why he is one of the perpetually successful people he talks so often about.

The Eight-Point Portfolio Checkup

Motivated by Ken Blanchard's simplification theme, I offer readers the following handy checklist of eight items you need to make sure you are wise when it comes to your investments. This compilation of investing principles is a list that is actionable now and something you can use on a regular basis.

1. Review your asset allocation

The first component to review in your portfolio is the overall allocation of stocks versus bonds. Generally, in preretirement situations, you should have no less than an 80% allocation to stocks.[28] A strong case can be made that in the long term (defined as an investment horizon of over five years), stocks not only provide a higher expected return but also are actually safer than bonds. If your tolerance for risk is not quite as high, you might reduce equity exposure.

If you are already retired, the amount you hold in short-term bonds should be based on a simple formula that uses your annual withdrawal needs times 5. This calculation is based on the fact that the Standard & Poor's 500 Index has not had a four-year downturn since the Great Depression.[29] This gives us the confidence to essentially ignore stock market volatility. This five-year short-term bond portion of your allocation will theoretically get you through most any down market cycle on the equity side with one year to spare.

More conservative investors could reasonably use a longer year multiple to make them feel more comfortable. But believing market cycles as I do, this is not necessary. Keep in mind that even if a five-year downturn in equities does occur, it is unlikely that every stock asset class will lose value simultaneously. One or two asset classes typically are headed up even when most are not. (Even during one of the worst bear markets in history from March 2000 to October 2002, the small U.S. value asset class gained 16.1% as represented by the Russell 2000 Value Index.) This gives you the opportunity to rebalance periodically, which means you will replenish the bond portion of your portfolio with the stock classes that have grown. So even though five years of needed income is recommended, they will likely never be spent down by utilizing this rebalancing technique.

2. Avoid underallocating to international markets

A common mistake that individual investors make is underallocating to foreign equity markets. International exposure for both preretirees and retirees should equal somewhere between 25 and 40% of your total equities. Even a 50% allocation of the equity portion of your portfolio to international stocks is not out of the question given the fact that approximately 60% of the total capitalization on the planet now resides outside of the United States.

International markets tend to move at a different pace than U.S. markets. In 2006, we saw a good example of this as the MSCI EAFE Index grew 26.8% while the S&P 500 Index grew 15.8%.[30] Likewise in 2007, the EAFE grew at more than twice the rate of the S&P at 11.6% versus 5.5%, and U.S. small caps came in behind the international index at −1.5% for the year.[31] The weak dollar, which many would usually consider a bad thing, has made for some nice returns overseas in recent years. Without exposure to these markets, your portfolio missed out.

3. Avoid fixed income allocations over five years' duration

In any interest rate environment, short-term bond mutual funds are called for. *Short-term* is defined as two years in duration or less. I rarely see any reason for individual investors to go beyond a five-year duration with their fixed income allocations. Bonds should be considered tools to dampen volatility and provide for cash flow needs only. Bonds should not be used for interest rate plays in order to try and guess which way the rate is going.

It is amazing how much effort is expended in bond brokerage houses trying to build ladders to the sky with fixed income instruments. They play on the fears many investors have concerning stocks and create other risks that are rarely defined—the main one being inflation risk. Longer-term bonds inject unnecessary risk into a portfolio with little or no reward. Remember, use bonds for cash flow and liquidity and let equities provide the long-term growth you need.

4. Avoid underallocation to small-cap stocks

Another common trend in individual portfolios is underallocating to small company stocks. I joke often that if I really had the intestinal fortitude I claim to have, I would put all my money in small-cap value stock and check it every 15 years or so. (For the 15-year period 1993 through 2007, small-cap value stocks returned 12.46% annualized, excluding the 29% loss in 2008.)[32]

Since 1926, we have seen small-cap stocks outpace large-cap stocks by approximately 2% per year on average.[33] But alas, few if any humans have the kind of stomach for the volatility that comes with those returns, so we superdiversify and win anyway. But in spite of the higher risk, preretirees should have somewhere between 30 and 40% of their equity allocation—both domestic and international—in small company stocks. Retirees should likewise maintain 25 to 35% in small companies. The higher risk means higher returns. This is the governing precept of investing.

5. Avoid underallocation to value stocks

There is a perception that growth stocks are the place to be because that is precisely the goal of investors—to have their portfolios grow. This "growth" nomenclature does a disservice to investors in that it takes away from the fact that "value" stocks actually outperform growth stocks over the long run. Perhaps value stocks are not as exciting to talk about as the go-go growth stocks with their hot products or services. However, if the objective is to increase value of a portfolio, value stocks fit the bill. You should maintain 50 to 70% of your stock allocation in value stocks with the remaining invested in "blend" asset classes as opposed to a dedicated growth category. The blend will capture enough of the growth companies to satisfy a prudent allocation.

6. Consider taxes

There are four simple rules to follow when considering taxes in your investment accounts:

- You should *rarely* pay taxes on short-term capital gains because these gains are taxed at ordinary income tax rates. If you do, it is possibly because your money manager is picking and timing the market—a big bad no-no.
- Use tax-managed mutual funds in taxable accounts when possible. The added tax efficiency means a higher return.
- Bonds should usually be held in tax-deferred accounts as the income they earn is taxed at ordinary income tax rates. Retirees may need to hold some bonds in taxable accounts for cash flow purposes.
- Use mutual funds with turnover ratios that are generally in the 20 to 40% range. Anything higher once again indicates the presence of those evil twin brothers: picking and timing.

7. Assess mutual fund fees

The average stock mutual fund fees (expense ratios) for your portfolio should not exceed 0.40%. The average stock fund fee in the marketplace in 2007 was around 1.32%.[34] As you can see, there is a great disparity in the mutual fund arena. Emerging market funds and often small-cap funds will be somewhat higher because of the transaction fees and lower market liquidity. That is why the average expense ratio of all the funds in your portfolio is the correct measurement to use. Bond fund fees should stay below 0.30%. Mutual funds that exceed these parameters are telltale signs of retail funds that use your money to pay for their huge advertising and marketing costs. As a current shareholder of such a fund, why would you care to subsidize the fund's acquisition of new clients by paying higher fees so the fund can increase its revenue?

8. Assess your advisor

- You should always work with an advisory firm that is independent. This means the firm is not associated with a "big-brother" brokerage firm that looks over its shoulder and markets the hot investment of the week to that firm and thus to you.

- The firm should also be set up as a fee-only and direct-pay brokerage. This means every dollar it makes comes directly from you—the client. It also means it does not accept "soft dollars" or rewards such as exotic vacations or other perks from mutual fund companies or fund custodians. The name at the top of your advisor's paycheck should only be yours.

- Look for the Certified Financial Planner (CFP) abbreviation after your advisor's name. This is the highest standard of knowledge and conduct in the financial industry. This qualification makes it more likely that your advisor will be willing to act in a fiduciary manner in the advisory relationship. And get this relationship spelled out in writing. This will put a higher standard of accountability on your advisor.

- Check to see if the firm uses a team approach in managing its business. There are extraordinarily talented people in the financial business, one of whom you may want to call "your guy." But his departure from the firm for any of a variety of reasons including health problems or death could leave you alone. A team approach assures you of some continuity. And it also allows the old "two heads are better than one" method to benefit you and your family.

- Finally, ask the advisor if she uses the same strategy for all of her clients. In other words, does she recommend the same type of investments (that is, asset class passive investing) for all of her clients? If the answer is yes, then you can be assured that you will not be getting the "investment of the week" recommendation when your portfolio is invested.

All eight points of this portfolio check-up can be achieved by finding an independent fiduciary advisor who provides a written *investment policy statement* to guide you through the investing process. By also using a passive asset class approach, most of these points will occur automatically, alleviating unnecessary worries about your investments.

Money and Happiness with Arthur Brooks

Arthur C. Brooks is a professor of public administration and the director of the Nonprofit Studies Program at Syracuse University's Maxwell School of Citizenship and Public Affairs. He is a regular guest on the radio program, and he has published many articles and books on the connections between culture, politics, and economic life in America. He speaks frequently in the United States, Europe, and Asia, and he is a regular contributor to the *Wall Street Journal* editorial page.

Professor Brooks is what I would call a "happiness expert." His latest book, *Gross National Happiness*, gives true meaning to what

Thomas Jefferson penned in the Declaration of Independence concerning "the pursuit of happiness." I believe we can all learn a great deal by sitting at the feet of Arthur Brooks as he discusses how and why we should be more content with our lives in America.[35]

During our September 2008 visit,[36] I mentioned to Professor Brooks that sometimes good financial decisions make us uneasy emotionally. I asked him to expound on the concept of what he calls the "comparative effect."

"I've been looking at happiness and money for years. I'm an economist, so I want to know, does money buy happiness? My priest always told me no and so did my mother, but I'm like everybody else. I want to figure it out for myself. So when you look at the data, you find that when you personally get richer, as long as you don't start in abject poverty, you actually won't get happier as you get richer. What will happen is, as you get richer, you will tend, on average, to feel like a more successful person, and that will make you happier. But you can get success without the money. You can do it through your family. You can do it through volunteering. You can do it through a satisfying career that doesn't pay very much. It just happens that money often goes along with success.

"The interesting thing is, however, you find that inevitably in America, and in countries all around the world, that you want more money than everybody else. It feels good, according to a lot of researchers on this subject, to have more than others. [So] a lot of people have concluded that the comparison effect is really important.

"But once again, that's not completely supported by the data. Most people want to feel like they have meaning in their lives. They want to feel that they're successful in creating value. Simply put, when people do well in their careers, they tend to feel like they have more of those things, and that's the reason why people who have more tend to feel happier than those who have less. They feel like more successful people.

"As a matter of fact, if you ask two people 'How successful do you feel in life?' they will be equally likely to be happy people even if one earns eight times as much as the other. So in other words, it's not really the comparison in money. It's the comparison in the feeling of success. If you want to give your kids or yourself greater happiness, do something that matches your skills and passions and that fulfills you, notwithstanding the money. The money will usually follow according to the data, but the money is not the key thing."

Brooks's answer made me think about the ironies involved in the dealing with money on the psychological side as he does. Professor Brooks says in his book, "Work, not leisure, makes us happy. Ninety percent of Americans like their jobs, and 70% of Americans say that they would continue to work even if they were financially independent." I wanted to know if he thought this was the case here in the United States, or was it the same all over the world. Especially in regard to retired Americans. We work our entire careers trying to get to the leisure, and yet his research is telling us that it's better to work because that's where the happiness lies.

Another area of interest that Brooks has dealt with extensively is charity. I knew he had taken the position that individuals, not government, offer the best solution to social ills as key factors in how much people give. I wanted our listeners to consider the reason for his position.

"I told you that money doesn't buy happiness, and it really doesn't, but there's one exception to that rule. I can offer your listeners a thousand dollars of happiness right now, but don't send it to me. Send it to your favorite charity.

"One of the things that we find is when people give money away charitably, you actually see differences in brain function. They lower their stress levels. They increase their endorphins that make them feel a slight buzz, but they immediately become happier. People who get into a pattern of giving their money away and their time away, for that matter, or their blood or anything else they have of value, can permanently boost their happiness above their baseline cheerful level. No joke. This is a great way to buy happiness.

"And what it suggests to us is that we get into a public policy environment as some would like us to get into in which public policy makers say, 'Charity is just evidence that the government is not doing its job. Charity is just evidence that we have unmet need. If the government did its job, we wouldn't need any charity in the first place.' That's completely wrong. The data that we plowed out on voluntary giving [indicate] that the day we stop giving is the day that we start getting poorer, unhappier, and unhealthier."

In his previous book, *Who Really Cares*, Brooks indicated that we could actually increase the GDP if people gave more to charity.[37] He stated that for every $100 a person gives in a year, he or she would earn on average another $375 in income. I asked him to expand on this concept and to tell us if the numbers had changed any given the tough economy we were experiencing.

"I tend to find that there's a personal multiplier—that when people give, they do get richer. It sounds kind of like magic or religion or something, but in truth what we find is people have these neurochemical effects. People tend to lower their stress and become more effectively joyful in their jobs and in their lives, and these are people who tend to be more successful and make more money.

"So there's real earth-bound psychological and neurochemical reasons why when people give, they become more effective. Consequently, they tend to earn more money over the long run. But there's also good data now showing that there's a multiplier effect for the macroeconomy, that when Americans give, it's not just a multiplier of $2.75 for every $1 that Americans give. On the contrary, it's more like $19 for the American GDP for every dollar that's given away, which is extraordinary when you think about it.

"When individuals give, they get, you know, between $3 to $4 of it on top of what they gave. But a much larger percentage just goes right into jobs and growth and the ability of Americans to prosper, and that tells us two big things. Number 1, charitable giving is a great investment opportunity and something that nobody should ignore. People who have a balanced investment portfolio need to be thinking about philanthropy to some extent or another as a smart investment decision.

"But even beyond that, charitable giving is a patriotic act. It's something that you can do that helps others, which helps your country, and helps yourself. It's a little miracle."

Arthur C. Brooks is one of those guests that truly inspire me to be a better person. May we all at the same time learn how to invest our money wisely—and also remember that we are the richest when our pleasures are the simplest.

The Market Return Benchmark (MRB)

When someone mentions the "stock market," most people immediately think of the S&P 500 Index or maybe the Dow Jones Industrial Average. These familiar indexes have become synonymous with "the market" even though combined they represent only approximately 12% of all U.S. stocks.[38] And those indexes don't even consider international stocks, which make up about 60% of the world capital markets.[39]

Indexes made sense 50 years ago because they were easy to calculate and track. Although they consisted of only a small sample of stocks, they gave us a general indication of where the market was heading. Over the last six decades, however, investing has been revolutionized by the advent of computers and modern portfolio theory (MPT). We now know that proper investing requires 10 to 12 different asset classes. So why do Wall Street and the financial media continually insist on referencing only a few?

Amazingly, Wall Street has made little effort to provide individual investors with a true benchmark representing the market as a whole. The industry can constantly come up with new products to sell consumers, but it hasn't devised a simple benchmark for fairly and accurately measuring a portfolio's performance. I believe the reason it has not accomplished this simple chore is because Wall Street doesn't want you to really know how it is doing. But investors need some way to measure portfolio return against the extended capital market system. That is why in 2004 we developed a tool to do just that: the *Market Return Benchmark* (MRB).[40]

In Figure 8-1 you can see a sample makeup of the MRB versus the S&P 500 Index. It was designed to give a basic allocation

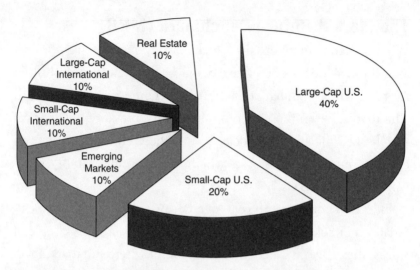

Figure 8-1 Sample Return History of the Market Return Benchmark

of a 100% equity portfolio. Keep in mind that it is a comparison tool for the stock portion of your portfolio only. It represents basic diversification among the six major asset classes: large-cap U.S. and international, small-cap U.S. and international, emerging markets, and real estate. There is a 65/35% ratio of large-cap to small-cap stocks (counting emerging markets as half large and half small) and a 2/1 ratio (60/30%) of U.S. to international stocks (excluding real estate).

Your portfolio should also contain asset subclasses such as small-cap value and small-cap emerging markets. Therefore, a live portfolio will have more asset classes represented. Some asset class investors also prefer a heavier weighting in small- versus large-cap or international versus U.S. holdings. A more nuanced allocation is the result of a personal written financial plan that should include an investment policy statement.

My hope is that this new measuring tool will shift your investing paradigm to include all of the appropriate asset classes to more accurately measure your portfolio success. Go to www.market returnbenchmark.com for updated results.

Three Timeless, Universal Investing Principles

I end each of my radio programs with the statement, "We hope you have learned something today about creating wealth without worry." The ultimate goal of *The Investing Revolution* is to educate investors on how to let go of the anxiety concerning their money and get on to the really important things in life. We want investors to take pleasure in the journey. The following three simple, yet timeless and universal investing concepts can change your financial outlook and thus change your life for the better as well.

Principle 1. Free Capital Markets Are Immortal

To contrast this fact, we can look at money managers and the human element that is inherent to them. First of all, managers make mistakes, as all of us mortals do. Even the big-name investing gurus like Peter Lynch and Warren Buffett, who have experienced extraordinarily unusual runs of good fortune, have also had their share of losses. (By the way, these are the only two money managers I could think of with such exceptionally good anomalistic records. Only two out of thousands that have come down the pike. How many more can you name?)

The market, on the other hand, is always right. It always reflects the compilation of current prices as set by the market. Think it is wrong sometimes? Then whom do you call to argue about it?

Where do you make your appeal? How do you question it or file a complaint? There is nowhere to do that; consequently, even when you disagree, the market is still always right. Once investors accept this fact, they can stop fretting over what to do next. Embrace the market as a partner that eventually brings only success.

Managers are also ambitious—and they should be. Aren't you? They want to climb the ladder of success and make a better life for themselves and their families just as you and I do. So when they experience a good year and thus have an opportunity to be more successful, they move on to somewhere or something else. When they make their move, any "expertise" they may have goes with them. Unfortunately, humans also get seriously ill, or step in front of the bus at just the wrong time, or even get burned out. Circumstances of this nature can happen quickly to any of us.

But the market? She's always there working—24/7. She's taking in all the data, setting prices based on the immutable law of supply and demand all over the world, in every time zone, in every form of capital market—from the freest entrepreneurial form to the fledgling state-guided form. Some might argue that she may occasionally get sick. In fact, a recession might be considered the market's flu bug. It is occasionally annoying and uncomfortable, but it is not long-lasting or fatal. It always recovers. Cast your lot with the permanency and constancy of the free capital market and not with time and chance.

Principle 2. Maintain a Perpetual Investment Time Horizon

The way you should think about your investment time horizon is the same way institutional investors think of theirs. How? Long, long term. Consider this: How often do institutions become insolvent?

When is the last time a scholarship endowment folded? They don't. And one reason this is the case is that the boards that serve them take their fiduciary responsibilities very seriously. Because of this, institutions have a perpetual investment time horizon. Since our feet are indeed made of clay, we do not have the need to plan for forever (financially that is). I suppose that one good thing about this fact is that we don't have to worry about managing our money forever. Eventually, your loved ones or a cause you feel deeply about will inherit whatever you leave behind. But even though you don't live forever, having an unending investment time horizon is the best way to manage your money.

One of the biggest problems with individual investors is that they manage their money with short-term thinking and short-term worries. They fail to realize or remember that all investment dollars should be considered long term in nature. After all, just because you retire at 60 or 65 does not mean that your money is retiring too. Hopefully, one or both of you will live another 25 or 30 years. That is long term in the financial world. Any individual year, or two, or three may see a downturn. But in the longer timeframe (five years or more), things will go fine. That is what institutional fiduciaries know already. In fact, the passive asset class approach we advocate started in the institutional arena long before it was rolled out to individual investors in the early 1990s. Investors need to adopt a prudent, fiduciary, perpetual attitude of investment management.

Principle 3. All Portfolios, Including Yours, Should Be Managed Passively

Your portfolio's makeup should not be based on market conditions or—as is the case all too often—on your investment advisor's current or new proprietary product lines of mutual funds, annuities, or stock offerings. You should be advised by firms that use the same tried and proven strategy for each and every client. Of course, the percentages within asset classes may be dissimilar based on differing ages, family circumstances, retirement time horizon, health, and so on. But as far as the strategy itself, a passive asset class approach that harnesses the power of free capital markets is the only way to create wealth without worry consistently. Don't be reduced to accepting the portfolio solution of the day.

During our April 2008 interview of Professor Ken French, he stated, "People [and institutions] whose job it is to question what they can really do for their constituents focus totally on cost and realize the best thing is to go passive."[41]

You too must "own the market." Own capitalism. It is the greatest economic invention of all of human history. You have been blessed to live in a time when you can literally own it via the vehicle of institutional asset class mutual funds. The best time to superdiversify using these remarkable tools is always right now. You no longer have to be paralyzed with indecision because of market fluctuations. Instead, owning the market will allow free markets to work for you while you work (or play) at something else.

The ancillary benefits of this approach are also significant: You can now stop watching markets. By allowing markets to do the work, you can eliminate the time-consuming stressful activity of watching market ups and downs and economic forecasts. This in turn allows you to avoid emotional mistakes that often accompany market-watching activity. Now that you understand that timing and picking decisions are futile anyway, what's the point?

You can also do something more worthwhile. Consider all the time and energy that has now been freed up for really important things. Never again should you be a slave to market or economic news. This affords a great opportunity to reevaluate the things in life that are important to you and your family.

These three principles can change your financial life—and thus other aspects of your life as well. They are straightforward and appropriate for each individual investor. Their simplicity and universal nature are not mainstream conventional wisdom in the investment world. On one level, this is surprising, but on another level, it is expected. Wall Street wants codependency. It wants to enable you to the point of your relying on it. That's another paradox of the financial realm. And it's another reason why you should join *The Investing Revolution*.

Bottom Line

It is no wonder that money is mentioned more times in the Bible than any other subject. Economic issues are threaded unceasingly through our entire lives. There is no avoiding them. You must embrace them. My sincere desire is that something you have read in this final chapter has motivated you to do better. Manage your portfolio better, think about money more clearly, and define in your own life some principles that you can live by that will improve not only your life but all the lives you come in contact with—and eventually leave behind.

EPILOGUE

This book was not designed to be a how-to instructional manual. Yet I have mentioned throughout that the passive asset class investing methodology is unequivocally the best way for you to invest your money. My first book, *Wealth Without Worry*, covers the basics of the asset class portfolio (ACP) strategy in detail. I highly recommend that you read it to get the full appreciation for how the strategy works. At any rate, I could not leave you hanging without some additional information, so I have included the following for your consideration.

Building a portfolio using active management is tantamount to building a house upon the sand that will cause it to eventually collapse. In contrast, the asset class portfolio (ACP) strategy entails building your investment house upon solid ground that can withstand the economic storms that befall it. How? You build it on the bedrock economic system of free capital markets.

This discussion is designed to give you a better idea of how you can implement an ACP strategy.

It is one thing to buy stocks when you realize that the stock market is the only place to be in order to beat inflation and attain real growth. It is quite another to do it properly.

I have mentioned diversification throughout this book, but how is proper diversification actually achieved? The key is superdiversification, so called because it transcends, or passes beyond, the limits of commonly defined diversification.

Diversification is a concept to which nearly all investment advisors give lip service. Unfortunately, few actually ever apply diversification correctly. Classic examples of improper diversification were seen in the mid- to late 1990s when the buying of large U.S. stocks—particularly technology stocks—was all the rage. The media and most brokers and advisors were telling investors that the new world economy had changed things. Consequently, investors were inclined to be overly weighted in the hot sectors or the flavor of the day. The tech bubble burst in 2000, which quickly brought the investors back to reality.

Diversification is the most critical and yet most misunderstood element of investing. You may believe you have proper diversification because you have multiple individual securities or mutual funds in your portfolio, but your belief may not be warranted. Having dozens or even hundreds of securities in your portfolio does not mean it is properly diversified. In actuality, it takes thousands of securities drawn from all the major asset classes— about 12,000 to be more specific.

This broad and deep asset class diversification mitigates the losses in bad markets. I call this "the giant portfolio stop-loss effect." Now, technically there is no such thing as buying a stop-loss on an entire portfolio, as is possible with an individual stock position. But a superdiversification strategy can basically achieve the same ends, and it can provide a safety net of sorts. Superdiversification also allows an opportunity to share in the market return when the bull market runs again.

The building blocks, or tools, used to accomplish superdiversification are known as institutional asset class funds (IACFs). They allow investors to superdiversify among all the companies in a particular asset class, starting again with the first dollar.

The concept for IACFs was born out of modern portfolio theory (MPT). The theoretical foundation for MPT was published by Harry Markowitz in 1952.[1] Along with two associates, Markowitz won the Nobel Prize in Economics in 1990 for his work on the subject. Other academicians naturally gravitated to this logical process.

Interestingly, multi-million-dollar institutional investors, such as pension plans and scholarship funds, have used both asset class mutual funds and modern portfolio theory for decades. Their fiduciary responsibility is to protect the investments placed in their trust. To meet that obligation, they have used these approaches in an effort to reduce the various risks to which their funds are exposed.

In the early 1990s, enterprising individuals implemented the MPT methods by creating the asset class funds now available for individual investors through independent registered investment advisors (RIAs). Now these same techniques are available for anyone who is interested in the preservation of capital and its steady, long-term growth.

Institutional asset class mutual funds are designed to deliver the investment results of an entire asset class, such as large U.S. value stocks or small international stocks. These asset class funds are best suited to create efficient portfolios that promote superdiversification.

Institutional asset class funds use what we refer to as a portfolio "filter" when determining which securities should be held in a particular fund. Generally, this methodology is designed to eliminate candidates rather than select candidates as active managers do. (That is why we call active managers "stock pickers.") This subtle, yet critical, difference is the foundation of passive asset class investing. It is the key ingredient that eliminates the human element in money management that so often derails the most disciplined of individual investors. By using objective filtering criteria instead of subjective selection, the consistency of the asset class portfolio approach to investing is achieved.

With the asset class portfolio approach, you do not mine data to find the best performers because the institutional asset class funds simply represent the market in the purest form. There is no picking of stocks or funds based on their past performances. The strategy affords basically one alternative—there is no choice or pick to make. We use institutional asset class funds, which provide market return. Period. There are no empty promises of beating the market or getting rich quick. It is simply the best way to invest and thus benefit from the free market system that has made our country great. When you apply this approach to your investment program, you too can enjoy the peace of mind that comes from doing the right thing with your money. I hope you will learn more about asset class investing so that you can implement the last investment strategy you will ever need.

Appendix

BOB McTEER DELIVERS FREE MARKET COMMON SENSE

There are those unique individuals we cross paths with in life that know more about a subject than we can ever hope to know—yet they relay their wisdom in a way that is understandable and practical. Bob McTeer is a gentleman and a scholar in every sense. His adoration for capitalism comes through immediately once you get him started talking about financial matters. He is a frequent guest as well as guest host on *The Investing Revolution*, and here I share some of his sensible and instructive perspectives on money and the workings of the free market economy.[1]

Bob is a distinguished fellow at the National Center for Policy Analysis (NCPA) where he covers macroeconomic issues including monetary policy, fiscal policy, and tax and education policy. Prior to joining the NCPA in January 2007, Bob was the chancellor of the Texas A&M University System (my alma mater). Before becoming chancellor, Bob had a 36-year career with the Federal Reserve System, during which time he spent 14 years as president of the Federal Reserve Bank of Dallas. As a Fed policymaker, Bob gained a national reputation as an independent voice and a maverick, dissenting from the Alan Greenspan majority twice in 1999 and once in 2002. His dissents and his outspoken views and plain talk got him the labels the "Lone Star Loner" and the "Lonesome Dove." (He says he's been called worse.)

During one visit on our show, Bob told us that his free market views in general, and his vigorous support of free trade in particular, earned the Dallas Fed its reputation as "The Free Enterprise Fed."[2] During an on-air visit in April 2008, we talked about the moral hazard at the Fed. Bob seems to always enjoy illustrating an issue as opposed to defining it. He was in true form as he helped our listeners get a grasp of what the moral dilemmas are at the Fed.

"The whole concept of moral hazard is sort of new in the popular vocabulary these days. When people are at a football game, let's say the Aggies are playing the Longhorns [in Texas], if somebody wants to see better, he can stand up and see better. But if everybody stands up to see better, it won't work. So the problem is that what's true for individuals isn't necessarily what's true for all individuals collectively. Or if you translate it into the economy—take farming, for example. If the farmer has a better crop this year, he's going to be better off. But if all farmers have a better crop this year, prices will fall. What a farmer really wants and needs is a good crop in a bad crop year."

In another interview, Bob showed again why he has a reputation of being able to boil down economics to understandable elements. I questioned him about the unusual economic wisdom he employed—that is, "If you're sure of yourself, go with what you see. If you're uncertain, assume the glass is half full." He explained that at the Dallas Fed, especially in the second half of the 1990s, the economy was just really performing so, so well, and it was exceeding everybody's expectations. "It just seemed like if you bet against it, you lost, and your odds were much better as an optimist then they were as a pessimist. So I told my economists, you know, call them like you see them, but if you don't have a clear view, if you are uncertain and if you're halfway guessing, I'd rather you go ahead and guess on the optimistic side just because the odds are higher that way."

Imagine that. An economist with an optimistic outlook, a rare occurrence to be sure. The joke goes, ask 15 economists and you'll likely get 30 different answers ("on the other hand . . ."). It is easier for them to either give noncommittal either-or explanations or take half-empty-glass positions. That way, when things go poorly, they can say "I knew it," and when things go well, they can avoid being held accountable for their pessimistic outlook. Economists who take an optimistic approach risk losing credibility the first time they miss their prediction. I appreciate Bob's more forthright, "call it like he sees it" approach.

In our many discussions, Bob shared with us a primer on economics, some of which Bob had included in an article he wrote in the late 1980s. Excerpts from that primer follow.[3] I share these thoughts from this unsung hero of *The Investing Revolution* because they contain timeless wisdom from which we all could benefit.

On free markets:

"In a free market system, the government doesn't organize, direct, and control economic activity. If the government doesn't, who does?

Who decides what is to be produced, and how, and in what quantities and quality, and who gets the fruits of production?

"The answer is that you and I decide these important questions by the way we spend our money. The market system features consumer sovereignty, meaning that the consumer is king. We decide what will be produced by casting dollar votes for the things we want and by not spending on the things we don't want."

On profits:

"The profit motive translates consumer demand into production. Nobody does consumers a favor. Producers are simply trying to earn a profit, just as consumers are seeking their best deal. Profit is the driving force of capitalism—it is the incentive for production, the reward for anticipating or reacting to consumer preferences correctly, and the source of capital for expansion. All market participants respond to the millions of price signals sent out daily to correct both incipient shortages and surpluses. Each responds to the participant's own self-interest, but in doing so, he or she contributes to a rational and efficient outcome."

On competition:

"Market prices, in conjunction with the profit motive and competition, also determine how production is organized. To maximize profits, producers will seek the least costly inputs and the most efficient production methods. They don't have to be directed to hold costs down; in a competitive environment, their survival depends on it.

"With competition driving down prices to average costs in the industry, firms with higher-than-average costs will experience losses. If they don't have enough market power to raise prices, cost reduction becomes the only alternative to going out of business. This market discipline encourages a constant search for new efficiencies. Efforts to thwart that process may protect individual producers but only at the expense of consumers and the efficiency of the overall economic system."

On income:

"The market system also determines who gets the goods and services that are produced. Of course, the people who buy them get them. But the real question is, who earns how much income from the nation's production and thus has the dollars to spend on it.

"To make a long story in price theory short, workers and owners of other factors of production in a competitive environment will tend to receive incomes based on their marginal contributions to the nation's output. Businesses, in following their profit motive, have a financial incentive to continue hiring workers as long as they expect each worker hired to add more to the firms' revenues than to their costs. The more productive people, in terms of the market value of their contribution, will earn more than less productive people and will be able to claim a larger share of that output. In a competitive environment, workers and other productive resources are paid the value of their marginal output."

On work and reward:

"The link between work and reward is another major driving force of capitalism. Working smarter is rewarded as much as working harder. So is seeking out new products or services, or new markets or new techniques, since it is market value that is rewarded more than hours worked or units produced. The market system encourages creativity and risk taking by rewarding their success. Imagine the difference in a system where everyone works for the state.

"Whom you work for makes all the difference. In a free enterprise system, you work for yourself. You get to keep your earnings—after taxes, of course. You can acquire private property with your earnings, enhance its value, and pass it on to your children if you wish. You may change jobs or firms or locations. Everyone is free to pursue his or her own interests rather than the interests of the nation."

On "the invisible hand":

"You may ask, isn't that selfish? The answer is yes. But Adam Smith showed us more than 200 years ago in *The Wealth of Nations* that pursuit of self-interest in a competitive market economy is, as if by some "invisible hand," consistent with promoting the public interest. Each of us can work where we get the highest wage, shop where we get the lowest price, and borrow where we get the lowest rate. In all these transactions, we face counterparts with the opposite motivation, but the outcome of all the bargaining is rational and efficient. Prices are established that coordinate the millions of daily transactions and bring order out of chaos."

On freedom of choice:

"The point is that a modern economy is very complicated. Billions of decisions and/or choices have to be made daily. The task is simply too complicated for governments or planning boards. Who better to make these decisions than the people most intimately involved—people who know their unique circumstances better than anyone else?"

On the role of government:

"Free enterprise is characterized by voluntary exchange and private property rights. In the private sector, exchanges made voluntarily presumably leave both parties better off. That presumption is absent in government transactions since they are not entirely voluntary. An element of coercion is involved, even if the tax laws and spending priorities are determined through democratic processes. (If you question the coerciveness of government, consider how you feel on April 15.) Property rights and individual liberty are compromised when governments demand a share of a person's property or income for their own use.

"Most advocates of free enterprise agree that government has a role to play, although many regard it as a necessary evil. Some services, such as national defense, a court system, and a police force, can be provided only collectively and are generally regarded as proper functions of government. At the other end of the spectrum, however, are functions that many regard as inconsistent with individual liberty. These might include programs to redistribute income or to advance the cause of one group at the expense of others. The latter would include subsidies, protection from competition, and the like. When the government can legally rob Peter to pay Paul, there is great potential for abuse.

"There will always be an abundance of worthy causes seeking government sponsorship. But the test should not only be whether the cause is worthy but also whether government is the appropriate entity to deal with it. National priorities and government priorities are two different things. To say that national defense should have a large share of the federal government's budget and child care or decent housing should not is not to denigrate the importance of the latter. Such a statement simply recognizes that child care and housing concerns can best be handled at the individual or family level while national defense cannot.

"In a world of finite resources, a decision by the government to undertake a new project is a decision to forgo others. Each dollar spent by the government is a dollar not spent by its former owner—the taxpayer—on something he or she deemed important. Collective decision making preempts individual decision making. Since governments get their funds from the people, helping one group or cause can be done only at the expense of another group or cause.

"In addition to comparing and evaluating the outcomes of such choices, we must be concerned that at some point the confiscation of private income for public purposes will inhibit the creation of wealth that is to be shared. The bottom line is that while limited government is necessary and consistent with an essentially free economy, there are limits to how large the size and scope of government can grow without killing the goose that lays the golden egg."

Amen, Bob, and Amen! May you live a long and fruitful life in the cause of free enterprise.

ENDNOTES

Chapter 1

1. John Bogle, Vanguard Group, "Capitalism," September 16, 2005, and "Common Sense Investing," March 23, 2007, interviews by Jim Whiddon and Lance Alston, hosts of *The Investing Revolution*, WBAP 820 AM.

2. John Bogle, *The Battle for the Soul of Capitalism: How the Financial System Undermined Social Ideals, Damaged Trust in the Markets, Robbed Investors of Trillions, and What to Do about It*, Yale University Press, New Haven, Conn., 2005.

3. Arthur Levitt, former chairman of Securities & Exchange Commission (1993–2001), "Economics in the U.S.," February 17, 2006, interview by Jim Whiddon and Lance Alston, hosts of *The Investing Revolution*, WBAP 820 AM.

4. Burton Malkiel, *A Random Walk Down Wall Street*, 5th ed., Norton, New York, 1973.

5. Burton Malkiel, "Another Random Walk," August 12, 2005, interview by Jim Whiddon and Lance Alston, hosts of *The Investing Revolution*, World Talk Radio.

6. Burton Malkiel, *From Wall Street to the Great Wall: How Investors Can Profit from China's Booming Economy*, Norton, New York, 2008.

7. Burton Malkiel, "Irrational Complacency?" *Wall Street Journal*, April 30, 2007.

8. Eugene F. Fama, University of Chicago, "Efficient Capital Markets: A Review of Theory and Empirical Work," *Journal of Finance*, May 1970.

9. Eugene F. Fama, University of Chicago, "Efficient Markets," April 13, 2007, interview by Jim Whiddon and Lance Alston, hosts of *The Investing Revolution*, WBAP 820 AM.

10. William J. Bernstein, *The Intelligent Asset Allocator: How to Build Your Portfolio to Maximize Returns and Minimize Risk*, McGraw-Hill, New York, 2001.

11. William J. Bernstein, *The Four Pillars of Investing: Lessons for Building a Winning Portfolio*, McGraw-Hill, New York, 2002.

12. William J. Bernstein, *A Splendid Exchange: How Trade Shaped the World*, Atlantic Monthly Press, New York, 2008.

13. William J. Bernstein, "A Historical Perspective on Trade and Commerce," August 1, 2008, interview by Jim Whiddon and Lance Alston, hosts of *The Investing Revolution*, WBAP 820 AM.

14. Edmund S. Phelps, Columbia University, Nobel Laureate, The Sveriges Riksbank Prize in Economic Sciences in Memory of Alfred Nobel 2006, nobelprize.org/nobel_prizes/economics/laureates/2006/.

15. Edmund S. Phelps, Columbia University, Nobel Laureate, "Entrepreneurial Culture: Why European Economies Lag behind the U.S.," OpinionJournal.com, *Wall Street Journal Online*, February 12, 2007, www.opinionjournal.com/editorial/feature.html?id=110009657.

16. Edmund S. Phelps, Columbia University, Nobel Laureate, "Entrepreneurial Culture," February 15, 2008, interview by Jim Whiddon and Lance Alston, hosts of *The Investing Revolution*, WBAP 820 AM.

17. Manuel Álvarez-Rivera, "General Election Results: Parliamentary Elections in the United Kingdom," May 5, 2005, Election Resources on the Internet, www.electionresources.org/uk/house.php?election=2005.

18. Steven Landsburg, "Why Europeans Work Less Than Americans," *Forbes*, May 23, 2006, www.forbes.com/2006/05/20/steven-landsburg-labor_cx_sl_06work_0523landsburg.html.

19. Ibid.

20. Ibid.

21. Edward C. Prescott, Nobel Laureate, "Why Do Americans Work So Much More Than Europeans?" *Federal Reserve Bank of Minneapolis Quarterly Review*, July 2004, pp. 2–13.

22. Edward C. Prescott, Nobel Laureate, "Equity Premiums," July 29, 2007, interview by Jim Whiddon and Lance Alston, hosts of *The Investing Revolution*, WBAP 820 AM.

23. Organisation for Economic Co-operation and Development (OECD) "Evolution of GDP," *OCED Factbook* 2007, Paris, 2007, pp. 32–33.

24. Prescott, "Why Do Americans Work So Much More Than Europeans?"

25. Ibid.

26. Dinesh D'Souza, "Free Marketeers," October 9, 2008, interview by Jim Whiddon and Lance Alston, hosts of *The Investing Revolution*, WBAP 820 AM.

27. Dinesh D'Souza, www.dineshdsouza.com/more/about.html, July 17, 2008.
28. Dinesh D'Souza, *The Enemy at Home: The Cultural Left and Its Responsibility for 9/11*, Doubleday, New York, 2007.
29. Dinesh D'Souza, *The Virtue of Prosperity: Finding Values in an Age of Techno-Affluence*, Touchstone, New York, 2000.

Chapter 2

1. Lu Zheng, "Maybe Investors Aren't Stupid After All: Oft-Cited Study Is Revised," *Wall Street Journal*, March 31, 2004.
2. Yuka Hayashi, "Funds Closed at Brisk Pace in 2003," *Wall Street Journal*, March 4, 2004.
3. Ibid.
4. Ibid.
5. Morningstar, "Mutual Funds Created 2005 to 2007," Morningstar Principia Pro Database, July 10, 2008, www.morningstar.com.
6. Kathy Shwiff, "Merrill Lynch to Revamp Its Stock-Rating System," MarketWatch.com, *Wall Street Journal*, May 14, 2008, www.marketwatch.com/news/story/merrill-lynch-revamp-its-stockrating/story.aspx?guid=%7BE04AC479%2D5E1F%2D4E94%2D9540%2DB3E106200530%7D&siteid=rss.
7. Diya Gullapalli, "Firms Pressure Mutual Fund Messenger," WSJ.com, *Wall Street Journal*, May 15, 2008, online.wsj.com/article/SB121081974352994349.html.
8. Ibid.
9. Ibid.

10. Morningstar, "2003 One-Year Performance: Wyoming Fund," Morningstar Principia Pro Database, July 10, 2008, www.morningstar.com.

11. Morningstar, "2003 One-Year Performance: D.U.M.B. Funds," Morningstar Principia Pro Database, July 10, 2008, www.morningstar.com.

12. Standard & Poor's, "Historical Prices of S&P 500 Index, January 1, 2003, to December 31, 2003," www2. standardandpoors.com/portal/site/sp/en/us/page.topic/ indices_500/2,3,2,2,11,31,2003,0,0,0,0,0,0,0,0,0,0.html.

13. Standard & Poor's, "Historical Prices of S&P 500 Index, January 1, 2003, to December 31, 2006," www2. standardandpoors.com/portal/site/sp/en/us/page.topic/ indices_500/2,3,2,2,11,31,2006,0,0,0,0,0,0,0,0,0,0.html.

14. Standard & Poor's, "Historical Prices of S&P 500 Index, January 1, 2003, to December 31, 2007," www2. standardandpoors.com/portal/site/sp/en/us/page.topic/ indices_500/2,3,2,2,11,31,2007,0,0,0,0,0,0,0,0,0,0.html.

15. *Wall Street Journal*, "Claymore Plans to Cut Its EFTs by about Half," February 2, 2008, p. R2.

16. John Stossel, *20/20, Friday Special Editions with John Stossel*, ABC News, WFAA, Dallas, Texas.

17. John Stossel, *Myths, Lies, and Downright Stupidity: Get Out the Shovel—Why Everything You Know Is Wrong*, Hyperion, New York, 2006.

18. John Stossel, *20/20*, ABC News, "Economics (Myths and Lies)," June 30, 2006, interview by Jim Whiddon and Lance Alston, hosts of *The Investing Revolution*, WBAP 820 AM.

19. Gene Fama Jr., Dimensional Fund Advisors, "Dimensional Fund Advisors," December 8, 2006, interview by Jim Whiddon and Lance Alston, hosts of *The Investing Revolution*, WBAP 820 AM.

20. Diya Gullapalli, "Falling off an ETF Seesaw," *Wall Street Journal*, May 10–11, 2008, p. B1.

21. James ("Jim") Whiddon with Lance Alston, *Wealth Without Worry: The Methods of Wall Street Exposed*, Brown Books, Dallas, 2005.

Chapter 3

1. Jennifer Saba, "NAA Reveals Biggest Ad Revenue Plunge in More Than 50 Years," *Editor & Publisher*, March 28, 2008.

2. Yahoo! Finance, "Dow Jones Industrial Average (^DJI) Historical Prices, January 1, 2008, to July 30, 2008," finance.yahoo.com/q/hp?s=%5EDJI&a=00&b=1&c= 2008&d=06&e=30&f=2008&g=m.

3. Weston J. Wellington, Dimensional Fund Advisors, "Dimensional Fund Advisors," March 30, 2007, and February 8, 2008, interviews by Jim Whiddon and Lance Alston, hosts of *The Investing Revolution*, WBAP 820 AM.

4. Nelson D. Schwartz and Julie Creswell, "Stocks to Grow With," *Fortune*, August 16, 1999.

5. Google Finance, "S&P 500 Index, July 14, 1999, to June 13, 2008," finance.google.com/finance?q=INDEXSP%3A.inx.

6. Google Finance, "AIG—American International Group, Inc., July 14, 1999, to June 13, 2008," finance.google.com/ finance?q=aig.

7. Google Finance, "BMY—Bristol-Myers Squibb Co., July 14, 1999, to June 13, 2008," finance.google.com/finance?q=bristol.

8. Google Finance, "CSCO—Cisco Systems, Inc., July 14, 1999, to June 13, 2008," finance.google.com/finance?q=csco.

9. Google Finance, "F—Ford Motor Company, July 14, 1999, to June 13, 2008," finance.google.com/finance?q=f.

10. Google Finance, "HD—The Home Depot, Inc., July 14, 1999, to June 13, 2008," finance.google.com/finance?q=HD.

11. Google Finance, "IBM—International Business Machines Corp., July 14, 1999, to June 13, 2008," finance.google.com/finance?q=ibm.

12. Google Finance, "TYC—Tyco International Ltd., July 14, 1999, to June 13, 2008," finance.google.com/finance?q=tyc.

13. Google Finance, "JNJ—Johnson & Johnson, July 14, 1999, to June 13, 2008," finance.google.com/finance?q=jnj.

14. Google Finance, "UAUA—UAL Corporation, July 14, 1999, to June 13, 2008," finance.google.com/finance?q=NASDAQ%3AUAUA.

15. Floyd Norris, "As WorldCom Stock Falls, a Debit Rises," *New York Times*, February 2, 2002, query.nytimes.com/gst/fullpage.html?res=9C05E4D9143DF931A35751C0A9649C8B63.

16. Dimensional Fund Advisors (DFA), "Balanced Strategy: Equity 100% Equity," *Matrix Book 2007*, DFA Securities, Inc., c/o Dimensional Fund Advisors, Santa Monica, Calif., 2008, p. 58.

17. Ibid.

18. *Hormel Foods Corp. v. Jim Henson Prods.*, 73 F.3d 497 (2d Cir. 1996), Harvard Law School, cyber.law.harvard.edu/metaschool/fisher/domain/tmcases/hormel.htm.

19. Morningstar, "26-Year Returns," Morningstar Principia Pro Database, July 10, 2008, www.morningstar.com.

20. Morningstar, "Stocks on U.S. Exchange," Morningstar Principia Pro Database, July 10, 2008, www.morningstar.com.

21. Morningstar, "Average Turnover on Fund Universe," Morningstar Principia Pro Database, July 10, 2008, www.morningstar.com.

22. *Wall Street Journal*, "2007 Best on the Street Analysts Survey," May 21, 2007, online.wsj.com/public/resources/documents/best2007-stocks.htm.

23. James ("Jim") Whiddon with Lance Alston, *Wealth Without Worry: The Methods of Wall Street Exposed*, Brown Books, Dallas, 2005, p. 49.

24. Morningstar, "Fidelity Magellan," Morningstar Dimensional Returns 2.0, March 31, 2008, www.morningstar.com.

25. Morningstar, "Magellan Fund to Close," *CNN Money*, August 27, 1997, money.cnn.com/1997/08/27/mutualfunds/magellan/.

26. Morningstar, "Fidelity Magellan," Morningstar Dimensional Returns 2.0, January 1, 1999, www.morningstar.com.

27. *CNN Money*, "Fidelity's Magellan Reopens for Investors," January 14, 2008; and Jon Kamp, "For Magellan Fund, Some Costly Choices," *Wall Street Journal*, October 1, 2008.

28. Morningstar, "Magellan YTD Return," Morningstar Quicktake, September 30, 2008, quicktake.morningstar.com/fundnet/snapshot.aspx?Country+USA&Symbol=FMAGX.

29. Pat Dorsey, "Stock Star Rising Performance Update," Morningstar, October 21, 2005, news.morningstar.com/ articlenet/article.aspx?id=146529&_qsbpa=y.

30. Raymond Fazzi, "Fund Returns: Theory vs. Experience," *Financial Advisor Magazine*, August 2006, www.fa-mag.com/ component/content/article/1460.html?issue=71&magazine ID=1&Itemid=27.

31. Ibid.

32. Ibid.

33. Ibid.

34. Ibid.

Chapter 4

1. Federal Aviation Administration (FAA), "NTSB Accident and Incident Data Systems," September 1, 2008, www.asias.faa.gov/ portal/page?_pageid=56,398034,56_398144&_dad=portal&_ schema=PORTAL.

2. Standard & Poor's, "Historical Returns, January 1, 1926, to December 31, 2007," S&P Compustat Point in Time Database, October 9, 2008. (Standard & Poor's is a division of the McGraw-Hill Companies, New York.)

3. National Bureau of Economic Research (NBER), *U.S. Business Cycle Expansions and Contractions*, NBER, 1050 Massachusetts Avenue, Cambridge, Mass.

4. Dow Jones Indexes, "The Dow Performance at the Onset of Major National Security Events," Dow Jones & Company, New York, October 7, 2008, www.djindexes.com/mdsidx/ index.cfm?event=showavgevents.

5. Standard & Poor's, "Historical Returns, January 1, 1926, to December 31, 2007."

6. Eugene F. Fama, University of Chicago, "Efficient Capital Markets: A Review of Theory and Empirical Work," *Journal of Finance*, May 1970, pp. 383–417.

7. Standard & Poor's, "Historical Returns, January 1, 1926, to December 31, 2007."

8. Remarks by Chairman Alan Greenspan, Annual Dinner and Francis Boyer Lecture of the American Enterprise Institute for Public Policy Research, Washington, D.C., December 5, 1996.

9. Justin Lahart, "Bernanke's Bubble Lab: Studying Market Manias," *Wall Street Journal*, May 16, 2008.

10. Daniel Gross, "Bubbles," June 6, 2007, interview by Jim Whiddon and Lance Alston, hosts of *The Investing Revolution*, WBAP 820 AM.

11. Daniel Gross, *Pop! Why Bubbles Are Great for the Economy*, HarperCollins, New York, 2007.

12. Dimensional Fund Advisors (DFA), "Balanced Strategy," p. 60.

13. Tom Randall, "Forests Burn While Clinton-Gore Administration Fiddles," Heartland Institute, *Environment and Climate News*, April 2000, www.heartland.org/policybot/results.html?artId=9800.

14. Robert Samuelson, "Recessions and Inflation," July 20, 2007, interview by Jim Whiddon and Lance Alston, hosts of *The Investing Revolution*, WBAP 820 AM.

15. Robert Samuelson, "The Upside of Recessions," *Newsweek*, April 2007.

16. Dow Jones Indexes, "Dowdata Printable Decade Chart, 1960 to 1969," Dow Jones & Company, New York, October 7, 2008, www.djindexes.com/mdsidx/index.cfm?event=showavg Decades&decade=1960.

17. Dow Jones Indexes, "Dowdata Printable Decade Chart, 1980 to 2009," Dow Jones & Company, New York, October 2, 2008, www.djindexes.com/mdsidx/index.cfm?event=showavg Decades&decade=2000, www.djindexes.com/mdsidx/ index.cfm?event=showavgDecades&decade=1990, and www.djindexes.com/mdsidx/index.cfm?event= showavgDecades&decade=1980.

18. Dow Jones Indexes, "The Performance of the Dow Jones Industrial Average after Major World Events," Dow Jones & Company, New York, October 7, 2008, www.djindexes.com/ mdsidx/index.cfm?event=showavgevents.

19. National Bureau of Economic Research (NBER), *U.S. Business Cycle Expansions and Contractions.*

20. Morningstar, "Growth of $10,000: Holding MSCI EAFE GR USD from January 1, 2007, to December 31, 2007," Morningstar Principia Pro Database, June 27, 2008, www.morningstar.com.

21. Standard and Poor's, "Historical Returns, January 1, 1926, to December 31, 2007."

22. Standard and Poor's, "Historical Returns, January 1, 1990, to December 31, 2007.

23. Morningstar, "Vanguard Small Cap Index Fund from January 1, 1990, to December 31, 2007," Morningstar Principia Pro Database, June 27, 2008, www.morningstar .com.

24. Dimensional Fund Advisors (DFA), "Balanced Strategy."

25. Jeremy J. Siegel, "The Resilience of American Finance," *Wall Street Journal*, September 18, 2008, p. B2.

26. Standard and Poor's, "Historical Returns, January 1, 1926, to December 31, 2007."

27. Ibid.

28. Ibid.

29. Ibid.

30. Ibid.

31. Dow Jones Indexes, "The Performance of the Dow Jones Industrial Average after Major World Events."

Chapter 5

1. Nick Murray, *Simple Wealth, Inevitable Wealth*, rev. 3rd ed., Nick Murray Company, Mattituck, N.Y., 2007, www.nickmurray.com.

2. Center for Research in Security Prices (CRSP), "Annualized Returns 1926 to 2007: Small Cap, Large Cap, Long Term, 30-Day, January 1, 1926, to December 31, 2007," CRSP Custom Data Set, Center for Research in Security Prices, Chicago Graduate School of Business (GSB), University of Chicago, 105 West Adams Street, Chicago, Ill.

3. Ibid.

4. Standard & Poor's, "S&P 500 Index Monthly Returns, January 1, 2003, to January 31, 2003," www2.standardandpoors.com/spf/xls/index/monthly.xls.

5. Murray Coleman, "Small World, Big Winners," Market Watch, Wall Street Journal, January 2, 2008,

www.marketwatch.com/news/story/
international-fund-managers-put-emerging/story.aspx?guid=
%7b8AFB5F10-CEE1-43C7-9ACF-8DD2D0D48A31%7d&
print=true&dist=printMidSection.

6. Dow Jones Indexes, "Dow Jones Indexes Price History,
   March 11, 2003," Dow Jones & Company, New York,
   June 30, 2008, www.djindexes.com/mdsidx/index.
   cfm?event=indexHistory.

7. Carolyn Cui, "Precious-Coin Market May Lose Its Luster,"
   Wall Street Journal, May 4, 2008, p. B1.

8. Dow Jones Indexes, "Dow Jones Indexes Price History,
   February 1, 2007, to October 31, 2008," Dow Jones &
   Company, New York, June 30, 2008, www.djindexes.com/
   mdsidx/index.cfm?event=indexHistory.

9. Dow Jones Indexes, "Dow Jones Indexes Price History,
   November 1, 2007, to March 31, 2008," Dow Jones &
   Company, New York, June 30, 2008, www.djindexes.com/
   mdsidx/index.cfm?event=indexHistory.

10. Susan Lee, "As Good as Gold?" *Forbes*, October 10, 2008.

11. Jeremy J. Siegel, *Stocks for the Long Run*, 4th ed.,
    McGraw-Hill, New York, 2008.

12. Jeremy J. Siegel, "Back to the Basics: Tried and True
    Investing," March 28, 2008, interview by Jim Whiddon and
    Lance Alston, *The Investing Revolution*, WBAP 820 AM.

13. Gene Fama Jr., vice president of Dimensional Fund Advisors,
    "Dimensional Fund Advisors," December 8, 2006, interview
    by Jim Whiddon and Lance Alston, hosts of *The Investing
    Revolution*, WBAP 820 AM.

14. Carolyn Cui, "Precious-Coin Market May Lose Its Luster."

15. Dimensional Fund Advisors (DFA), "Balanced Strategy: 100% Equity: Total Returns," *Matrix Book 2008*, DFA Securities, Inc., c/o Dimensional Fund Advisors, 1299 Ocean Avenue, Santa Monica, Calif., 2008, p. 60.

16. Morningstar, "Growth of $10,000: Holding Dow Jones Industrial Average from January 1, 1980, to October 31, 2007," Morningstar Principia Pro Database, June 30, 2008, www.morningstar.com.

17. Catherine S. McBreen and George H. Walper, Jr., *Get Rich, Stay Rich, Pass It On: The Wealth-Accumulation Secrets of America's Richest Families*, Penguin Group, New York, 2007.

18. George H. Walper, Jr., "The Secrets of the Millionaire Mindset," April 25, 2008, interview by Jim Whiddon and Lance Alston, *The Investing Revolution*, WBAP 820 AM.

19. Standard & Poor's, "Historical Monthly Returns, January 1, 1926, to December 31, 2007," S&P Compustat Point in Time Database, October 9, 2008. (Standard & Poor's is a division of the McGraw-Hill Companies, New York.)

20. Ibid.

21. Standard & Poor's, "Sector Returns 2007," S&P Compustat Point in Time Database, October 9, 2008. (Standard & Poor's is a division of the McGraw-Hill Companies, New York.)

22. Jane Bryant Quinn, *Making the Most of Your Money*, 1st ed., Simon & Schuster, New York, 1991, pp. 796–799. Quinn is also the author of the book *Smart and Simple Financial Strategies for Busy People*, Simon & Schuster, New York, 2006.

23. Jane Bryant Quinn, "The Call of the Wild, Absolutely Awful Investments," April 4, 2008, interview by Jim Whiddon and Lance Alston, hosts of *The Investing Revolution*, WBAP 820 AM.
24. Quinn, *Making the Most of Your Money*, p. 794.
25. Ibid., p. 671.
26. Jane Bryant Quinn, "Cash Savings, Undervalued until the Economy Tanks," *Washington Post*, March 30, 2008.

Chapter 6

1. Ronald Reagan, "Remarks on East-West Relations at the Brandenburg Gate in West Berlin," June 12, 1987, Ronald Reagan Presidential Library.
2. Organisation for Economic Co-operation and Development (OECD), "Evolution of GDP," *OECD Factbook* 2007, Paris, 2007, pp. 32–33.
3. Robert E. Litan, "Emerging Markets," July 6, 2007, interview by Jim Whiddon and Lance Alston, hosts of *The Investing Revolution*, WBAP 820 AM.
4. William J. Baumol, Robert E. Litan, and Carl J. Schramm, *Good Capitalism, Bad Capitalism, and the Economics of Growth and Prosperity*, Yale University Press, New Haven and London, 2007, p. 1.
5. Ibid., pp. 1–14.
6. Organisation for Economic Co-operation and Development (OECD), "Evolution of GDP."
7. Morningstar, "Growth of $10,000: S&P and MSCI EAFE GR USD from January 1, 2007, to December 31, 2007,"

Morningstar Principia Pro Database, June 27, 2008, www.morningstar.com.

8. Kim R. Holmes, Edwin J. Feulner, and Mary Anastasia O'Grady, "2008 Index of Economic Freedom," Heritage Foundation and Dow Jones & Company, Inc., Washington, D.C., 2008, www.heritage.org.

9. Ibid.

10. Ibid.

11. MSCI Barra, *Emerging Markets: A 20-Year Perspective*, New York, September 17, 2008, www.mscibarra.com/products/indices/em_20/.

12. Heritage Foundation, "Economic Freedom Holding Steady, 14th Index of Economic Freedom Shows," Heritage Foundation press release, Washington, D.C., January 15, 2008, www.heritage.org/Press/NewsReleases/nr011508a.cfm.

13. MSCI Barra, *Emerging Markets*.

14. Ibid.

15. Ibid.

16. Ibid.

17. Paul van Eeden, "Can China Really Save the World?" *MoneyWeek*, September 18, 2006, www.moneyweek.com/file/18446/can-china-really-save-the-world.html.

18. Ibid.

19. Burton Malkiel, "The Chinese Market Considered," *Journal of Indexes*, February 2008.

20. Kenneth Lieberthal, *Governing China: From Revolution Through Reform*, 2d ed., Norton, New York, 2003.

21. Ibid.

22. Malkiel, "The Chinese Market Considered."
23. MSCI Barra, *Emerging Markets*.
24. T. Boone Pickens, "Great Ideas on Energy," September 22, 2008, interview by Jim Whiddon and Lance Alston, hosts of *The Investing Revolution*, CNN HLN 1190 AM.
25. T. Boone Pickens, *The First Billion Is the Hardest: A Reflection on a Life of Comebacks and America's Energy Future*, Crown Business, New York, 2008.
26. Marvin Zonis, "Capital Deepening and Nonbalanced Economic Growth," Daron Acemoglu and Veronica Guerrieri, *Journal of Political Economy*, vol. 116, no. 3, 2008 (DOI: 10.1086/591152).
27. Marvin Zonis, University of Chicago, "Global Economy," April 27, 2007, interview by Jim Whiddon and Lance Alston, hosts of *The Investing Revolution*, WBAP 820 AM.
28. Mohamed El-Erian, *When Markets Collide: Investment Strategies for the Age of Global Economic Change*, McGraw-Hill, New York, 2008, pp. 36–50.
29. Mohamed El-Erian, "Signals within the Noise," August 26, 2008, interview by Jim Whiddon and Lance Alston, *The Investing Revolution*, WBAP 820 AM.
30. President Ronald Reagan's second inaugural address, January 21, 1985, Ronald Reagan Presidential Foundation and Library, www.reaganfoundation.org/reagan/speeches/speech .asp?spid=22.

Chapter 7

1. Barry Schwartz, "Decision Making," March 17, 2006, interview by Jim Whiddon and Lance Alston, hosts of *The Investing Revolution*, WBAP 820 AM.

2. Barry Schwartz, *The Paradox of Choice: Why More Is Less*, HarperCollins, New York, 2004.

3. Jason Zweig, "Neuroeconomics and Market Volatility," January 25, 2008, interview by Jim Whiddon and Lance Alston, hosts of *The Investing Revolution*, WBAP 820 AM.

4. Jason Zweig, *Your Money & Your Brain: How the New Science of Neuroeconomics Can Help Make You Rich*, Simon & Schuster, New York, 2007.

5. Matthew Lieberman, University of California, Los Angeles, June 4, 2008, lieber.bol.ucla.edu/Lieberman/titleAP.html.

6. Charles Mackay, *Extraordinary Popular Delusions and the Madness of Crowds*, Three Rivers Press, a division of Random House, New York, 1980, p. 2.

7. Peter M. DeMarzo, Ron Kaniel, and Ilan Kremer, "Diversification as a Public Good: Community Effects in Portfolio Choice," *Journal of Finance*, vol. 59, no. 4, 2004, 1677–1716.

8. Peter M. DeMarzo, "Market Analysts and Weathermen," February 22, 2008, interview by Jim Whiddon and Lance Alston, hosts of *The Investing Revolution*, WBAP 820 AM.

9. Peter L. Bernstein, "Risk," June 13, 2007, interview by Jim Whiddon and Lance Alston, hosts of *The Investing Revolution*, WBAP 820 AM.

10. Peter L. Bernstein, *Against the Gods: The Remarkable Story of Risk*, Wiley, New York, 1996, p. 91.

11. Ibid., p. 37.
12. Standard & Poor's, "Historical Returns, January 1, 1929, to December 31, 2007," S&P Compustat Point in Time Database, October 9, 2008. (Standard & Poor's is a division of the McGraw-Hill Companies, New York.)
13. Ibid.
14. Ibid.
15. Standard & Poor's, "Annual Returns, December 31, 1988, to December 31, 2007," S&P Compustat Point in Time Database, October 9, 2008. (Standard & Poor's is a division of the McGraw-Hill Companies, New York.)
16. Standard & Poor's, "Annual Returns, January 1, 2003, to October 31, 2007," S&P Compustat Point in Time Database, October 9, 2008. (Standard & Poor's is a division of the McGraw-Hill Companies, New York.)
17. NBC, *Deal or No Deal*, Season 3, hosted by Howie Mandel, KXAS 32.
18. Richard H. Thaler, "Probability versus Possibility," May 23, 2008, interview by Jim Whiddon and Lance Alston, hosts of *The Investing Revolution*, WBAP 820 AM.
19. Richard H. Thaler and Cass R. Sunstein, *Nudge: Improving Decisions about Health, Wealth, and Happiness*, Yale University Press, New Haven, Conn., 2008.
20. Thierry Post, Martijn J. Van den Assem, Guido Baltussen, and Richard H. Thaler, "Deal or No Deal? Decision Making under Risk in a Large-Payoff Game Show," *American Economic Review*, vol. 98, no. 1, March 2008, ssrn.com/abstract=636508.

21. NBC, *Deal or No Deal*, Season 3, Episode 322, KXAS 32, December 7, 2007.

22. Ori Brafman, "Spam versus Technology," August 8, 2008, interview by Jim Whiddon and Lance Alston, hosts of *The Investing Revolution*, WBAP 820 AM. Ori Brafman and Rom Brafman, *SWAY: The Irresistible Pull of Irrational Behavior*, Doubleday Business Press, New York, 2008.

23. Ori Brafman and Rod A. Beckstrom, *The Starfish and the Spider: The Unstoppable Power of Leaderless Organizations*, Penguin Group, New York, 2006.

24. Gary S. Becker, "Human Capital," December 14, 2007, interview by Jim Whiddon and Lance Alston, hosts of *The Investing Revolution*, WBAP 820 AM.

25. Gary S. Becker, The Sveriges Riksbank Prize in Economic Sciences in Memory of Alfred Nobel 1992, nobelprize.org/ nobel_prizes/economics/laureates/1992/.

26. Becker, "Human Capital."

27. Gary S. Becker and Kevin M. Murphy, *Social Economics: Market Behavior in a Social Environment*, Belknap Press of Harvard University Press, Cambridge, Mass., and London, 2000.

28. Tim Harford, "Economics Undercover," September 23, 2008, interview by Jim Whiddon and Lance Alston, hosts of *The Investing Revolution*, WBAP 820 AM.

29. Tim Harford, *The Undercover Economist: Exposing Why the Rich Are Rich, The Poor Are Poor—and Why You Can Never Buy a Decent Used Car!* Oxford University Press, New York, 2006.

30. Tim Harford, *The Logic of Life: The Rational Economics of an Irrational World*, Random House, New York, 2009.

Chapter 8

1. Jonathan Clements, "A Cool Million No Longer Buys You a Lux Retirement," *Wall Street Journal*, July 3, 2007, p. B2.

2. *Tampa Bay Online*, "$1 Million Just Isn't What It Used to Be," July 1, 2007, www.tbo.com/news/money/MGB50JGAJ3F.html.

3. Dimensional Fund Advisors (DFA), "Balanced Strategy: 100% Equity: Total Returns," *Matrix Book 2008*, DFA Securities, Inc., c/o Dimensional Fund Advisors, 1299 Ocean Avenue, Santa Monica, Calif., 2008, p. 60.

4. Jonathan Clements, "A Cool Millionaire," July 29, 2005, interview by Jim Whiddon and Lance Alston, hosts of *The Investing Revolution*, WBAP 820 AM.

5. Dimensional Fund Advisors (DFA), "Balanced Strategy."

6. Social Investment Forum, "Socially Responsible Investing Facts," "What is SRI?" Social Investment Forum, Washington, D.C., June 10, 2008, www.socialinvest.org/resources/sriguide/srifacts.cfm.

7. Morningstar, "Socially Responsible Investors, December 31, 2007," Morningstar Principia Pro Database, July 10, 2008, www.morningstar.com.

8. Bruce Piasecki, *World, Inc.: When It Comes to Solutions— Both Local and Global—Businesses Are More Powerful Than Government. Welcome to World, Inc.*, Sourcebooks, Naperville, Ill., 2007.

9. Ibid.

10. Ibid.

11. Teri Roden, "The Mutual Fund That Plays Politics," *BusinessWeek*, May 2, 2007, p. 47.

12. Morningstar, "Average Expense Ratio, SRI Funds, December 31, 2007," Morningstar Principia Pro Database, July 10, 2008, www.morningstar.com.

13. Penelope Wang, "For Do-Good Funds, an Ethical Dilemma," *CNN Money*, March 22, 2007.

14. Tersia Booyzen, "Global Standards for Multinational Corporations," *CNET Networks*, March 2004.

15. Ibid.

16. Charles Piller, "Money Clashes with Mission," *Los Angeles Times*, September 18, 2007.

17. Morningstar, "Five Year Returns, SRI Funds in 2007," Morningstar Principia Pro Database, July 10, 2008, www.morningstar.com.

18. Morningstar, "Average Turnover Ratio, SRI Funds in 2007," Morningstar Principia Pro Database, July 10, 2008, www.morningstar.com.

19. Morningstar, "Average Expense Ratio, SRI Funds in 2007," Morningstar Principia Pro Database, July 10, 2008, www.morningstar.com.

20. John J. Havens and Paul G. Schervish, "Why the $41 Trillion Wealth Transfer Estimate Is Still Valid: A Review of Challenges and Questions," Boston College Center on Wealth and Philanthropy, Social Welfare Research Institute (SWRI), Boston, January 6, 2003, www.bc.edu/swri/.

21. Arthur C. Brooks, *Who Really Cares: The Surprising Truth about Compassionate Conservatism—America's Charity Divide: Who Gives, Who Doesn't, and Why It Matters*, Basic Books, New York, 2006.

22. Rod Zeeb, Heritage Institute, "Inheritance," October 6, 2006, interview by Jim Whiddon and Lance Alston, hosts of *The Investing Revolution*, WBAP 820 AM.

23. Ken Blanchard, "Eight-Point Portfolio Check-Up," June 6, 2006, interview by Jim Whiddon and Lance Alston, hosts of *The Investing Revolution*, WBAP 820 AM.

24. Ken Blanchard and Spencer Johnson, *The One Minute Manager: Increase Productivity, Profits, and Your Own Prosperity*, William Morrow, New York, 1982.

25. Ken Blanchard, Don Hutson, and Ethan Willis, *The One Minute Entrepreneur: The Secret to Creating and Sustaining a Successful Business*, Doubleday, New York, 2008.

26. Mike Hoffman, "Interview with Ken Blanchard: In Tough Times, Focus on Fairness," *Inc.* magazine, May 2008.

27. Kerry Hannon, "One Minute Entrepreneur Has Bite-Sized Words of Wisdom," *USA Today*, May 22, 2008.

28. Dimensional Fund Advisors (DFA), "Balanced Strategy," p. 58.

29. Standard & Poor's, "Historical Returns, January 1, 1929, to December 31, 2007," S&P Compustat Point in Time Database, October 9, 2008. (Standard & Poor's is a division of the McGraw-Hill Companies, New York.)

30. Morningstar, "2006 International Markets and U.S. Markets Comparison, Monthly Performance S&P, MSCI EAFE Index, January 2006, to December 2006," Morningstar Principia Pro Database, July 10, 2008, www.morningstar.com.

31. Morningstar, "2007 International Markets and U.S. Markets Comparison, Monthly Performance S&P, MSCI EAFE Index, January 2007 to December 2007," Morningstar

Principia Pro Database, July 10, 2008, www.morningstar .com.

32. Morningstar, "2007 International Markets and U.S. Markets Comparison, Monthly Performance DFA U.S. Small Cap Value, April 1993 to December 2007," Morningstar Principia Pro Database, July 10, 2008, www.morningstar.com.

33. Morningstar, "2007 International Markets and U.S. Markets Comparison, Monthly Performance S&P, CRSP 1-2 Index, CRSP 6-10 Index, January 1926 to December 2007," Morningstar Principia Pro Database, July 10, 2008, www.morningstar.com.

34. Investment Company Institute (ICI), "Mutual Fund Fees and Expenses," *2008 Investment Company Fact Book*, 48th ed., June 10, 2008, http://www.icifactbook.org/ fb_sec5.html.

35. Arthur C. Brooks, *Gross National Happiness: Why Happiness Matters for America—and How We Can Get More of It*, Basic Books, New York, 2008.

36. Arthur C. Brooks, "Charitable Giving," December 22, 2006, and September 25, 2008, interviews by Jim Whiddon and Lance Alston, hosts of *The Investing Revolution*, WBAP 820 AM.

37. Brooks, *Who Really Cares*.

38. Morningstar, "S&P," Morningstar Principia Pro Database, July 10, 2008, www.morningstar.com.

39. Diane Farrell, Susan Lund, and Alexander Massary, *Mapping the Global Capital Markets Third Annual Report*, McKinsey & Company, New York, January 2007,

www.mckinsey.com/mgi/publications/third_annual_report/
index.asp.

40. James ("Jim") Whiddon and Lance Alston, *Wealth Without Worry: The Methods of Wall Street Exposed*, Brown Books, Dallas, 2005, p. 125. *Authors' note:* The Market Return Benchmark (MRB) is not an investment product. You cannot invest in the benchmark directly. The Market Return Benchmark is designed to be used as an educational tool that will allow investors to measure the performance of their portfolio against a diversified 100% equity portfolio representing exposure to multiple asset classes. The MRB is updated 25 days after the end of each month. This information should not be construed as an offer to sell or buy any investment product or as specific advice to any individual.

41. Ken French, Dimensional Fund Advisors (DFA), "The Cost of Active Management," April 18, 2008, interview by Jim Whiddon and Lance Alston, hosts of *The Investing Revolution*, WBAP 820 AM.

Epilogue

1. Harry M. Markowitz, "Portfolio Selection," *Journal of Finance*, March 1952, pp. 77–91.

Appendix

1. Bob McTeer, former president and CEO of the Federal Reserve Bank of Dallas, "The Fed's Tool Box," October 5,

2007, interview by Jim Whiddon and Lance Alston, hosts of *The Investing Revolution*, WBAP 820 AM.

2. Bob McTeer, former president and CEO of the Federal Reserve Bank of Dallas, "Everyday Economics," April 11, 2008, interview by Jim Whiddon and Lance Alston, hosts of *The Investing Revolution*, WBAP 820 AM.

3. Bob McTeer, former president and CEO of the Federal Reserve Bank of Dallas, "Free Market Primer," Maryland Council on Economic Development, www.BobMcTeer.com, 1989.

GLOSSARY

active management The system of investment management that is dependent on successfully predicting market and security movements (timing) and security selection (picking).

asset allocation A portfolio strategy that involves periodically rebalancing the portfolio in order to maintain a long-term goal for asset allocation.

asset class investing The method of constructing a portfolio to reliably deliver the returns of a specific asset class—that is, a group of securities that share common risk and return characteristics. No subjective forecasting of market or economic conditions is involved, and no attempt is made to distinguish between undervalued and overvalued securities.

bear market A prolonged period in which investment prices fall 20% or more over at least a two-month time period, accompanied by widespread pessimism.

brokerage commission A fee paid to a stockbroker by a client for the purchasing or selling of shares in the stock market. Large corporations are under constant pressure to help improve the bottom line, and as a result, they have introduced new types of fees for individual investors. It is important to read over your account agreement and fee summaries to make sure that none of these fees take you by surprise. Although these fees are not broadcast when you first open an account, they can, after a couple months, cause significant detriment to your portfolio.

bull market A prolonged period in which investment prices rise faster than their historical averages.

capitalism An economic system in which property is owned by either private individuals or corporations.

capital market A marketplace in which companies and governments can raise long-term funds through selling securities. The capital market includes the stock market and the bond market.

Certified Financial Planner (CFP) A certification designation for financial planners conferred by the Certified Financial Planner Board of Standards. To receive authorization to use the designation, the candidate must meet education, examination, experience, and ethics requirements and pay an ongoing certification fee. A qualified investment professional who assists individuals and corporations meet their long-term financial objectives by analyzing the clients' status and setting up a program to achieve the clients' goals.

cub market A market that has a downturn between 5 and 20%.

data mining Obtaining information about customers or groups of customers from a data warehouse and using that information for marketing or other purposes.

direct pay Money paid exclusively from a client directly to an advisory firm for financial advice. Direct pay is different from the entrenched Wall Street system of indirect payments, subsidies, and sales commissions.

dollar-weighted return The rate of return that would make the present value of future cash flows plus the final market value of an investment or business opportunity equal the current market price of the investment or opportunity.

D.U.M.B. fund A hypothetical mutual fund family (Diversified United States Mutual Fund Balderdash) that we created using a single criterion that would have allowed us to beat every actively managed fund in the Morningstar database of funds.

economic dynamism A characteristic of a marketplace consisting mostly of fast-growing, entrepreneurial companies. The ability of firms to innovate and get to market faster is becoming a more important determinant of competitive advantage. Likewise, the ability of metro economies to rejuvenate themselves through the formation of new, innovative companies is a key in determining their economic vitality.

efficient analyst paradox The logical conclusion that the work of many highly skilled securities analysts will ensure efficient market prices, thus making those same skilled analysts unable to consistently find undervalued stocks.

efficient capital market A market in which security prices fully reflect all relevant information that is available at the time about the fundamental value of the securities.

efficient market theory An investment theory that states that it is impossible to "beat the market" because stock market efficiency causes existing share prices to always incorporate and reflect all relevant information.

Fama-French three-factor model A factor model that expands on the capital asset pricing model (CAPM) by adding size and value factors in addition to the market risk factor in the CAPM. This model considers the fact that value and small-cap stocks outperform markets on a regular basis. By including these two additional factors, the model adjusts for the outperformance tendency, which is thought to make it a better tool for evaluating fund manager performance.

fear tax The cost of something considered in terms of an opportunity given up and the benefits that could have been received from that alternative opportunity. A fear tax is like a lost-opportunity cost.

fiduciary An advisor acting in the best interests of his or her client and disclosing any real or implied conflicts of interest. This is generally a higher standard than is customary in the financial services industry.

fiduciary duty A legal relationship between two or more parties, most commonly a "fiduciary" or "trustee" and a "principal" or "beneficiary." The legal duty of a fiduciary is to act in the best interests of the beneficiary.

Financial Industry Regulatory Authority (FINRA) The largest nongovernmental regulator for all securities firms doing business in the United States. The FINRA was created in July 2007 through the consolidation of the National Association of Securities Dealers (NASD) and the member regulation, enforcement, and arbitration functions of the New York Stock Exchange (NYSE).

free market An economic market in which supply and demand are not regulated or are regulated with only minor restrictions.

fund drift The drift of a fund away from its stated investment objective or between two or more other investment styles. A fund that is drifting may still be operating within its stated investment objectives.

fund incubation A strategy that many Wall Street managers use in order to highlight one specific fund from a pool of many, newly introduced funds from a specific fund company.

giant portfolio stop-loss effect A beneficial effect caused by the superdiversification found in a market return portfolio (MRP), which tends to limit volatility during down markets.

growth stock Stock of a company that is growing earnings and/or revenue faster than its industry or the overall market.

herd mentality A mindset in which people are influenced by their peers to adopt certain behaviors, follow trends, and/or purchase items.

hindsight bias The inclination to see events that have occurred as more predictable than they in fact were before they took place.

incubator fund A fund that is offered privately when it is first created. Investors in this type of fund are usually employees associated with the fund and its family members. Incubation allows fund managers the ability to keep a fund's size small, while testing different investment styles, before the fund is available to the public and subject to restricting rules and regulations.

independent advisor An advisor who is not employed or related in any way to brokerage houses, banks, or other financial institutions that may profit from the advisor's being offered incentives for recommending particular products. An independent advisor will be associated with a fee-based registered investment advisor (RIA) firm.

in-perpetuity bias As related to securities markets, the propensity to presume that once a market trend in prices is established (up or down), values will continue in that direction forever.

institutional asset class fund (IACF) A mutual fund designed to deliver the investment results of an entire asset class—such as large-cap U.S. value stocks or small-cap international stocks. These asset class funds are best suited to create efficient portfolios that promote superdiversification.

investment policy statement (IPS) A formal statement with a description of the investment philosophy that will be utilized for a given fund, retirement plan, or other investment vehicle.

loss-plus-tax trap The dilemma created when an investor seeks to avoid current long-term capital gains taxes on long-term investments instead of paying the taxes currently and implementing the consistent portfolio investment approach known as the *market return portfolio* (MRP). This hesitation can lead to a loss of value in the securities held as well as an eventual tax on the remaining gain when the security is sold—thus creating a double-loss situation.

market return Nothing more and nothing less than the return readily available when investors efficiently harness the power of capital markets.

Market Return Benchmark (MRB) A measurement designed to be a broad indicator of the success of the equity portion of a portfolio. The Market Return Benchmark is designed for individual investors. In contrast, all other indexes were created as benchmarks for money managers.

market return portfolio (MRP) A portfolio that is constructed with the objective of earning market return by using low-cost, no-load institutional asset class mutual funds.

market return portfolio (MRP) future value A portfolio's estimated worth on a specified future date.

market risk The risk that the value of an investment will decrease due to moves in market factors. The four standard market risk factors are the following:

- *Equity risk:* The risk that stock prices will change.
- *Interest rate risk:* The risk that interest rates will change.
- *Currency risk:* The risk that foreign exchange rates will change.
- *Commodity risk:* The risk that commodity prices (for example, grains or metals) will change.

market timer A money manager who assumes he or she can forecast when the stock market will go up and down.

modern portfolio theory (MPT) Research in finance over the last 50 years that relates to the risk and return characteristics of various asset classes when they are combined to create investment portfolios. Academicians such as Harry Markowitz, William Sharpe, Merton Miller, Franco Modigliani, and Eugene Fama are some of the major contributors to this field of research.

National Association of Securities Dealers (NASD) An industry organization representing persons and companies involved in the securities industry in the United States. It is also the primary self-regulatory organization (SRO) responsible for the regulation of its industry, with oversight from the Securities and Exchange Commission (SEC). [*See also* Financial Industry Regulatory Authority (FINRA).]

National Association of Securities Dealers Automated Quotations (Nasdaq) system An American stock market, with approximately 3,200 companies. The Nasdaq lists more companies and on average trades more shares per day than any other U.S. market.

National Bureau of Economic Research (NBER) Founded in 1920, a "private, nonprofit, nonpartisan research organization" dedicated to studying the science and empirics of economics, especially the American economy. NBER is well known for providing start and end dates for recessions. Furthermore, of the 31 American winners of the Nobel Prize in Economics, 16 have been NBER associates. Also, three of the past chairs of the Council of Economic Advisers have been NBER associates.

no-load fund A mutual fund whose shares are sold without a commission or sales charge, which the fund is able to do because the shares are distributed directly by the investment company. Since there is no cost for you to enter a no-load fund, all of your money is working for you. Most studies show that load funds don't outperform no-load funds.

passive investing An investment strategy involving limited ongoing buying and selling actions. Passive investors will purchase investments with the intention of long-term appreciation and limited maintenance.

portfolio filter Objective criterion used in screening stock selections for mutual funds.

portfolio risk The risk that is related to a portfolio or a grouping of assets.

purchasing power The value of a particular monetary unit in terms of the goods or services that can be purchased with it.

rate of return The gain or loss of an investment over a specified period, expressed as a percentage increase over the initial investment cost. Gains on investments are considered to be any income received from the security, plus realized capital gains.

rebalancing The process of realigning the weightings of the assets in a portfolio.

reconstitution An adjustment or series of adjustments resulting in additions to and/or deletions from the list of stocks that make up a given index.

registered investment advisor (RIA) An entity (an individual or firm) that is registered with either its respective state government or with the Securities and Exchange Commission depending on the amount of investment assets under its management.

risk The variability of returns from an investment.

risk management analysis A technique designed to quantify the impact of uncertainty in the markets, resulting in a plan of action to minimize the consequences of risk.

rolling time period Annualized average return period ending with the listed year. Rolling returns are useful for examining the behavior of returns for holding periods similar to those actually experienced by investors.

sector A distinct part, or niche, of a nation's economy.

Securities and Exchange Commission (SEC) A federal government board, consisting of five members, that is charged with regulating the public offer and sale of securities.

securities market An exchange where securities trading is conducted by professional stockbrokers.

speculation Engagement in business transactions involving considerable risk, especially trading in commodities, stocks, and so on, in the hope of profit from changes in the market price.

superdiversification A high degree of diversification that occurs when institutional asset class funds (IACFs) are used to construct a portfolio. IACFs provide broad and deep representation of the capital markets.

survivorship bias Specifically in the context of mutual funds, the tendency for poor performers to be removed from the fund while strong performers are kept in it. This practice results in an overestimation of past returns.

tactical asset allocation Portfolio strategy that allows active departures from the normal asset mix according to specified objective measures of value. Often called *active management*, this strategy involves forecasting asset returns, volatilities, and correlations. The forecasted variables may be functions of fundamental variables, economic variables, or even technical variables.

time-weighted return A rate-of-return measure of portfolio performance that gives equal weight to each period included in the study regardless of any differences in amounts invested in each period.

total return When measuring performance, the actual rate of return of an investment or a pool of investments over a given evaluation period. Total return includes interest, capital gains, dividends, and distributions realized over a given period of time.

utility In economics, the total satisfaction received from consuming a good or service.

value stock Stock sold by a company with a low price/book ratio or a low price/earnings ratio. Historically, value stocks have enjoyed higher average returns than growth stocks (stocks with high price/ book or price/earnings ratios) in a variety of countries.

variability The quality, state, or degree of being variable. Also used to describe market fluctuations.

volatility A statistical measure of the dispersion of returns for a given security or market index. Volatility can be measured by using either the standard deviation or the variance between returns from that same security or market index.

written financial plan A plan for spending and saving future income. This plan allocates future income to various types of expenses, such as rent or utilities, and it also reserves some income for short-term and long-term savings. A financial plan also acts as an investment plan, which allocates savings to various assets expected to produce future income, in addition to establishing an estimation of cash needs during retirement.

zero-sum game A game in which the sum of the winnings by all the players is zero. In a zero-sum game, a gain by one player must be matched by a loss by another player. Poker is a zero-sum game if the house does not take a cut as a charge for playing.

RECOMMENDED READING AND *THE INVESTING REVOLUTION* GUESTS

Books

The books below represent the writings of guests on *The Investing Revolution*. While some of their investing philosophies may vary from our own, the thoughts and works of these authors have earned our great respect.

Axelrod, Alan, *Profiles in Audacity: Great Decisions and How They Were Made*, Sterling Publishing, 2005.

Becker, Gary S., *Human Capital: A Theoretical and Empirical Analysis with Special Reference to Education*, National Bureau of Economic Research, 1993.

Bee-Gates, Donna, *I Want It Now: Navigating Childhood in a Materialistic World*, Palgrave Macmillan, 2006.

Belsky, Gary, *Why Smart People Make Big Money Mistakes and How to Correct Them*, Fireside, 1999.

Bernstein, Peter, *Against the Gods: The Remarkable Story of Risk*, Wiley, 1998.

Bernstein, Peter, *Capital Ideas Evolving*, Wiley, 2007.

Bhagwati, Jagdish, *In Defense of Globalization*, Oxford University Press, 2004.

Blanchard, Ken, and Spencer Johnson, *The One Minute Manager*, William Morrow, 1982.

Blodget, Henry, *The Complete Wall Street Self-Defense Manual: A Consumer's Guide to Intelligent Investing*, Atlas Books, 2007.

Bogle, John, *The Battle for the Soul of Capitalism: How the Financial System Undermined Social Ideas, Damaged Trust in the Markets, Robbed Investors of Trillions, and What to Do About It*, Integrated Publishing Solutions, 2005.

Bogle, John, *Bogle on Mutual Funds*, Dell Publishing, 1994.

Bogle, John, *The Little Book of Common Sense Investing; The Only Way to Guarantee Your Fair Share of Stock Market Return*, Wiley, 2007.

Boortz, Neal, and John Linder, *The FairTax Book*, HarperCollins, 2005.

Brooks, Arthur C., *Who Really Cares: The Surprising Truth about Compassionate Conservatism—America's Charity Divide: Who Gives, Who Doesn't, and Why It Matters*, Basic Books, 2006.

Chancellor, Edward, *Devil Take the Hindmost: A History of Financial Speculation*, Penguin Group, 2000.

Clements, Jonathan, *You've Lost It, Now What? How to Beat the Bear Market and Still Retire on Time*, Portfolio, 2003.

Cowen, Tyler, *Discover Your Inner Economist: Use Incentives to Fall in Love, Survive Your Next Meeting, and Motivate Your Dentist*, Dutton/Penguin Group, 2007.

DeMarzo, Peter, *Corporate Finance*, Addison-Wesley, 2007.

DeMarzo, Peter, *Fundamentals of Corporate Finance*, Addison-Wesley, 2008.

Eisenberg, Lee, *The Number: Do You Know Yours?* Free Press/Simon & Schuster, 2006.

El-Erian, Mohamed, *When Markets Collide: Investment Strategies for the Age of Global Economic Change*, McGraw-Hill, 2008.

Ellis, Charles D., *Winning the Loser's Game: Timeless Strategies for Successful Investing*, McGraw-Hill, 2002.

Fama, Eugene, *Foundations of Finance: Portfolio Decisions and Securities Prices*, Basic Books, 1976.

Farrell, Paul, *The Millionaire Code: A Smarter Approach to Making Millions*, Wiley, 2005.

Folbre, Nancy, *U.S. Economy: A Compact and Irrelevant Guide to Economic Life in America*, New Press, 2006.

Frank, Robert, *The Economic Naturalist: In Search of Explanations for Everyday Enigmas*, Basic Books, 2007.

Friedman, Benjamin, *Moral Consequences of Economic Growth*, Random House, 2005.

Galford, Robert, *Your Leadership Legacy: Why Looking Toward the Future Will Make You a Better Leader Today*, Harvard Business School Publishing, 2006.

Gratzer, David, *The Cure: How Capitalism Can Save American Health Care*, Encounter Books, 2006.

Gross, Daniel, *Pop! Why Bubbles Are Good for the Economy*, HarperCollins, 2007.

Harford, Tim, *The Undercover Economist: Exposing Why the Rich Are Rich, the Poor Are Poor, and Why You Can Never Buy a Decent Used Car*, Oxford University Press, 2006.

Homer, Christopher, *The Politically Incorrect Guide to Global Warming and Environmentalism*, Regnery Publishing, 2007.

Hughes, James, *Family Wealth: Keeping It in the Family*, Bloomberg Press, 2004.

Jansen, Eric, *Americans' Bubble Economy: Profit When It Pops*, Wiley, 2006.

Kay, John, *Culture and Prosperity: The Truth About Markets, Why Some Nations Are Rich But Most Remain Poor*, HarperCollins, 2004.

Kay, John, *Everlasting Lightbulbs: How Economics Illuminates the World*, Antony Rowe, 2004.

Khanna, Tarun, *Billions of Entrepreneurs: How China and India Are Reshaping Their Futures, and Yours*, Harvard Business School Press, 2008.

Levine, Ross, *Rethinking Bank Regulation: Till Angels Govern*, Cambridge University Press, 2006.

Levitt, Arthur, *Take on the Street: What Wall Street and Corporate America Don't Want You to Know*, Pantheon Books, 2002.

Litan, Robert, *Good Capitalism, Bad Capitalism, and the Economics of Growth and Prosperity*, Yale University Press, 2007.

Lott, Jr., John R., *Freedomnomics: Why the Free Market Works and Other Half-Baked Theories Don't*, Regnery Publishing, 2007.

Mahar, Maggie, *Money Driven Medicine: The Real Reason Health Care Costs So Much*, HarperCollins, 2006.

Malkiel, Burton, *A Random Walk Down Wall Street: The Best and Latest Investment Advice Money Can Buy*, Norton, 1996.

Manning, Robert, *Credit Card Nation: The Consequences of America's Addiction to Credit*, Basic Books, 2001.

Marks Jarvis, Gail, *Saving for Retirement without Living Like a Pauper or Winning the Lottery*, Financial Times Press, 2007.

Mauboussin, Michael, *More Than You Know: Finding Financial Wisdom in Unconventional Places*, Columbia University Press, 2007.

Nofsinger, John R., *Investment Madness: How Psychology Affects Your Investing . . . And What to Do About It*, Financial Times/Prentice Hall, 2001.

Opdyke, Jeff, *The Wall Street Journal. Complete Personal Finance Guidebook*, Three Rivers Press, 2006.

O'Rourke, P. J., *On the Wealth of Nations*, Grove/Atlantic, 2007.

O'Shaughnessy, Lynn, *The College Solution: A Guide for Everyone Looking for the Right School at the Right Price*, Financial Times Press, 2008.

Perle, Liz, *Money, A Memoir: Women, Emotions and Cash*, Henry Holt, 2006.

Phelps, Edmond S., *Rewarding Work: How to Restore Participation and Self-Support to Free Enterprise*, Harvard University Press, 1997.

Pickens, T. Boone, *The First Billion Is The Hardest*, Crown Business, 2008.

Prescott, Edward C., *Barriers to Riches*, First MIT Press Edition, 2002.

Quinn, Jane Bryant, *Making the Most of Your Money*, Simon & Schuster, 1997.

Quinn, Jane Bryant, *Smart and Simple Financial Strategies for Busy People*, Simon & Schuster, 2006.

Reicht, Robert, *Supercapitalism: The Transformation of Business, Democracy, and Everyday Life*, Knopf, 2007.

Reingold, Dan, *Confessions of a Wall Street Analyst*, HarperCollins, 2006.

Samuelson, Robert, *Untruth: Why the Conventional Wisdom Is (Almost Always) Wrong*, AtRandom, 2001.

Schwartz, Barry, *The Paradox of Choice: Why More Is Less*, Harper Perennial, 2002.

Shiller, Robert J., *Irrational Exuberance*, Princeton University Press, 2005.

Shiller, Robert J., *The Subprime Solution: How Today's Global Financial Crisis Happened and What to Do About It*, Princeton University Press, 2008.

Siegel, Jeremy, *Stocks for the Long Run*, 4th ed., McGraw-Hill, 2007.

Silber, William, *When Washington Shut Down Wall Street: The Great Financial Crisis of 1914 and the Origins of America's Monetary Supremacy*, Princeton University Press, 2007.

Solin, Dan, *Does Your Broker Owe You Money?* Silvercloud, 2004.

Solin, Dan, *The Smartest Investment Book You'll Ever Read*, Perigee, 2006.

Stossel, John, *Myths, Lies, and Downright Stupidity: Why Everything You Know Is Wrong*, Hyperion, 2006.

Swedrow, Larry, *Rational Investing in Irrational Times: How to Avoid the Costly Mistakes Even Smart People Make Today*, St. Martin's Press, 2002.

Swedrow, Larry, *The Successful Investor Today*, St. Martin's Press, 2003.

Swedrow, Larry, *Wise Investing Made Simple*, Charter Financial Publishing, 2007.

Tapscott, Don, and Anthony D. Williams, *Wikinomics: How Mass Collaboration Changes Everything*, Penguin Group, 2007.

Thaler, Richard H., *Nudge: Improving Decisions About Health, Wealth, and Happiness*, Yale University Press, 2008.

Thredgold, Jeff, *EconAmerica: Why the American Economy Is Alive and Well*, Wiley, 2007.

Town, Phil, *Rule #1: The Simple Strategy for Successful Investing in Only 15 Minutes a Week*, Crown Publishing, 2006.

Updegrave, Walter, *We're Not in Kansas Anymore: Strategies for Retiring Rich in a Totally Changed World*, Crown Publishing, 2004.

Walper, Jr., George H., *Get Rich, Stay Rich, and Pass It On*, Penguin Group, 2007.

Waymire, Jack, *Who's Watching Your Money: The 17 Paladin Principles for Selecting a Financial Advisor*, Wiley, 2004.

Weiner, Eric, *What Goes Up: The Uncensored History of Wall Street*, Little, Brown, 2005.

Wheelen, Charles, *Naked Economics: Undressing the Dismal Science*, Norton, 2002.

Zeeb, Rod, *Beating the Midas Curse*, Heritage Institute Press, 2005.

Zonis, Marvin, *The Kimchi Matters: Global Business and Local Politics in a Crisis-Driven World*, Agate, 2003.

Zweig, Jason, *Your Money & Your Brain: How the New Science of Neuroeconomics Can Help Make You Rich*, Simon & Schuster, 2007.

The Investing Revolution Guests

A partial lineup of guests previously interviewed on *The Investing Revolution* and excerpts from most of the interviews listed can be found on our Web site at www.theinvestingrevolution.com.

Axelrod, Alan, "Historical Decisions," June 23, 2006.

Barone, Michael, "Capitalism," August 24, 2007.

Barr, Colin, "Wall Street: Five Dumbest Things This Week," September 23, 2005.

Baum, Caroline, "John Galt and the Financial System," May 2, 2008.

Becker, Gary S., "Human Capital and Marriage Happiness," December 14, 2007.

Bee-Gates, Donna, "Kids and Money," January 5, 2007.

Belsky, Gary, "Big Money Mistakes," December 17, 2004.

Bernstein, Peter, "Risk," July 28, 2006.

Bernstein, Peter, "Risk Evolving," June 13, 2007.

Berstein, William J., "A Historical Perspective on Trade and Commerce," August 1, 2008.

Berry, Dave, "Congress," September 30, 2005.

Bhagwati, Jagdish, "Globalization," December 2, 2005.

Blanchard, Ken, "Eight-Point Portfolio Check-Up," May 30, 2008.

Blodget, Henry, "What's on Wall Street," February 9, 2007.

Bogle, John, "Capitalism," September 16, 2005.

Bogle, John, "Common Sense Investing," March 23, 2007.

Bogle, John, "We Have Had Enough," January 22, 2009.

Bosworth, Barry, "India's Economy," September 15, 2006.

Brafman, Ori, "Spam versus Technology," August 8, 2008.

Brooks, Arthur C., "Charitable Giving," December 22, 2006, and September 25, 2008.

Brown, Jonathan, "The Cuban Economy," May 9, 2008.

Bullard, Mercer, "Fund Democracy," June 17, 2005.

Chancellor, Edward, "Speculative Bubbles," January 13, 2006.

Clements, Jonathon, "A Cool Millionaire," July 29, 2005.

Cooper, Ken, "Investing In Your Health," December 10, 2008.

Covey, Stephen, "Follow the Leader," November 24, 2008.

Cowen, Tyler, "Science versus Art: Investing and Financial Planning," August 17, 2007.

DeMarzo, Peter, "Market Analysts and Weathermen," February 22, 2008.

d'Eon, Joe, "Coping with Mandatory Retirement," September 28, 2007.

Dillon, Joe, "Optimal Health," May 5, 2006.

Drucker, David, "The Secret Is Out," May 16, 2008.

D'Souza, Dinesh, "Capitalism Prevails," September 30, 2008.

Eisenberg, Lee, "Retirement by Numbers," January 6, 2006.

El-Erian, Mohamed, "Signals within the Noise," September 26, 2008.

Ellis, Charles, "Market Timing," February 3, 2006.

Ellis, Charles, "Walls Come Tumbling" December 19, 2008.

Fama, Eugene, "Efficient Markets," April 13, 2007.

Fama Jr., Gene, "Dimensional Fund Advisors," December 8, 2006.

Farrell, Paul, "The Millionaire Code," June 15, 2005.

Farrell, Paul, "Millionaires," July 13, 2007.

Finke, Michael, "Capital Gains," June 27, 2008.

Folbre, Nancy, "Field Guide to the U.S. Economy," November 10, 2006.

Foley, Jay, "Identity Theft," June 1, 2005.

Frank, Robert, "Psych Meets Eco," May 24, 2007.

Fredoso, David, "Bailouts or Handouts," November 28, 2008.

Freeman, Congressman John, "Mutual Fund Reform," October 7, 2005.

Freidman, Benjamin, "Morality and Economics," November 11, 2005.

French, Ken, "The Cost of Active Management," April 18, 2008.

Frieden, Jeff, "Economic Globalization," December 7, 2007.

Fryer, Congressman Kevin, "Mutual Fund Overlap," June 3, 2005.

Galford, Robert, "Pressure Testing Your Advisor," March 14, 2008.

George, Ron, "Football Players and Investing," October 25, 2005.

Goldbart, Stephen, "Sudden Wealth," April 20, 2007.

Gratzer, David, "Health Care," March 9, 2007.

Gross, Daniel, "Bubbles," June 6, 2007.

Harford, Tim, "Economics Undercover," December 9, 2005, and September 23, 2008.

Harvey, Lou, "Investing," November 18, 2005.

Holtz-Eakin, Douglas, "Pensions," October 28, 2005.

Horner, Christopher, "Global Warming," March 16, 2007.

Hughes, James, "Succession Planning," February 29, 2008.

Jaffe, Chuck, "Lump of Coal Awards," December 29, 2006.

Janzen, Eric, "Alternative Investments," June 21, 2007.

Johnson, Sam, "Social Security," June 10, 2005.

Kay, John, "Real Estate," August 31, 2007.

Khanna, Tarun, "China and 1B Investors," July 4, 2008.

Kiplinger, Knight, "*Kiplinger's*," December 1, 2006.

Kotlikoff, Laurence, "The Coming Generation Storm," July 22, 2005.

Kruetzer, David, "Oil and Gas," June 20, 2008.

Laibson, David, "Hidden Fees," March 2, 2007.

Lerach, Bill, "Securities Law," April 22, 2005.

Levine, Ross, "Foreign Markets," March 31, 2006.

Levitt, Arthur, "Economics," February 17, 2006.

Lieberthal, Ken, "Chinese Economy," August 19, 2005.

Linder, John, "Fair Tax," October 14, 2005.

Litan, Robert, "Emerging Markets," July 6, 2007.

Lott, Jr., John R., "Free Markets," August 3, 2007.

Lusardi, Annamaria, "Financial Literacy," October 13, 2006.

Luscombe, Marc, "Taxes: President's Tax Panel," December 16, 2005.

Luskin, Donald, "Can an Investment Benchmark Save Social Security? (MRB)," September 14, 2007.

Ma, Jeff, "Baseball and Luck," September 26, 2006.

Mahar, Maggie, "Health Care," August 25, 2006.

Malkiel, Burton, "A Random Walk Down Wall Street," August 12, 2005.

Mankin, Charles, "Oil," September 2, 2005.

Manning, Robert, "Credit Cards and Debt," November 4, 2005.

Marks Jarvis, Gail, "Know What You Need: How Financial Planners Evaluate Your Needs (IRA Decisions, Allocations)," October 19, 2007.

Mauboussin, Michael, "Complexity Theory and Finances: Do They Fit Together?" November 16, 2007.

McPherson, David, "Investing Primer," January 4, 2008.

McTeer, Bob, "The Fed's Tool Box," October 5, 2007.

McTeer, Bob, "What's on the Mind of the Fed?" April 11, 2008.

Murray, Alan, "CEO Compensation," April 7, 2006.

Nofsinger, John, "Chinese Investors," April 6, 2007.

Odean, Terrance, "Behavioral Finance," August 5, 2005.

Opdyke, Jeff, "Life Transactions," August 10, 2007.

O'Rourke, P. J., "Wealth of Nations," January 26, 2007.

O'Shaughnessy, Lynn, "Economics: Myths and Lies," June 23, 2006.

O'Shaughnessy, Lynn, "Education Planning for the Crunch," July 18, 2008.

Perle, Liz, "Women and Money," March 10, 2006.

Phelps, Edmund S., "Entrepreneurial Culture," February 15, 2008.

Pickens, T. Boone, "Great Ideas on Energy," September 22, 2008.

Pike, Bill, "Energy and Gas," June 6, 2008.

Poterba, James, "Economics and Demographics," May 26, 2006.

Prescott, Edward C., "Equity Premiums," July 29, 2007.

Preston, Alan, "Health Care in America," November 30, 2007.

Quinn, Jane Bryant, "The Call of the Wild, Absolutely Awful Investments," April 4, 2008.

Reicht, Robert, "The Free Market Debate," October 12, 2007.

Reingold, Dan, "Wall Street: Confessions of an Analyst," February 10, 2006.

Romer, Todd, "Kids and Finance," May 13, 2005.

Rosato, Donna, "Financial Scams," July 14, 2006.

Sahadi, Jeanne, "In the Media," December 15, 2006.

Samuel, Larry, "Millionaires (Different Types)," August 4, 2006.

Samuelson, Robert, "Recessions and Inflation," July 20, 2007.

Schlaes, Amity, "Depression Lessons," January 10, 2009.

Schkade, David, "Money and Happiness," October 20, 2006.

Schwartz, Barry, "Decision Making," March 17, 2006.

Shiller, Robert, "Housing Bubble," August 19, 2005.

Shiller, Robert, "Digging into Subprime," October 6, 2008.

Siegel, Dr. Marc, "Bird Flu," March 3, 2006.

Siegel, Jeremy, "Back to the Basics: Tried and True Investing," March 28, 2008.

Silber, William, "When Washington Shuts Down Wall Street," February 2, 2007.

Sinquefield, Rex, "Dimensional Fund Advisors," August 18, 2006.

Smith, James, "Immigration," May 19, 2006.

Smith, Ray, "Renting versus Owning," March 25, 2005.

Solin, Dan, "Investing," May 27, 2005.

Solin, Dan, "Practical Investing," November 3, 2006.

Stossel, John, "Economics (Myths and Lies)," June 30, 2006.

Swedrow, Larry, "The Investor's Big Mistake," January 18, 2008.

Tapscott, Don, "Efficient Markets," June 29, 2007.

Tetlock, Philip, "Experts," July 7, 2006.

Thaler, Richard H., "Probability versus Possibility," May 23, 2008.

Thredgold, Jeff, "Outlook 2008," October 26, 2007.

Torbenson, Eric, "Airline Stocks: Performance versus Potential," January 13, 2006.

Town, Phil, "Rule No. 1," May 19, 2006.

Updegrave, Walter, "Market Return Benchmark and Market Averages," January 11, 2008.

Valliere, Greg, "Greenspan/Bernanke," January 27, 2006.

Walker, Graham, "Rock, Paper, Scissors," April 28, 2006.

Wallison, Peter, "Mutual Fund Reform," May 4, 2007.

Walper, Jr., George H., "Affluent Investors Index," May 20, 2005.

Walper, Jr., George H., "The Secrets of the Millionaire Mindset," April 25, 2008.

Warsh, David, "Sink or Swim Economics," December 21, 2007.

Waymire, Jack, "Finding Advisors," April 1, 2005.

Weiner, Eric, "Wall Street: History," October 25, 2005.

Weiner, Glenn, "Trust in America Survey," January 20, 2006.

Wellington, Weston J., "Dimensional Fund Advisors," March 30, 2007.

Wellington, Weston J., "Dimensional Funds and Emerging Markets," February 8, 2008.

Wheelen, Charles, "Econ 101," May 18, 2007.

Williams, Walter, "Economics in Everyday Life," September 1, 2006.

Wray, David, "401(k)s," November 17, 2006.

Yip, Pamela, "From an Advisor," November 2, 2007.

Zeeb, Rod, "Inheritance," October 6, 2006.

Zonis, Marvin, "Global Economy," April 27, 2007.

Zweig, Jason, "Neuroeconomics and Market Volatility Risk and Diversification," January 25, 2008.

INDEX

ABOUT THE AUTHOR

James N. Whiddon is founder and CEO of JWA Financial Group, Inc., and a popular host of a syndicated talk radio show. He has been named repeatedly one of the fastest growing Aggie Business Leaders and one of Dallas's Best Financial Planners, and his firm has been named a "Wealth Master" by *Bloomberg Wealth Manager* five years running. Whiddon is also a well-known source of financial planning and money management wisdom among viewers of CNBC, CNN Money, and Investment News, as well as readers of the *Wall Street Journal, Chicago Tribune,* and *Financial Advisor.*